No. 1074
$9.95

How to Build Your Own Vacation Home

By Charles R. Self

TAB BOOKS

BLUE RIDGE SUMMIT, PA. 17214

FIRST EDITION

FIRST PRINTING—DECEMBER 1978

Copyright © 1978 by TAB BOOKS

Printed in the United States of America

Library of Congress Cataloging in Publication Data

Self, Charles R
    How to build your own vacation home.

    Includes index.
    1. Second homes. 2. House construction—Amateurs' manuals. I. Title.
TH4835.S44   690'.8'7   78-10563
ISBN 0-8306-9862-0
ISBN 0-8306-1074-X pbk.

Other TAB books by the author

872 *Wood Heating Handbook*
892 *Do-It-Yourselfer's Guide to Chainsaw Use & Repair*
949 *Do-It-Yourselfer's Guide to Auto Body Repair & Painting*

Contents

Introduction

Today's reasons for building or buying a vacation home have grown a great deal over those in past years. With the ever increasing price of land, the spiraling costs of almost any kind of construction, and the ever present and ever fluctuating inflation, vacation homes today may seem an unaffordable luxury to those of us locked into lower middle class and middle class income brackets. But in many cases, we can still find reasonably priced land in desirable locales. And in just as many cases, starting with a smaller vacation home, with fewer amenities, we can erect the basic structure ourselves. In doing so we can end up with a place for relaxation and enjoyment at one-third to one-half the price similar structures would cost in or around a city.

Some estimates show as many as 250,000 Americans each year joining the ranks of those with second or vacation homes. The reasons are many: the pressures of city or suburban living are becoming extreme, the vacation home serves as an investment and a strong hedge against inflation, and the basic quality of getting away from things is something most of us have been led to believe is desirable. And for most vacation home owners, this last statement holds true. A few will start the home, finish, move in and sell out in a year or two. The life of ease and mild sports isn't for them.

Fewer people would move out so quickly if more thought were given to the style of life actually enjoyed instead of the style of life, though never tried, they think they may enjoy. In other words, if you're not sure about living in an area, using the recreational facilities there, and actually having a good time, try it first on a rental basis for a year or two. Don't jump in until you know either how deep the water is, or how well you can swim. You probably won't lose your shirt, but you will expend a lot of energy and money and time doing something you don't like, and most of us have enough of that sort of thing to contend with during our nonrecreational time.

While site and locale selection is a very personal thing, I have included some information on the subject, for there are more or less standard considerations pertaining to such things as drainage, rocky outcrops, accessibility, and such that each of us must pay some attention to. It's up to you to figure out if you are willing and able to pay the premium for lakefront property, or prefer sitting by a stream back in the woods. Too, you must decide on the amenities: if you build far, far back in the woods or up the side of a mountain, the cost of installing everything from basic electrical service to plumbing to telephones goes up in relation to your distance from the nearest populous area, as does the time of installation increase with distance from population centers. With each decision to build a vacation home, such factors need to be considered, and are certain to multiply as you take steps to put plans in action.

Today, cheap land is almost nonexistent. Almost everywhere, land costs a minimum of $500 an acre, or very near that, with prices going rapidly upwards so that lakefront, ski slope front, and other such types of land can cost as much as $15,000 an acre, and sometimes even more. More savings are needed to purchase the land; more savings are needed to purchase the house, the materials, or the kit for construction. But a quarter of a million people a year manage to at least get started and most of them finish. It is possible, in part because we now have a vast selection of materials, kits, and tools that never before were available. You can build a log cabin from kit or scratch, you can build almost any style of frame vacation home you desire, you can build of brick or masonry, and you can erect a home of steel. In some areas, it is still legal to put up sod houses.

This book will cover the basics for log cabins, both kits and from scratch, as well as frame home building from the ground up or from the various companies who supply vacation home kits, which are prefabricated and rather simple to assemble in relation to starting a home from scratch.

While I recommend that the person who knows little of masonry work hire a subcontractor for any foundation work; basic instructions for cement block foundations will be covered. The same recommendation would hold true for plumbing, wiring, and heating if any is needed. Still, we'll look at plumbing to a small extent, and wiring. Heating will be covered in only one aspect—wood.

Along the way, the book will cover the various tools needed, along with techniques of use and safety conditions for most such tools. For example, the chainsaw. It is easy to use, popular, and very profitable today; however, a chainsaw can become one of the most dangerous tools the average person is ever likely to be exposed to if not used properly and carefully. By the time you finish reading this book, I hope you'll be able to select the skills you have and add the described techniques to build your own home.

Should you choose to hire a professional builder to do all the work, the methods contained in this book will at least give you insight into the various processes, and may allow you to save money where possible and avoid short-cuts in areas where they're not desirable.

Charles R. Self, Jr.

Chapter 1
Selecting the Locale

In all probability, you will already know the type of recreation that appeals most to you and your family. If you love skiing, then your second home should be located at least near some good ski runs of the type you like best. If fishing is your aim, look for an area that has many streams or lakes; homes for hunters should be located in or near game areas. Water skiers want to get as close to larger bodies of water as possible. Someone who wants to sit and read Thoreau may just wish to get as far from other people as possible. There are vacation home communities with lots, erected homes, and such available for just about all of the types of recreation one may desire, from crafts to sports. A careful look needs to be taken at as many as possible of those which fall within the family's areas of interest.

Next in consideration is the cost. Plots located in already developed vacation communites are going to be more expensive than plots located in undeveloped areas. Plots close to major skiing, or other mass recreation types, areas will be more expensive than plots located near nothing more than the side of a lone mountain and well away from any town. Don't expect to find a great deal of land going for $500 per acre anymore. Most probably, the land you wish to buy, if removed from settled or heavy recreation areas, will start at $1,500 per acre and go rapidly up. Land in close is more likely to start at $5,000 per acre, possibly even $10,000.

Next in the top three considerations is the distance the vacation home site is from home and work. While you may love the idea of sitting on top of one of the Rockies and singing along with John Denver, there isn't much point to owing such property if you have to have a 3-week vacation to reach it. Most vacation homes are so expensive that we are best off utilizing them as often as possible. Too, care and general upkeep is simpler if we're close enough to drive up on a regular weekend without getting so tired as to be unable to move the next day. In other words, with today's speed limits, try to keep the vacation home within no more than about a 250-mile radius of home. Less distance is better but not always possible with population pressures as they now are. Probably ideal distance would be a vacation home from which you could commute to work, but work could not commute to you.

With today's roads and speed limits, 250 miles will take about 4.5 to 5 hours of driving time, which would allow you to get there by no later than 10 PM on a Friday. This is with proper planning and assuming you can actually get away from work at 5 PM. And it is also assuming you don't get caught in major traffic jams each Friday. Probably more realistic planning would be a midnight time of arrival. You can still get a decent night of sleep, with all of Saturday to relax and the next to pack, relax, and return. A shorter distance is better and cheaper as the gas and car wear and tear costs will go down as distance drops.

TYPES OF LOCALES

Generally, there are four types of vacation home sites that are desirable: waterfront, rural, winter sports area, and mountain. Each of these presents advantages and disadvantages. We must remember, too, that types are often combined; winter sports areas are often in the mountains, mountains often drop down to lakefront property, and so on.

Waterfront property provides its owners with chances for swimming, water skiing, sailing, motorboating, fishing, and many variations on the basic themes. It also tends to be hard to find in a reasonable price range, unless very far from everything. Areas that are not remote may easily be overcommercialized. I won't list the places I've lived or visited that have rapidly become undesirable as more and more people moved in while the locals got greedier for their cash; it happens often.

Interior property, property not actually on the waterfront, may often be a better buy, but when buying make sure of several things. First, do you have lake rights with an unimpeded right of way? Next, what is the tide or high water situation? Add to this queries about the local insect population and its density, prevailing winds, rainfall, and legal checks on types of buildings.

Snow or winter sports country is available in many guises. Planned communities abound in mountainous areas, while unplanned communities continue to build across the country where heavy snows are available for many months. Generally, snow country is only one type of mountain country with the added fun and problems of greater population density and heavy snowfall. Skiers tend to congregate possibly because ski runs are so expensive to build, and just as possibly because the sport involves a great many gregarious people.

Mountain country in the United States can cover a very wide area, from the small bumps in the foothills of the Ozarks to some of Alaska's towering giants. The advantages can be found in privacy: the higher up and more rugged the terrain, the more privacy. Disadvantages include sometimes extreme privacy, the difficulty of building on rugged, rocky terrain subject to heavy erosion, more extreme weather than down on the flatland, difficult access, the need

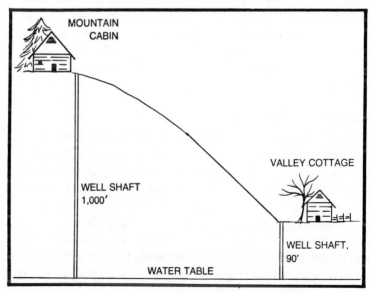

Fig. 1-1. Mountain country can cause expensive water problems.

for a deeper well (Fig. 1-1), the probability of great expense to bring in electricity and phones, and possible poor access in bad weather.

Rural property in the United States is widely available, possibly more so than at any other time in history, as many small farmers are calling it quits each year. While the major parts of their land are often taken by large, corporate farmers, smaller plots with houses or outbuildings are often retained or sold individually to the many urbanites eager for a place out of the smog. Because I have just moved from rural New York to rural Virginia, some of the advantages are totally obvious. By leaving New York, I got out of a resort area where prices reached Manhattan levels on most all items, from sales taxes to blue jeans. By moving from the foothills of the Catskills to the foothills of the Blue Ridge Mountains, I retained the rolling landscape I love. By the same token, by not going farther south, I also kept the four seasons, something I hadn't even realized I needed until I spent most of one winter in Florida and the next two in Hawaii. Yet if I had wished, I could have located rural areas in the United States that would offer flatland, as I did some 5 years ago around Whitewater, Wisconsin, or most any other feature I might desire, including mountains of moderate size. One of these days, I'll try the spots I've missed in this country. Generally, rural areas have somewhat more relaxed building codes, so that the choice of house is wide. In some cases, it isn't even necessary to have a licensed electrician inspect wiring you have done. While it may not be legally required, I believe safety demands such a check. While a few areas don't bother too much with the latest in National Electrical Codes, I would sooner drive over my foot than not follow them as a minimum safety standard.

SELECTING YOUR LAND

Land selection, based on family needs and wants, covers many areas. First, important beyond all else, is the type of land desired as described above. If you don't enjoy your vacation home, there's little point in building it. After that, you must consider the basic site imperatives, such as availability of water, electricity, phone lines, and the need for installation of septic fields and wells. Too, you need to check for prevailing winds. It's much better to site a house slightly over the brow of a hill and out of direct winter blasts when possible, but a coppice of trees can also be used to break winds in winter. If there is no information around on drainage, you will have to run percolation tests on the land. We'll assume that you've already checked for swampy areas.

SITING THE VACATION HOME

While the individual site will dictate much of the placement for any house, some thoughts can be kept in mind that add to enjoyment and economy in heating and air conditioning. Once the septic field and well locations are known, the next thing to consider in home siting is drainage around the house (Fig. 1-2). Look for natural drainage areas that could run right through the foundation of the house. These natural drainage areas could be simple gullies directing rain runoff to the foundation. In such cases, they are rather easily modified to keep dampness problems away. In other cases, the natural drainage could come from creeks, again fairly easily diverted, or underground seeps and springs, neither of which are easy to handle. Check carefully beforehand or building expense and related problems will increase rapidly. In some areas, the natural drainage is in subsoil spots so that there is little or no indication of what's there until the foundation is at least partly dug. If the drainage area is bad enough, it will often pay to resite the house rather than try to channel or contain the water runoff. In others, proper preparation of the foundation can eliminate most problems. In spots where the natural drainage is so heavy, and the house so situated as to be a poor candidate for relocation, a sump pump could be required.

SUN AND WEATHER EXPOSURE

Using the lay of the land to protect a house from the elements is a technique that was well known to most of our forefathers and one

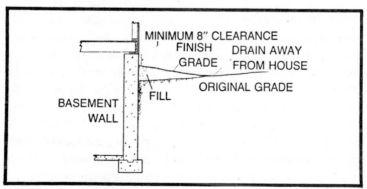

Fig. 1-2. Finish grade sloped for drainage.

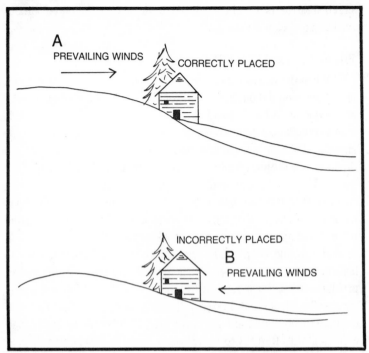

Fig. 1-3. A house built over the brow of a hill or knoll is protected from prevailing winds.

that is becoming even better known to many of us today. No longer should a house be stuck up on a knoll, surrounded by nothing but the local winds. With the cost of various heating fuels, this sort of house siting technique is not even sensible for areas in the far South, as it will run up air conditioning costs unmercifully. Generally, if flatland is all that's available, the existing tree cover should be used to provide shade and windbreaks wherever possible. In mountain or rolling country, situating a house so that the roof line is at least a few feet under the top of a hill is a good way to cut down on exposure to prevailing winter winds. Of course, you must select the hill so that it is positioned to block those winds; siting the house just over the brow of a hill when the winds whip up the other side of the valley most of the time is not a good way to work things. (Figure 1-3.) Siting a house all the way down in a deep valley is not a particularly good idea unless the prevailing winds run up or down the length of the valley, and can be blocked by some sort of windbreak. Basically, dropping a house entirely out of the wind adds to cooling costs in summer as there is no breeze to provide natural air conditioning in such areas. Still, it is essential to break the full force of winter winds.

Too, these days it is possible to add to the quality of house insulating by building the home at least partly into the hill, much as sod houses were built back in homesteading days. Many experiments are now being done with homes that are built partially or entirely in the ground, and so far the fuel savings have been very significant. Naturally such homes tend to lack the immense glass areas that provide a lot of light in a home; glass areas, though, are extreme sources of heat loss, even with double and triple glazing in use.

Most of the problem of heat loss through windows can be solved by siting a home so that the major glass areas face south, with the north wall free, or almost free, of large windows. South facing windows with good overhang from the roof allow the low slanting winter sun to shine in the house, while the hotter, higher angled summer sun is cut mostly out, at least during the hottest parts of the day.

If no other natural barriers are to be found to break up strong prevailing winds, you can easily plant a row of evergreens. Still, evergreens tend to also cut down on summer breezes so that interspersing with deciduous trees of some type is often a good idea. The leaf dropping deciduous trees can also be used as summer shade for the house when planted to the south, east, or west. Because these trees drop their leaves in fall, the winter sun is allowed to shine through and provide some heat.

MISCELLANY IN HOUSE SITING

To start this list of miscellany, we can consider the view you'll be seeing from the rooms you use most. While the differences in surrounding views will be extreme for different kinds of vacation homes, you can easily consider the major points of appeal to you around the plot on which you're building—possibly a mountain in the backyard, a lake just down the hill, or a large pond. Decide just where you'd like to place a particular room so that the major feature of the terrain is visible at the best times of day. Or you may prefer to provide a view for the dishwasher and have the most spectacular or interesting piece of terrain located so that it can be seen from the kitchen window. If the house is also sited so that the view falls into the sunset or sunrise, this is an added benefit, though it is limited by the direction of the terrain to be viewed. As, for example, a north lying slope would never be caught in the full glow of a sunrise or sunset.

Too, the house should be placed so that whoever does the shopping, toting of luggage and such doesn't have to carry the load up 70 steps or a long, steep hillside full of rocks. Generally, the closer we can drive to the kitchen door, the happier we will be when unloading the car time arrives. Little things such as this can add a great deal to everyone's enjoyment of a home, whether primary or vacation style.

Another point to consider is if the area in which the home is built tends to be very messy, such as at the seashore with a lot of sand to be tracked in, or near a lake, pond, or stream where a great deal of mud, leaves, and other debris could easily be carried into the house, situate the house so that some sort of vestibule is either right at or adjacent to the main entrance. This can cut the time involved in cleaning the house by a remarkable amount, and any vacation home should be as chorefree as possible if full enjoyment is to be had by all.

While I realize the above siting instructions are very general, there is really no other way to go about such things without knowing the specific piece of property selected for the construction of a home. Major pitfalls can be avoided by adhering to the following checklist:

1. Select a home site that suits the family's recreational needs.
2. Check carefully for locations of the well and septic fields, including a percolation test.
3. Check for the direction of prevailing winds.
4. Make sure there is some way available of protecting the home in winter from those prevailing winds without shutting off summer breezes.
5. Check carefully for site drainage where the house is to stand. Few of us enjoy having water fill a basement.
6. Use the sun and weather exposure naturally available to provide the warmest house in winter and the coolest in summer possible.
7. Add natural elements, such as trees, to help nature protect the house from the elements.
8. Site for the best possible view of the terrain features.
9. Build for convenience of house chores.

Chapter 2
Tooling Up for Home Building

Tools are something the novice home builder either fears or enjoys so much that undertooling and overtooling are the major problems in building many houses. One makes the job unnecessarily hard, while the other adds unneeded expense to the work. I can sympathize with the person who overtools quite easily as my major addiction is to hardware stores and tool catalogs. My spare cash tends to go for tools that may be used once in my lifetime. Much like the gun nut, I am a tool nut. For that reason, as I go through the list of tools used in homebuilding, I will, as often as possible, try to specify whether or not a tool is essential to the job at hand. As an example, while a circular saw of 7¼-inch capacity is nearly essential in home building today, there is seldom any need for one of the huge 10¼-inch models also available unless you choose to erect a plank and beam house. At the same time, I will attempt to cover the safe and efficient use of most of the tools.

THE BASIC TOOL KIT

Without the following tools, no home today would get built. In fact, with no other tools, a home can be built, using some old fashioned substitutes for other tools. For example, a level can be made with a piece of transparent plastic hose partially filled with water, while a plumb line of more than fair accuracy is easily made by hanging a rather heavy nail from a piece of cord. The essential tools

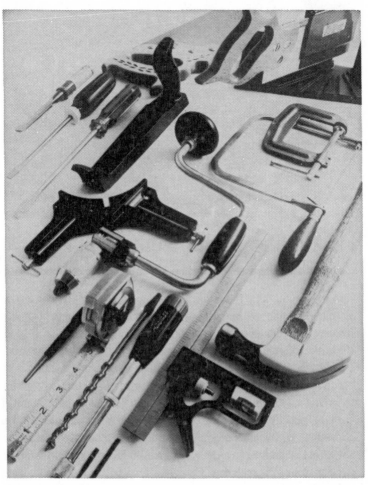

Fig. 2-1. Tools for home building. (Courtesy of Stanley Tools.)

are a crosscut saw with eight or ten teeth per inch, a claw hammer weighing at least 16 ounces and a combination square. While these really are all the tools you would need to build a frame home, the amount of work would be prodigious and time-consuming, so that a decent series of power tools and other hand tools will become nearly as essential in order that the job go as rapidly as possible (see Fig. 2-1).

HANDSAWS

Handsaws (Fig. 2-2) come in many varieties, from the sharp nosed keyhole saw to the gap toothed bucksaw used for sawing wood for fires. For housebuilding uses, several will do the job better than a single one. For general work where a power saw isn't suitable—and there'll be more of these jobs than you would think—a crosscut saw of good quality, with eight teeth per inch will speed up work. Generally, a hand ripsaw isn't useful in homebuilding. A backsaw, along with a miter box, is another form of the basic crosscut saw, and should be selected with fine teeth, either eleven or thirteen per inch. The backsaw and miter box are used for fine work on trim, and anyplace where accurate miters are needed during construction. Select the best you can afford, but don't go overboard as miter boxes, with backsaws included, can range from a low of about $15 to a high of well over $150 (Fig. 2-3). Try for a midrange of about half or a bit less of the top figure. If you don't wish to buy a backsaw and miter box, select a small wood miter box for a few dollars and get a crosscut saw with ten or twelve teeth per inch. The backsaw will do a finer job, but is not essential if great care is used. The finer teeth on the crosscut saw will, by the way, slow down the work.

Keyhole and compass saws are very similar in looks and application but shouldn't be confused. A keyhole saw (Fig. 2-4) is used for making internal cuts in heavy material by making a drilled hole for a starting point. Because the blade is wider than that of a compass saw, it is unsuitable for use in cutting curves. The compass saw, with its narrower blade will provide you with the ability to cut moderate curves in heavy material.

A coping saw looks very much like the classic hacksaw but has a higher arched back and a narrower blade. It is used for cutting curves in lightweight material and for trimming molding to fit exactly (Fig. 2-5). Also, coping saws have the blades mounted with the teeth pointing toward the handle so that they cut on the pull stroke instead

Fig. 2-2. Standard handsaw. (Courtesy of Stanley Tool Works.)

Fig. 2-3. Backsaw in metal miter box. (Courtesy of Stanley Tools.)

of the push stroke. The reason for this is simple since the blade and frame of a coping saw are light enough to give and break if push stroke cutting is used.

For cutting tubing, whether plastic or metal, and for cutting pipe, a hacksaw is indispensable. The frame and blade are much heavier than those in a coping saw. Most cutting is done on the push stroke, using both hands on the saw. In contrast, you use only one hand on the coping saw. Blade selection is of great importance here, as too many teeth per inch will make cuts in thick material unnecessarily hard, while too few teeth per inch will tend to tear up light stock instead of cutting it neatly. For heavier material, including soft steel, iron, brass, bronze copper, and aluminum select a fourteen-teeth-per-inch blade, and make sure that at least two teeth rest on the stock to be cut. If two teeth don't fit on the stock, select an eighteen-teeth-per-inch blade. When tubing of medium wall thickness, and medium weight sheet metal need to be cut, look for a blade with twenty-four teeth per inch. For fine stock, such as thin wall copper tubing and sheet metal similar to that used in guttering, select a hacksaw blade with thirty-two teeth per inch.

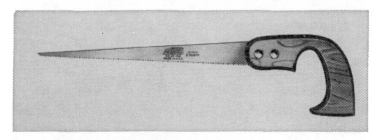

Fig. 2-4. Keyhole saw. (Courtesy of Stanley Tools.)

SAW CARE AND SHARPENING

Of course, the saws with replaceable blades are not sharpened. The blades are simply discarded and replaced with fresh ones when dull. Handsaws of the crosscut, rip, and backsaw types though will need occasional sharpening to make the work go easily. Generally, my recommendation is for you to have a professional with power machinery do the job. A properly cared for wood saw will need sharpening few times during a single housebuilding job if at all. The job is a bit tedious and time consuming and forces the purchase of several special files that, while not overly expensive, add as much to your tool cost as a good sharpening by a pro.

Handsaw care is a simple matter. Check used wood for nails and make sure the blade doesn't hit them. Don't force the handsaw blade through a cut so that it buckles. Such treatment just about warrants

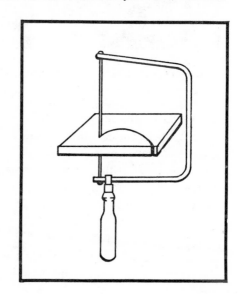

Fig. 2-5. Coping saw.

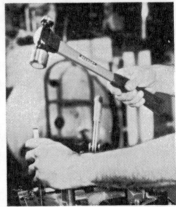

Fig. 2-6. Stanley line of fiberglass handled hammers. (Top) Rip claw hammer. (Lower left) Framing hammer. (Lower right) Ball peen hammer.

the saw will never again cut straight. Make sure any material being cut is supported far enough from the ground so that the tip of the saw doesn't hit and buckle. Store the saw correctly, either in a toolbox support or hanging from a nail inserted through the hole in the end of the blade. Don't lay the saw where something else will be set on top of it, either for a short time or a long time, as this can also cause the blade to buckle. Give the blade a light coat of a material known as Tri-Flon at the end of each working day. Tri-Flon is a synthetic carrier lubricant with micron size Teflon particles that adhere to the surface being lubricated. It not only keeps the blade from rusting, but provides a long lasting lubricant that can prevent buildup of pine resin.

24

HAMMERS

The variety of hammers is so great as to nearly defy description (Fig. 2-6). The most important hammer for the home builder is the nail hammer, also called a claw hämmer (Fig. 2-7). Even here, the variety of styles and weights can be confusing. And there are some points of preference that will vary from person to person with little or no rationale given or really needed. If the style suits use it. A claw hammer is not made for removing nails. The claw is there as a convenience for ripping small boards loose and pulling small nails gently. Basically, it is meant for driving nails. You need a nail puller or cat's claw bar to remove bent or otherwise wrongly driven nails.

Claw hammers come with three types of faces. For general nail driving, the flat face is fine. For work with wallboard where a dimple must be left without breaking the paper cover on the wallboard, a bell face is best. For rough framing work, a checkered face on the hammer will provide a more or less nonskid design to help speed up nailing of structural members.

Once you're past the face and claw, you move into hammer weights. Nailing hammers can weigh from as little as 7 ounces on up to 28 ounces. Generally, in home building, there will be little use for the hammers weighing less than 12 ounces, while most people won't want to bother with the 28-ounce framing hammers. While that heavier hammer will make driving large nails a one-shot deal, the weight is a lot to contend with for people who don't work as framing carpenters. For best results, I would recommend three hammers: a 12-ounce one for fine work, such as interior and exterior molding, a 16-ounce one for general nailing (siding, door and window frames,

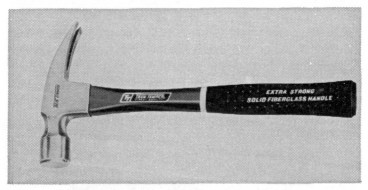

Fig. 2-7. True temper's 20-ounce framing hammer with straight claw.

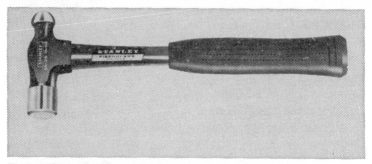

Fig. 2-8. Ball peen hammer. (Courtesy of Stanley Tools.)

etc.), and a 20- or 22-ounce framing hammer for the rough framing of the entire house. If you are stronger or weaker than the average, you should adjust the hammer weights accordingly. And be honest with yourself if you're on the weak side of average. Too heavy a hammer simply adds to the work. A fourth hammer, a 12- or 16-ounce bell face, will prove useful if you are doing the interior of your home in gypsum wallboard.

Hammer handles provide another area of selection. Once upon a time your choice would be one of several types of wooden handles, hickory usually. Now the choice encompasses hickory, which is tough and resilient, tubular steel, which is very rugged but lacks resiliency and may be more tiring for many people, solid steel, which offers much the same strength as tubular steel, and the same lack of resilience, and fiberglass. Fiberglass is my choice as it offers just about the same strength as steel, but also provides much of the resilience found in wooden handles.

Hammer quality can be a problem if you start searching among off brands to save a few bucks. To date, I've used, with no quality complaints, hammers from Stanley, True Temper, Sears, Wards, Millers Falls, and a couple of others. Feel of the hammers has varied, but the quality has always been fine: there's no sense in even trying to select an on-sale off-brand hammer to save three or four bucks as the tool will be in almost constant use during housebuilding. Get the best you can find. It will pay in the long run.

OTHER HAMMERS

Obviously, when I said that claw hammers were for nailing and light ripping work only, I cut out a lot of jobs that will sooner or later turn up. How do you drive a chisel if you don't use a hammer? Well, you use a hammer, but not a nailing hammer which was designed and built for the simple job of driving mild steel nails into wood. In fact, you do not use a nailing hammer to drive hardened steel masonry nails. Ball peen hammers are used to drive wood chisels and to drive masonry nails. Head selection and weight is somewhat similar to claw hammers, though there is a ball instead of the claw. Face design is different: ball peen hammers have a slightly crowned striking face. Use a ball peen hammer with a face 50 percent larger than the tool being struck (Fig. 2-8).

For masonry work, you'll find a bricklayer's hammer (Fig. 2-9) invaluable. Head weights will range from 10 to 24 ounces, and the face will be square with sharp corners. The face is also flat. The blade of the hammer has a sharp, hardened cutting edge. These hammers are never used to strike metal. Even when a bricklayer's or mason's chisel is used, a ball peen hammer must be used to strike it.

For striking use with hardened metals and masonry, you should always wear safety goggles, as hardened steel is prone to chipping if struck at the wrong angle; brick and rock are noted for throwing splinters (Fig. 2-10).

At times during the building of some houses, other types of hammers will be needed. Sledge hammers may be needed to break up rock and concrete, or to drive metal posts. These double face

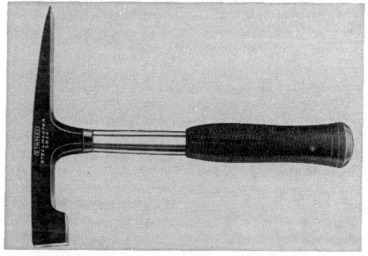

Fig. 2-9. Bricklayer's hammer. (Courtesy of Stanley Tools.)

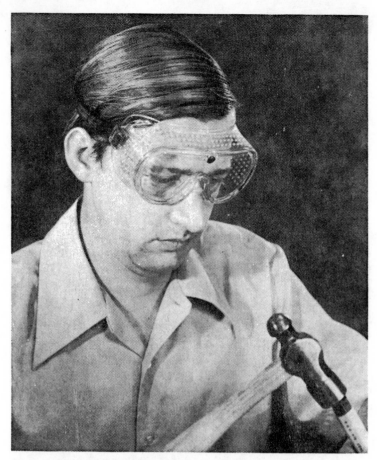

Fig. 2-10. Using striking tools requires precautions to prevent eye damage. Wear safety goggles. (Courtesy of Stanley Tools.)

hammers have head weights ranging from 2 to 20 pounds. Specialized stone sledges are used on rock and concrete, while general sledges are used only for wood and metal. Hand sledges can weigh up to 5 pounds and will have a 15-inch handle.

Hand drilling hammers, useful for driving star drills through a concrete or concrete block wall for pipe and wire entry are heavy with short handles. Head weights of this type from 2 to 4 pounds, and handles of no more than 11 inches.

SQUARES

Squares vary in style and purpose as well as in price and general usefulness. The most useful in house building is the combination square (Fig. 2-11), which, as its name states, combines both the try square, essential for testing corners for squareness and for drawing square lines when a board must be cut off, and the miter square. While the try square presents a 90-degree angle, the miter square gives you a 45-degree angle for times when such a measurement or

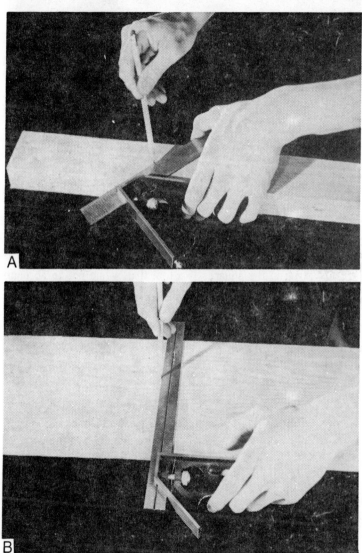

Fig. 2-11. The combination square. (A) Using the 45-degree angled edge for mitered corners. (B) Using the 90-degree angled edge for straight cuts. (Courtesy of Stanley Tools.)

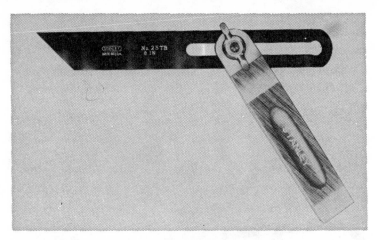

Fig. 2-12. The sliding T-bevel makes angled cut a simple matter. (Courtesy of Stanley Tools.)

cut is needed. A combination square will also serve as a level. Most have liquid level vials inserted at the correct angles useful for both vertical, plumb, operations and horizontal, level, work. It can be used as a straight edge with the frame removed and a depth gauge, handy for tracing longer lines for long rip cuts.

Next up in the squares is a tool that, while not an absolute essential to housebuilding, can make certain jobs a great deal easier. This is the sliding T-bevel (Fig. 2-12). The sliding T-bevel resembles a try square, except that the blade is adjustable to any angle. While a protractor can be used to set an already known angle to make marking simple, the sliding T-bevel has a more useful life. By inserting the tool in an area that needs an angle cut, then setting the slotted blade and tightening it down, you can transfer any angle needed to boards that need to be cut, saving a lot of measuring and figuring.

The framing square or rafter square (Fig. 2-13) is one of the most complex tools the do-it-yourself home builder will have to become familiar with. So accordingly, I'll have to do a rather lengthy, though I hope not too complicated, explanation of its uses. The rafter square is, more or less, a one-piece computer for determining the length of rafters once you have the basics down. As such, the *body* or *blade* of the square is the longer, wider leg. While no standard actually exists, most are 24 by 2 inches. The *tongue* is the shorter side, usually 16 by 1½ inches. The *heel* is the outside corner where the tongue and blade meet.

When you first pick up a rafter or framing square, you'll note that both the face, the side with the maker's name on it, and the back are stamped with columns of figures. To understand these figures you'll need an understanding of the terms used to describe roof structures.

1. The span of a roof is the distance between the outside edges of the supporting walls, expressed in unit of span.

Fig. 2-13. Use of the rafter or framing square is essential when framing roofs or building stairs. The lower portion of the figure shows rafter tables located on the face of the square. (Courtesy of Stanley Tools.)

Units of span are always 24 inches so that the framing defines the unit.

2. The rise of a roof is the vertical distance to the roof peak or ridge.

3. The run is the horizontal distance from the ridge to the outer edge of the vertical wall members. In an equal span roof, to which we'll confine ourselves here for simplicity's sake, the run equals half of the span.

4. The pitch is the ratio of the rise to the span. With an 8-foot rise and a 24-foot span, the pitch would be 1/3. For a 24-foot span, the pitch would be 1/3. For a 24-foot span with a 4-foot rise, the pitch would be 1/6. Pitch can also be expressed as inches of vertical rise per foot of run and this figure is needed if you are to use the rafter square to determine rafter length. Simply take the unit of span, 24 inches, and multiply it by the pitch ratio. In our first example, that would be 1/3 times 24 or 8 inches, while the second example, 1/6 times 24, would give 4 inches.

With this in mind, it becomes a relatively simple chore to find the length of rafter needed on an equal pitch simple gable roof. On the left end of the body is found the table for length of common rafters per foot of run. From that point, you simply move along to the rise of foot per run for your house. We'll use 8 inches for rise here. The figure directly under the 8-inch mark is 14.42 inches. With a 12-foot run, half of the 24-foot span, multiplication of 14.42 times 12 gives us 173.04. For all practical purposes, the rafter will be, to the nearest tenth of an inch, 173 inches; the job now amounts to marking the rafter, cutting, and checking the fit.

The rafter square is used to make the marks so that correct angle lines are possible. First the length of the rafter, plus any overhang, is laid out on the material. Then two small marking clamps are added at the correct spot on the rafter square. The job can be done without these marking clamps, but is made a lot easier and more accurate with them. Marking the cut at the ridge is done by laying the square on the rafter with the tongue facing your right and the heel towards you, while the length of the rafter is to your left. The markings, in this case 8 inches and 12 inches, are positioned on the rafter. Once set, you simply draw the square along until outer edge of the tongue meets the length marking at the rafter's center.

Now draw the angle along that outside edge and you have your angle cut. A notch will need to be cut if there is an overhang, but that is simply done by measuring the needed depth of the cut and angling it correctly to get the "bird's mouth" or cutout to fit on the top plate of the wall framing.

Once this first rafter is cut and checked for fit, every other rafter can be cut from its pattern, assuming an equal pitch roof is used. Where more complex roof shapes are desired, the rafter square will have to be used more often. Too, if a ridge board is used you must remember to take half the thickness of that ridge board off the top of each rafter.

LEVELS

Getting a house level and plumb can be quite a job without the correct tools. As I said earlier, you can quite easily use a piece of

Fig. 2-14. A good level is needed to do accurate work. (Courtesy of Stanley Tools.)

transparent hose partially filled with water to form a crude level. Much better, though, is the carpenter's level (Fig. 2-14), which provides not only greater accuracy, but also ease of transport from one part of the job to another. In general, a 6-foot level is best for most house framing jobs, but for spaces where the 6-footer won't fit, you'll also need a 2-foot level. Six-foot levels serve when you're plumbing or leveling doors, corner sections, and other large parts of the structure, while the 2-foot level will prove nearly essential to getting windowsills, doorsills, and such at the correct angle.

Generally, the longer the level you can use on any job, the greater the accuracy because the longer level tends to ride over surface irregularities, thus is less affected by them.

Care of levels is simple. Keep them clean and don't bang them around. If a level is banged around it will, sooner or later, lose its accuracy. The top grades of levels have adjustments to allow for this, but you must first find a perfectly level or plumb surface in order to make the adjustment.

WOOD PLANES

Wood planes if used correctly are extremely handy when the time comes to bevel, trim, or otherwise shape a piece of finish molding, clapboard, etc. See Fig. 2-15. For those times when you need to true up a door or a very long board, you'll want a jack plane; these run from about 20 inches to 2 feet long. Slightly smaller work is taken care of with fore planes, which run up to about 1.5 feet in size. A smoothing plane about 8 or 9 inches long will finish up the jobs started with the two larger planes. If end grain wood needs trimming, check out a block plane; in this case the blade is set at a different angle so that the end grain is only cut off, not torn up, as would happen with other planes. The block plane angle is 12 degrees, while planes for use in with-the-grain cutting are normally set at 20 degrees.

Planes must be kept sharp. Keep the bite as small as possible, and work smoothly along the board being trimmed so that the savings come off in long curls. For novice woodplaners, the smaller bite provides much easier control and less chance of gouging the wood badly.

OTHER CUTTING TOOLS

Somewhere along the line, you'll find yourself needing other cutting tools while working on most any house. Included in these will

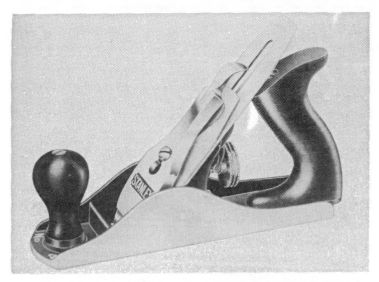

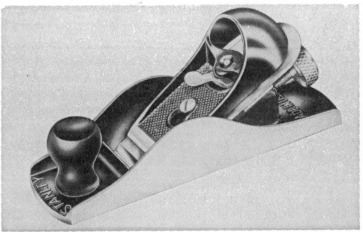

Fig. 2-15. Both the jack plane (top) and the block plane (bottom) are extremely handy tools when board edges need working. (Courtesy of Stanley Tools.)

be basic pocket knives, utility knives with replaceable blades, wood chisels, and such things as Stanley's Surform rasps.

Wood chisels are made in many widths, with different sets at the blade and different kinds of handles. You'll need a couple of rough work chisels for clearing holes in the framing when plumbing is run. The best sizes (Fig. 2-16) are probably about 1 and 2 inches wide. Finishing chisels can be handy in trimming molding. I would look for a ½-inch size and a 1-inch size to start.

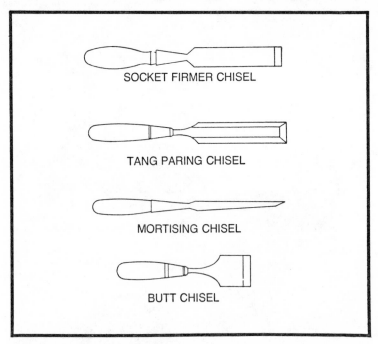

Fig. 2-16. Common types of wood chisels.

Stanley's Surforms (Fig. 2-17) are tools to reckon with. They can be used to work wood, plastics, and the softer metals, replacing many steps in rough files. These tools look something like cheese graters and come in a variety of sizes and shapes. I would suggest that you get at least one two-handled one, a foot or more long, and a couple of smaller models.

From this point on, hand tools spread on out. You'll need a nail set (Fig. 2-18) for working with flooring and finish molding, possibly a hatchet, and maybe a center punch. A few gluing clamps can prove handy in some house construction, as will pliers and a full set of screwdrivers.

To do your own plumbing and heating work you'll need pipe wrenches and basin wrenches (see Fig. 2-19 for a chain pipe wrench), as well as tubing benders, flaring tools, and some soldering equipment (Fig. 2-20).

One major need will be a hand auger or drill holder. Often electric drills can't be used in the early stage of construction, while at other times it is just plain simpler to run holes with a bit brace (Fig. 2-21) rather than run hundreds of feet of extension cord. Select a top quality ratchet bit brace and a series of good, wide range auger bits (Fig. 2-22), as well as a countersink, an expansive bit, and some masonry drills.

POWER TOOLS

Power tools deserve a great deal of consideration when getting ready to build a home. To start, they are generally a lot more expensive than are handtools of the nonpower type, so care in selection is even more important. And as a second point, the effort

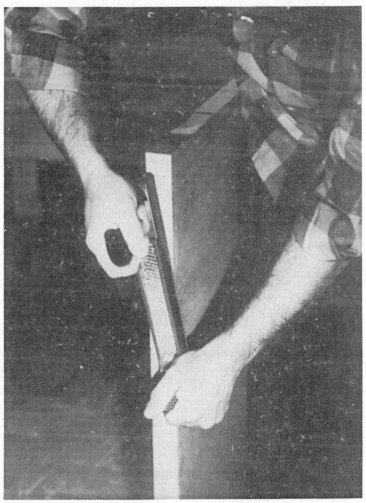

Fig. 2-17. For many rough smoothing jobs nothing beats Stanley's Surform tools.

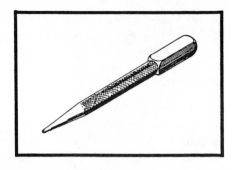

Fig. 2-18. Typical nail set.

any power tool can save over a nonpower tool is extreme. Anyone who has ever felled a tree with an axe and will testify to the efficacy of switching to a chainsaw. But consider the difference in price, too. The saw used may cost $10, with about the best single bit axe available going for around $20. Chainsaws range in price from about $85 on up past $500. Just which one do you need? Well, unless you're enamored of the log cabin section of this book, the odds are excellent you will not need a chainsaw for home building at all; though for later stages of working around the house, building fences, cutting firewood, and so on, a modest size chainsaw is a superb tool investment.

CIRCULAR SAWS

The electric circular saw is indispensable in building any home today. It speeds work over a handsaw and can be used with greater

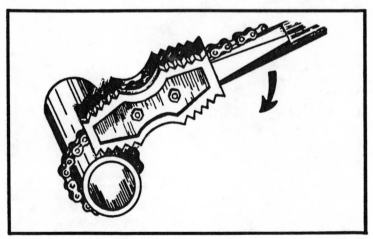

Fig. 2-19. Chain pipe wrench.

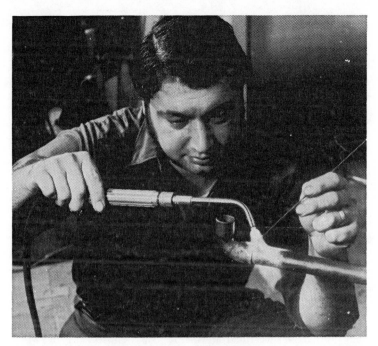

Fig. 2-20. A good propane torch saves much time when sweat soldering plumbing joints. This model has a tube from the propane tank so that all you have to support is the torch head. Notice that this particular job is being silver soldered instead of tin-lead soldered. (Courtesy of Airco.)

accuracy with a few attachments. It makes repeat and other types of multiple cuts a great deal easier, and also allows the use of jigs so that several pieces can be cut at one time. Doing this sort of work with a handsaw is almost like inviting your arm to drop off from exhaustion.

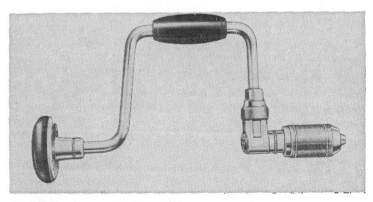

Fig. 2-21. Ratcheting bit brace. (Courtesy of Stanley Tools.)

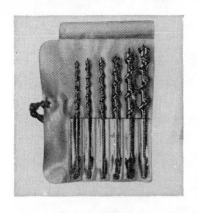

Fig. 2-22. Set of bits for a brace.
(Courtesy of Stanley Tools.)

Circular saws, though, present a price problem, too. They are available in a wide price range, no matter whether the maker is Skil or Sears. The price can range from a very inexpensive sounding $20, on up past $350. My own Skil 10¼-inch saw cost upwards of $220 several years ago. My smaller and more versatile Skil 7¼-inch one cost on the order of $60 a year later. In general, a good circular saw from Black & Decker, Rockwell, Sears, Montgomery Ward, Skil, or any other maker will run from $50 to $75 in the 7¼-inch size. I would recommend this size, or one near it, for almost all work. My 10¼-inch saw was bought for post and beam work which simply cannot be handled with lighter saws; the thing weighs 18 pounds or so and is very tiring after a half-hour's use (Fig. 2-23).

Circular saw blades come in many grades, styles, and sizes. Generally, for framing and other work a combination blade for both rip and crosscut work is a good idea; get at least half a dozen so you won't lose time while one or two are out for sharpening. Then, for working with plywood and flooring underlayment board, you'll need a very fine toothed blade known as a plywood blade. If you make or intend to make masonry cuts, get a masonry cutoff blade. Get at least one rip blade. That should pretty well cover any situation you're likely to run into.

RADIAL ARM SAWS

For work where greater accuracy than is possible with a hand-held circular saw is needed, you may wish to invest several hundred dollars in one of the most versatile shop tools around, the radial arm saw. The price range here is as wide as ever, with lighter models starting at about $250 and the industrial types reaching $1,000. Get a midrange 10-incher if you feel this sort of saw is needed. In most cases, it won't be, but if you practice a bit with the circular saw and find your cutoffs poor for squareness and true length, then the radial arm saw is not just a good investment; it is essential to a good job. Fortunately for anyone not wishing to set up a woodworking shop after building a home, such shop tools hold their value a great deal better than most handtools do.

ELECTRIC DRILLS

Welcome to the country of confusion. I just looked through Skil Corporation's newest dealer catalog and am stuttering a bit after spending more than 20 years using electric drills. You can now buy power drills that will do just about every job imagined, from the drilling of a 1/16-inch hole up to chiseling out a portion of a concrete wall. Of course, the more adaptable the drill is, the more expensive it also is, so you'll be repaid if you spend at least a little time examining your needs. In general, look for a ⅜- or ½-inch chuck, on a drill that

Fig. 2-23. Skil's 6½-inch 552 circular saw will provide enough depth of cut for almost any house building job. (Courtesy Skil Corp.)

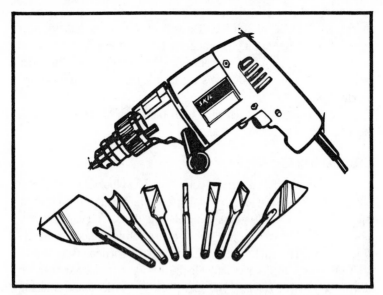

Fig. 2-24. Skil's 599 is an example of the sophistication possible in a tool once known as an electric drill. While still doing that job superbly, this model will chisel and do other jobs. (Courtesy of Skil Corp.)

offers trigger controlled variable speed and reversing. This will take you through most any job in house building that is really needed. Anything else on the drill is simply a luxury. Not all that long ago, in fact, the reversible and variable speed features were found on only the top of the line drills. Today, the electric drill is probably the single best tool buy around. Simple ¼-inch electric drills can now be bought for $10, while 15 years ago they would have cost at least twice that—inflation in reverse (Fig. 2-24).

For drill bits to go with your drill, pick up a ten-drill set, with a top size of ½-inch or so. These are wood and metal bits. Then pick up wood bits as you need them. If you start with an immense drill set, you'll find you seldom, if ever, use 90 percent of the bits, and if you get metal/wood bits over ½-inch in size, the price becomes prohibitive rapidly. A set of masonry drill bits can also prove handy when bathroom fixtures are installed. Get the best quality you can find, and buy only as needed here, too, as expense tends to be high.

CHAINSAWS

As I said earlier on, you don't generally need a chainsaw unless you are building a log cabin or plan to cut firewood for a fireplace or woodstove after the vacation home is finished. For those planning either, though, there are a few things to watch for in chainsaw buying. First, if heavy use, such as erecting a log cabin from trees you fell, is intended, do not under any circumstances get one of those 12-inch guide bar models. The engine will probably wear out just about the time your cabin is completed, and you'll go half crazy, at least, from constantly having to sharpen the chain. There are so few teeth on a 12- or 14-inch chain, that each is contacting the wood too frequently to stay sharp for long.

Next, consider the total use of the saw. If you plan to keep it for years, using it for a variety of jobs, get something on the order of a top-of-the-line consumer saw or the bottom of the particular company's professional chainsaw line. Consider your own strength and endurance when buying the saw, too. A heavy saw, one on the order of mine, the Homelite 360 with a 20-inch bar, can be extremely tiring for smaller people or those who use such a saw only once in a while. A smaller saw, with a 16-inch guide bar is probably best for most people, as it will be several pounds lighter and powerful enough to do 99 percent of the work needed with ease. Still, for those who can handle it and who wish to zip through logs, something on the order of the bottom-of-the-line professional saws will save time.

But such a saw costs money, and a fair amount of it. Of course, no chainsaw that is any good at all for major work is really cheap. Expect prices to start at about $150 and go up rather quickly, but paying $300 or more is seldom essential.

Chainsaws must be treated with respect. In the chapter on log cabins, I'll cover the proper ways to fell trees and use the saw for other operations so that the danger from that speeding set of steel teeth is reduced to a minimum.

MEASURING AND MISCELLANEOUS TOOLS

Accurate measurements are the secret of much of building ease and durability. To get these measurements, you'll need two tools which may seem redundant, a steel tape or fiberglass tape measure and a wood folding rule. One can substitute for another, but for greatest accuracy, each should be applied to the job for which it is intended.

The steel tape needs to be on the order of 50 feet in length; they're available up to 100 feet long. This tool is used for measuring

Fig. 2-25. A 50-foot measuring tape is an essential tool for laying out anything longer than a door. (Courtesy of Stanley Tools.)

the footings, outside and inside wall lengths, roof runs, and so forth (Fig. 2-25).

The folding rule is used to measure shorter distances, including windowsills, window and door rough openings, and so on. They are available in several styles, 8 or 6 feet long, usually with a 6-inch long metal extension, which enables you to use a 6-foot rule to measure a finished 78-inch door opening.

To add to these measuring tools, locate a chalk line for a marking tool. The chalk line is indispensable for jobs such as marking shingle courses, cuts over a foot or so long, rip cuts, floor layouts, and so on. I prefer the type that winds back into its own container which is filled with powdered chalk, although others prefer the style held in loops and dragged through a solid lump of chalk.

Mason's cord is also needed. This tough twine is used to indicate boundaries for footings, to keep concrete block and brick courses from running out of line, and so on.

A router is a tool that is extremely handy when the time comes to trim up laminated plastic countertops and so forth.

Trowels are for putting down tile adhesive, mortar, and other such jobs. Styles will vary as to intended use, so don't try to use a concrete surface trowel to lay mortar, nor a tile adhesive trowel for surfacing your basement floor. It won't work.

In the class of concrete and masonry tools, jointing tools give a finished look and a water resistant pack to mortar joints. Darbys and bull floats are used to provide a finish on floors.

A wide range of other tools may come in handy as you progress—carpenter's dividers, line levels, glass cutters, vises, and awls. If you find them necessary, I would suggest a look at possible future needs. If you see any kind of a future need for a tool, buy the absolute best quality you can afford. If there is no estimated need coming up anytime, then get the tool in the middle price range. Never, under any circumstances, buy a bottom of the quality and price line tool and expect it to do the job even once.

Buy good tools and take care and you'll get a good job. Buy cheap tools and take care and you may get a good job, but you better not place any money on it. An expert workman can often get by with junk tools, but the amateur or novice is much better off with top quality.

Chapter 3

The Owner Built Log Cabin

Log cabins are becoming more popular now than ever before. The reasons are so varied as to defy definition. First, construction ease with modern tools is rather good, though some of the longer logs can cause more than a few difficulties when being lifted into place; hoists and block and tackles can be substituted for arm and leg power, though. Second, the log home, if properly built and sealed, is inexpensive in relation to conventional framing methods; this does not necessarily apply when a prefabricated log home is erected, though. Third, energy is saved because the thick log walls provide good insulation. Fourth, a log cabin is extremely attractive in a rustic setting, and often in other settings if carefully designed and built. Fifth, once the logs are cut, peeled, and dried, erection is quick. Sixth,...why go on.

Starting to build a log cabin is like starting to build any other home. You must select a site on the land you own. Next, you must either design, or have designed, a home that will provide the necessary space and facilities. Once those two jobs are finished, you can look toward the type of foundation you wish to build and move on from there.

Log cabins are suited to almost any sort of foundation you care to imagine, whether it is pier style, crawl space, concrete block, or poured. Most economical is the pier style, with piers placed about every 8 feet under the cabin and floor joists resting on those; piers can be constructed of native stone or concrete blocks. You can also use driven piles, but that requires equipment you may not wish to hire or not be able to get into your site. Piers must extend below frostline and rest on footings twice the width of the pier to prevent frost heave and toppling (Fig. 3-1).

Once all of this is decided, laid out, and ready to go, you must locate the trees for your log cabin. If you're located in a rural area where the trees have been allowed to grow back to suitable size, you're in luck. If not, a search is going to be needed. In some areas of the United States, that search will prove unsuccessful, and, if you desire a log cabin, your only recourse will be a prefabricated style. In most areas, though, some looking will demonstrate the practicality of building your own log cabin. Pine trees of suitable size and length

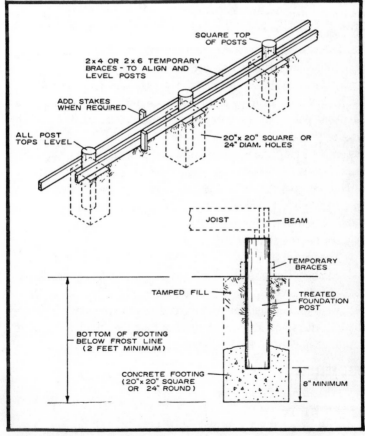

Fig. 3-1. Footings. As shown, footings should be below the frost line.

can usually be had for the payment of a modest stumpage fee (higher than the stumpage fee for firewood, of course, but still quite reasonable compared in any way to the cost of finished lumber). In fact, if you wish to avoid felling and moving trees to the site on your own, it is often possible to locate someone in most rural areas to do it for you. Those most likely to have the gear needed are people who cut pulp wood for a living, or people who cut and sell firewood. Full scale lumbermen are not likely to be interested in cutting a few dozen logs for you, but pulpwood cutters may, in a slack season, be willing to drop trees to order.

Once the trees are located, you'll need a way to move them, of course. Many farmers and almost all pulpwood cutters have the needed equipment, but you may have to spend a lot of time to get them to rent it to you. It is best, in most cases, to simply hire the equipment owner to move the wood, even if you have felled your own trees.

Selecting trees to fell for a log cabin is a bit of a job. Sizes are of exceptional importance, as are such things as overall length, straightness, and taper. In general, you're looking for trees, at least for the lower log courses in the cabin, of about the same size as a telephone pole, with about the same amount of taper. Length is a function of cabin size and of available transport; it is sometimes easier to section a cabin instead of trying to transport too many 40- or 50-foot logs). Straightness speaks for itself. If the logs are not fairly true, you'll have to do a lot fitting, shaving, and chinking to end up with plumb and level walls. While a certain amount of this work is to be expected, too much results in a really odd looking cabin that may not be safe to live in.

The type of wood used is of just as great importance as its shape and condition. Using some forms of oak is impossible, as durability in contact with anything more than air is poor. Most pines will serve very well, while locust or any of the cedars would be ideal. Unfortunately, cedars and locusts are seldom found in either the size or quantities needed. Look to the pines, preferably yellow.

TREE FELLING

While it might seem that your major chore in felling trees for a log cabin is to get the wood needed to build, your first consideration is one of safety. If a 1-foot thick pine drops on you, you won't be building anything.

Start by studying the tree. Things are simplified when cutting logs for a cabin since we're looking for straight trees. This cuts down on the chance of having a leaner kick back or fall the wrong way. But check the upper stories of the tree. See if there are obvious dead branches sitting on other limbs. These are called widowmakers for obvious reasons. Make sure the growth of branches is not so heavy on one side as to make felling in the direction needed difficult or impossible. Check for wind movement in the upper portion of the tree. Often when there is little wind at ground level, the tops of the trees will still be whipping around from winds up there. If such is the case, put off the felling for a time until the wind drops. Gusty wind has hurt more than one logger.

Check also for power lines and trees close by that might hang up your tree as it drops.

Now check the ground around the tree. Is the path chosen as an escape clear of brush and tangling vines or debris that might trip you up if a fast retreat is needed? If not, clear it. Now look to the area where your fuel and other equipment is sitting. Make sure it is well away from the drop zone. The same holds true for any vehicles in the area. I've only once seen someone drop a tree on their pickup truck, but that was enough grief for both of us—a 2-foot oak on the pickup bed, and a 4-mile walk to a main road (Fig. 3-2).

Too, any helpers or watchers should be well away from the drop zone. If two people are working at cutting down trees, keep them

Fig. 3-2. Locate an exit path before you start cutting. If necessary cut away all brush to insure a quick getaway. (Courtesy of Homelite.)

Fig. 3-3. Attention must be given to the distance any helper is from the intended direction of fall. (Courtesy of Homelite.)

well apart (Fig. 3-3). Each feller must be able to give full attention to his or her own tree to prevent the possibility of injury. Children should never be allowed unsupervised around a logging site.

Once all of this is taken care of, you can fuel the chainsaw, staying at least 25 feet from the spot where the saw will be started. Bring it over next to the tree to be felled before starting the saw.

If all else is safe, you can start your notch cut in the direction you wish the tree to fall. Make sure the center of the notch points exactly where the tree is to go unless adjustments to the fall are needed, as covered in a bit. Start the notch slant cut on the underside, with the straight cut to be on top. This is called an undercut or Humboldt notch and serves to save a bit of lumber, as well as making the needed end finishing cut only half a log wide, thus saving a bit of time, too.

As always, the backcut comes in about 2 inches above the top cut of the notch, which should be about 30 percent of the diameter of the tree deep. Leave at least 2 inches of the trunk uncut to serve as a hinge, and, if necessary, drive in a soft felling wedge (plastic, aluminum or wood), to force the tree over.

You may find some good trees on hillsides. Such trees pose problems of fall, of course, but these are moderately easy to handle by notching in the correct direction after making the checks covered already. But in many instances, such hillside trees will lean, and a standard notch, whether undercut or overcut will cause the stump to form what's known as a barber's chair. This ruins much timber, as it can split the trunk quite a long ways up, as well as being dangerous. A triple notch cures this problem. Make your first notch in the direction you wish the tree to fall. Now, come in from one adjacent side and make a notch about half the depth of the first notch. Do the same on the other side of the tree. These side notches must be as close to equal as possible and should never be more than half the depth of the main notch. They, like the main notch, can be either overcut or undercut. Now, bring the backcut in as usual (Fig. 3-4).

If you must move the fall of a tree out of its natural line, different measures are in order. The notch is started as usual, but the backcut is slanted in the direction you want the tree to fall. That is, the backcut not as deep in the direction of the desired fall than it is on the other side. If needed, felling wedges can be inserted in the backcut at the thin side (Fig. 3-5).

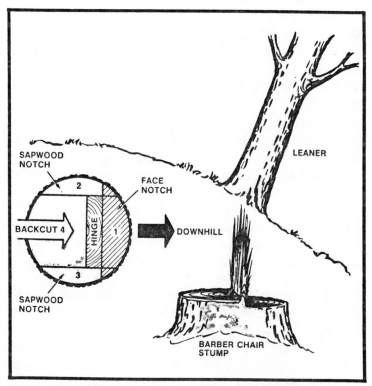

Fig. 3-4. When cutting leaners avoid splitting and barber chairs by making the face notch (1) as deep as is safe. Then make side notches (2 and 3) to cut through the sapwood before starting the back cut (4). (Courtesy of Homelite.)

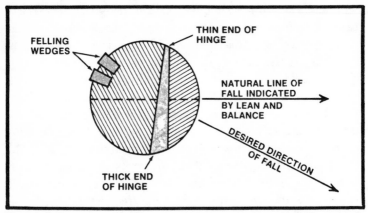

FELLING WEDGES

THIN END OF HINGE

NATURAL LINE OF FALL INDICATED BY LEAN AND BALANCE

DESIRED DIRECTION OF FALL

THICK END OF HINGE

Fig. 3-5. Felling a tree on a different line from the natural line of fall. (Courtesy of Homelite.)

LIMBING AND BUCKING DOWNED TREES

Once the tree is on the ground, your job is not over. Logs must be limbed and bucked into transportable lengths. Again, safety considerations are of greatest importance. When a log is being limbed, it is always best, when possible, to limb it from the side opposite. In other words, you stand on one side and cut on the other (Fig. 3-6).

Should the log fall on a hillside, do all limbing on the downhill side from a stance above the log. Too, any bucking cuts must be made from that uphill side (Fig. 3-7). If this isn't done, sooner or later a log will roll on you, which at best is an unpleasant situation as it can pin you, and at worst can cause severe injury.

Bucking stresses and obstructions on the ground can add to problems, as can saplings pinned by the fall of your tree. Your best bet is to leave a few supporting limbs so that stresses are easy to judge, and finish limbing after the log has been bucked to length.

A log supported at both ends, as in Fig. 3-8, will need two cuts to keep from splitting the log or trapping the saw's guide bar. The first cut, of about a third the tree's diameter, is made from the top. The second cut comes up from underneath. If the end of the log is unsupported, the first cut, once more about a third of the log's diameter, is made from underneath, and the rest of the cut comes down from the top (Fig. 3-9).

It is in making undercuts that obstructions become a problem. The ground may be littered with rocks, or other debris which can

LEAVE SOME SUPPORTING BRANCHES UNCUT. AFTER YOU HAVE BUCKED OFF THE LOG SECTIONS YOU CAN CUT OFF THESE LAST FEW LIMBS.

Fig. 3-6. As often as possible when limbing, stand on the opposite side of the trunk from the limbs you are cutting. (Courtesy of Homelite.)

USE WEDGE TO HOLD CUT OPEN

Fig. 3-7. Stand on the up hill side when cutting because the log may roll. Also keep your feet and body clear of the log section which may drop off or settle when cut. (Courtesy of Homelite.)

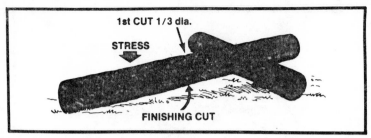

Fig. 3-8. A stressed log supported at both ends. Make two cuts as shown to avoid pinching the guide bar. (Courtesy of Homelite.)

rapidly ruin a chain. In such cases, you'll need to make boring cuts. Follow the steps shown in Fig. 3-10 and results will be good. Keep in mind that, as crazy as it seems, the chances of kickback are lessened if you have the throttle wide open before touching the nose of the bar to the log for a boring cut.

Spring poles (Fig. 3-11), present a different kind of problem. These saplings, if cut or released rapidly, can spring back and slap you silly or break bones. Cut the tree well away from any such spring pole and use a lever to maneuver the bucked log off the spring pole, making sure you're out of range of any whip.

LOG STRIPPING

There is a difference in aesthetic values concerning logs used in cabins, stripped or unstripped. The stripped log is favored for a great many applications for many reasons. First, after a time unstripped logs tend to harbor a rather large fleet of insects. Too, unstripped logs hold dust and lint making housecleaning more of a chore. Finally, logs that are unstripped can split or even rot as they don't dry evenly.

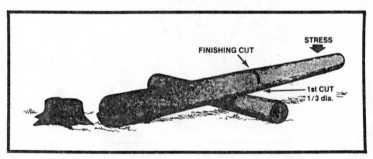

Fig. 3-9. Log supported at only one end. Make the cuts shown and keep your toes clear. (Courtesy of Homelite.)

OBSTRUCTION

1   ANGLE THE BAR AND CUT INTO
    LOG AS IN +2.

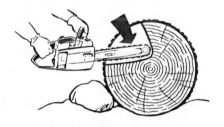

2   GRADUALLY MAKE THE BAR
    COME LEVEL

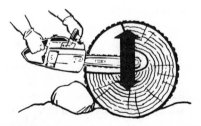

3   BORE STRAIGHT INTO THE LOG.
    THEN CUT UPWARD OR DOWNWARD
    AS REQUIRED.

Fig. 3-10. Step-by-step instructions for cutting a log on the ground located near rocks. Chainsaws are made for cutting wood, not rocks. (Courtesy of Homelite.)

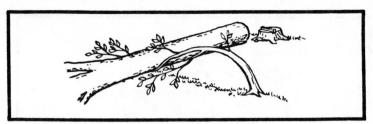

Fig. 3-11. Use caution when small saplings are caught under fell trees. You might get surprised. (Courtesy of Homelite.)

For those who prefer the unstripped logs, even with their disadvantages, at least partial stripping is a good idea. Select the log surfaces that will mate with other surfaces in the cabin, and peel the log along those lines. This not only prevents rot and checking and splitting problems, but will make the mating of logs easier, especially if you wish to groove the logs for a spline before fitting them (Fig. 3-12).

For those who don't want any of the hassles associated with unstripped logs, complete stripping is needed. Logs are most easily stripped by using a tool called a log stripping spud. To date, I have never seen a log spud in any hardware or building supply store, store, so your only recourse is to make one yourself.

Luckily, the job is not difficult, requiring only a single modification in a simple tool available in every hardware store in the United States and Canada. Pick up a gardening hoe, the type with a square blade, and apply heat right at the neck with a propane torch. Using a pair of pliers, bend the blade of the hoe until it is at a point just about 5 degrees past being on a straight line with the handle. You now own a bark peeling spud with a handle long enough to make the chore reasonably easy. You are also in a position to find out why many people leave logs unstripped; it's still a lot of work.

SEASONING THE LOGS

Building your own log cabin causes you to have to handle quite a few jobs that can be bypassed if prefabricated cabins are used. Seasoning the logs is one of those. Unseasoned wood will cause problems as it pulls away from chinking, window and door frames, moldings around floors and ceilings, and other spots. Wood shrinkage in the first year is fairly large. As Fig. 3-13 from the California Redwood Association shows, shortleaf pine has an overall shrinkage of 191 percent from green to oven dry, with an across the grain or tengential shrinkage of 205 percent. Thus some form of curing is needed, especially if you don't wish to have to virtually rebuild the cabin the second year of occupancy.

Since few kiln drying ovens of a size to handle logs exist for our possible use, and such use would add to expense anyway, our best bet is simple air drying which can drop moisture content of the wood down to about 20 percent. Kiln drying usually gets it down to 12 percent.

This takes time, quite a lot of it, as well as proper stacking techniques. First, expect to let completely peeled logs sit no less than 9 months, with a preference for a full year, before expecting them to be properly dried for building use. If the logs are only partially peeled, they must sit for a full year to 15 months before use.

But just flopping the logs on the ground is not practical. If ground drying is tried, many of the logs will rot and none will approach the proper drying level in the time specified. An open stack is needed.

OPEN STACKING

Start your open stack by locating several junk logs, wood you have no intention of using for anything. Make a line of these junk logs

Fig. 3-12. Ripping. Place the log to be ripped on two or more supports, holding it firmly in place with nail, end cradles, etc. For precision place a guide board beside the timber being ripped and make horizontal cuts using the guide board to support the saw as the blade progresses through the wood. Drive wedges in the kerf to prevent pinching. With a guide board it is possible to rip rough dimensional lumber for cabin flooring, siding, and other purposes. When ripping vertically be careful of your feet. (Courtesy of Omark Industries.)

on the ground, providing enough support for the first row of good logs so that no part of the good wood comes within a couple of inches of the ground.

Now, take the first row of good logs and lay it over the ground layer, leaving a log's diameter between each log laid out. The second row is done in the same way, but laid across that first row of good logs. The process continues on up as high as you need to go, or until this arrangement becomes so precarious you must start another pile.

The open spaces are essential so that air can pass between the logs and draw off moisture. If not enough space is left, the drying process will be retarded badly, so be as generous as your available space allows.

Over the top of each pile you should draw a tarp or plastic cover to keep snow and rain out. The tarp can be tied or weighted at the corners to prevent its blowing away in high winds.

Open air curing processes such as this are best started in the spring when breezes can be expected and left to extend right on up till the following spring. They also work best if you are able to locate a small knoll or hill to place the stacks, especially if the knoll is unshielded from prevailing winds.

Still, instead of dropping trees during the winter, it is usually best to lay them down in the fall, when the heat of the summer is past and the bitter breezes have yet to start. Too, sap levels are getting lower about then, so drying may be more rapid. Old timers say that if you leave unlimbed trees on the ground for several weeks that the leaves or needles will serve to transport a great deal of the moisture out of them with nothing else required. I have tried this technique for firewood when I've run out of dry wood, but never for building materials; it seems to work for firewood. This could help shorten curing time, though I wouldn't really want to have to depend on it.

Testing the logs for proper seasoning may seem difficult without a lot of fancy equipment, but about all you really have to have is an extra hickory handle for a sledge or axe, a baseball bat, or any other chunk of wood that is reasonably well dried.

Take your dry wood and give a log a sharp rap a foot or two back from both the butt and the tip. If you get a dull thump, then the wood needs more time before it will be as ready to use. If you get a ringing sort of sound, then your logs are about ready to go into your log cabin.

Commercial and botanical name of species	Trees tested	Specific gravity, oven-dry, based on volume when green	Weight per cubic foot		Shrinkage from green to oven-dry condition based on dimensions when green		
			Green	At 12 percent moisture content	Radial	Tangential	Volumetric (composite value)
1	2	3	4	5	6	7	8
	Number		*Pounds*	*Pounds*	*Percent*	*Percent*	*Percent*
Redwood (Sequoia sempervirens)	16	0.39	52	28	100	100	100
Cedar, Port Orford (Chamaecyparis lawsoniana)	14	.40	36	29	192	172	158
Cedar, eastern red (Juniperus virginiana)	5	.44	37	33	129	118	116
Cedar, western red (Thuja plicata)	15	.31	27	23	100	125	113
Cedar, northern white (Thuja occidentalis)	5	.29	28	22	88	118	103
Cypress, southern (Taxodium distichum)	26	.42	50	32	158	155	155
Douglas fir (Pseudotsuga menzesii) (Coast type)	34	.45	38	34	208	195	181
Douglas fir (Pseudotsuga menzesii) (Rocky Mountain type)	10	.40	35	30	150	155	154
Fir, lowland white (Abies grandis)	9	.37	44	28	133	180	157
Fir, noble (Abies nobilis)	9	.35	30	26	188	208	188
Fir, silver (Abies amabilis)	6	.35	36	27	188	250	212
Fir, white (Abies concolor)	20	.35	47	26	133	175	142
Firs, white (Average of four species)	45	.38	41	26	158	198	164
Hemlock, western (Tsuga heterophylla)	18	.38	41	29	179	198	179
Pine, loblolly (Pinus taeda)	10	.50	54	38	229	188	190
Pine, longleaf (Pinus palustris)	34	.55	50	41	221	188	185
Pine, northern white (Pinus strobus)	18	.34	36	25	96	150	124
Pine, shortleaf (Pinus echinata)	12	.49	51	38	212	205	191
Pine, sugar (Pinus lambertiana)	9	.35	51	25	121	140	118
Pine, western white (Pinus monticola)	14	.36	35	27	171	185	176
Pine, ponderosa (Pinus ponderosa)	31	.38	45	28	162	158	145
Spruce, Sitka (Picea sitchensis)	25	.37	33	28	179	188	173

Fig. 3-13. Average comparative properties of clear redwood compared with a number of other species. (Courtesy of California Redwood Association.)

Of course, this seasoning process may sound as if it wastes a great deal of time, but assuming you plan the building reasonably well, it doesn't waste quite as much as you would think. Assume your first felling, limbing, and bucking chores are taken care of late in the fall of one year. With everything stacked and curing, you can wander on home and await the coming of spring. When spring arrives, you can dig holes for the foundation, run temporary wiring lines to the site, and get the well in; that's assuming you plan to have a cabin with electricity and running water. Too, the winter slack time is excellent for going over your plans and making detail changes. Now, wait out the hot summer and start building in the fall.

ERECTING THE CABIN

When the foundation is ready (see the chapter on foundations for all types of vacation homes), the base logs are bored for the sill anchor bolts, then set in place. It is at this time that two techniques become necessary for proper construction.

First, logs will fit one on another a great deal better, with less need for chinking and filling, if the matching surfaces are plane. Second, corner notching is essential to any kind of cabin building.

To start, and to keep ahead of the log raising, plan the use of logs as you go along, but about three or four logs in advance of the one going into the wall. Lay the logs next to each other, as tightly as possible; then secure them to each other with devices known as log dogs. These are tools that expand and have bent points that drive a short distance into the logs to hold them tight. Take your chainsaw and run it between the logs, serving to match the surfaces where the cut is made. This process may need to be repeated several times before a flat surface is obtained on logs that have a fair number of knots and branches, or on logs that are otherwise not as straight as you might wish. Fit is improved at least 100 percent with this method, though purists may find it undesirable.

When the logs are laid up, take some glass wool and place a strip about 1 inch thick along the bottom log's flat top, and set the top log on that. As simply as that, you have just about totally eliminated the need for indoor chinking, cut drafts almost totally, and made sure your cabin will be snug and weathertight for many years; the glass wool used in insulation is a permanent, nonrotting material.

Notching the corners is a different skill, one that is essential, but that requires a little time and care to get right while not really being hard to learn. When the first two sill logs (the ones next to the foundation) are laid, you'll find you need to notch the end sill logs to fit over them. This method leaves those end sill logs about half a log higher than you have set the side sills. This is the reason that foundations for log cabins need the end foundation raised half a log's height along most of its length. By the way, wood rot and termite infestation will be cut considerably if you use formed sheet metal shields, as well as a layer of glass wool, between the sill logs and the top of the foundation. This will also seal out many floor drafts.

Using a carpenter's divider, after placing the logs for the end sills across the side sill logs, set the bottom point of the dividers about halfway down the side sill log. The top pointer of the dividers should then rest just at the start of the log resting at right angles across this one. Move the dividers up the curve of the bottom log, keeping pressure on the top arm of the dividers. This will provide you with your notch marking for the top log.

This notch marking procedure will be carried out at each and every notch to be made to allow for any irregularities in individual logs. Called a half-notch, this is about the most popular style for log cabins built by hand.

The A-notch or inverted-V notch requires a little more work but can be made in advance. In this case, both bottom and top logs have a part of the notch. The bottom log is marked for the width of the log to lie on top of it; then the log is cut to a depth of several inches. The combined notch depth, bottom and top log, should equal half the depth of the top log. The notch should be cut with a peak. The top log is marked and notched to fit that peak.

The curved half-notch is most easily made if the center of the notch is cut down with the chainsaw, and the rest is either chiseled or cut out with a small axe or hatchet.

While log walls will often stand alone, the best security is obtained by using spikes, driven with a 5-pound maul, to secure one log to another. If the logs are too thick for you to drive spikes through them, you may need to take a brace and bit and bore holes for dowels. Or bore holes part way through, then drive spikes using a metal drive pin to set the spikes into the bored hole. Spikes should be driven in each log, starting about 2 feet from the corners, moving along every 3 or 4 feet. This not only makes the logs more secure but helps to hold the log surfaces together, crushing the glass wool, and preventing drafts.

Glass wool, by the way, should be used in the notches just as it is along the walls, so that drafts can't blow in from the corners of the cabin.

Because of variations in log size, only one side of the log wall should be lined up and leveled. In almost every case, you'll be better served by making this the interior side of the wall, simply letting the exterior take on a rather rough and ready shaping. Use a plumb 2 by 4 to even up the inside of the wall, keeping a check on it until you're able to use toenailing to tack it to about the fifth or sixth course of logs.

There are two ways to arrange for windows and doors in log cabins. You can build the thing as a solid box, then make your cutouts, or you can frame out, rough frame, the window and door openings, and use short or trimmed lengths of logs to fill in the gaps. Generally, the solid box is the easiest way to go but a lot depends on the log lengths you are able to obtain.

A compromise closed box style is probably the best overall, as this allows setting in the door or a window, and prevents the need for ladders reaching over the walls as building progresses. Because you need to keep a rather constant check on the inside wall leveling, with no door cut you'll be clambering over the wall quite often, about every second log course, during erection. This is no real problem, but with several people working fairly hard, those log courses tend to go up rather quickly.

Decide, if it's not shown on your plans, where the door opening must be. Then select the 2 by 6s or 8s for the rough framing. Box these in the correct size, flatten the top of the sill log to the correct height, and spike in place. Use 45-degree angle corner bracing to keep the door's rough cutout frame plumb and level, along with a 1 by 6 or two running back to the interior of the cabin. Once the log courses are up to the 4-foot or 4½-foot level, and each course is spiked to the door frame, you can remove the bracing after checking for plumb and level, of course.

If the joists for the floor aren't in, you may have to brace the plumb braces to the interior (the 1 by 6s). Simply drive a stake into the ground at the base of the brace.

While the every 3-foot or 4-foot spiking isn't essential, for those of you who wish the extra security it provides, make sure you use a piece of carpenter's chalk to mark the site of each spike. If this isn't done, no matter how good you feel your memory is, you are certain to smack one of these spikes with the chainsaw chain when making window cutouts. A small mark is all that's needed, and these will weather away in a few weeks.

Log walls can be laid up to fairly good heights, but once the second story is started, some changes in structure are needed to support the floor joists; the top course of logs on the first story must be inlet to accept the ends of the joists for that second floor. A notch or inlet the width of the joist and several inches deep will be sufficient; depth will depend on the size of the wall logs, the width of the cabin, and the number of supporting walls, which must be at least partially erected before the second story log courses are started.

When rafters are to be put in place, more inletting is needed. This is a different kind, cut to match the bird's mouth on the rafter, or cut to match the end angle of the rafter if no bird's mouth is used (see Chapter 5 on roofing for the details of gable roof rafter design).

Once the roof is on, you've arrived at the time for cutting out the window openings. The first step is to nail 1 by 6s to the exterior face of the log wall, with the inside of those boards providing the outline of the window's rough opening. If the rough opening corresponds to an exact number of log courses, the job is simplified. If not, you'll make your cuts as shown in Fig. 3-14, then have to chisel away a portion of the top or bottom log to allow the window to fit with ease.

The exterior boards shown are left in place until the rough framing boards are nailed to the log ends. In all cases where doors or windows are installed, you must make sure that the rough opening is

Fig. 3-14. The simplest way to make cabin windows and doors is to disregard them until the walls are up, then mark off the areas where you want the openings. Bore through the top log and cut down to the desired depth. A flat sill and threshold can be achieved with a horizontal rip cut. (Courtesy of Omark Industries.)

plumb and square, or the doors and windows will, sooner rather than later, stick badly on opening and closing. I would recommend, too, that the idea of running a strip of glass wool about 2 inches thick and 2 or 3 inches wide, be continued here as it was between log courses and at the notches. Anything that can be done to stop drafts will make any home, vacation or otherwise, more comfortable and cheaper to own in these energy faltering days.

While it is possible to build one's own doors and windows, the extra steps and the complexities of construction can be a real pain for the amateur builder. My recommendation is that you make a quick check of lumberyards and building supply houses to get the cost of good quality windows, such as R.O.W., Andersen, or Marvin, with either double or triple glazing. Available in a very wide variety of styles, these prebuilt and ready to install windows need only some careful nailing to work properly for as long as most of us can expect to have to worry about them. They are also available unfinished, primed, and completely finished. Prices are rather high as compared to building one's own, but the savings in time and effort should more than make up for that.

By the way, people building vacation homes in the country, where heavy snow is likely, and who expect to spend at least a part of a winter in their cabins, should make absolutely certain that any doors installed open inwards. Should you be vacationing it up when a blizzard strikes, with a door that opens only to the outside, you could find yourself trapped until help comes. A door that opens inwards, with a shovel placed inside, is some assurance that if the worst arrives you can at least dig yourself out and see how you stand.

Log course ends can be left uneven for a total rustic look, axe trimmed for even more rustic look, or evened up with a chainsaw to make the exterior a bit neater looking. For those who wish to even things up, the job is reasonably simple. Get as straight a 1 by 4 as possible. Plumb it along the line you wish to trim and tack it to the corner. Now simply cut down the entire series of log course ends with your chainsaw.

A lot of nonsense goes on about the true log cabin, with interior joists made from adzed logs, set into the walls and so on, as well as rafters made in the same manner. More practical is the use of modern lumber products for such chores. The time of erection is cut phenomenally, and the job is eased quite a bit. No one who has never used an adze or broad axe really has any idea how much effort went into the older homes in this country; back in the days when labor was so cheap one farmhand spent the entire winter cutting firewood. Those old beams in many barns and homes are not pine, soft and easily workable, but most often chestnut or oak.

Floor joists for the first floor are first started with nailers along the sill logs. You may or may not need the bracing from extra piers or parts of the foundation, depending on the width of your cabin. In most cases, it will provide a much stronger floor.

If you really wish, you can go ahead with the so-called traditional insets of logs to use as joists. But don't expect the cabin to be up and ready in a single season if you do, as this sort of work, even with modern tools, requires a lot of handwork with chisels, broadaxe, and adzes if a good floor is to be laid on top. Actually, though, with the exception of the inlets, the logs can be flattened on one side simply by ripping along with a chainsaw. This method does cut the work, though it does not give the traditional look. It will be covered anyway once the floor is installed.

For second-floor joists, you may wish to do the work involved, as this could be attractive if the ceiling is left unfinished downstairs. In most cases, though, I would simply go about one size over on my joists, then use either a broadaxe or an adze to trim them down to give the effect of hand-hewn beams. This method is a lot simpler, quicker, and just as attractive. Local sawmills will be more than glad to supply as much rough-cut (unplaned) lumber as you need for this sort of work. Often you can supply the logs to the sawmill to cut costs a fair amount.

CHINKING

Chinking, even with glass wool laid between log courses, is a good idea. For best results, use a modern mortar made up heavy enough so that it will not sag when forced into the gaps between logs. If you don't wish to use mortar, then oakum is about the best bet for chinking. Go to a boatyard and pick this up, as it is a tarred hemp used for caulking wooden boats and ships.

Finishing the exterior of the log cabin is an individual decision. You can apply a stain, paint, or sealants. Or you can simply let it weather (not a good idea for more than 2 or 3 years). My suggestion would be a clear sealer/preservative that is listed as having at least 5 years durability, so that you won't have to spend a part of every or every other year refinishing.

Chapter 4
Conventional Framing Methods

While the log cabin expands in popularity as the second home or vacation home market grows, the conventionally framed home is still often the simplest to build, as logs are not always easy to locate in the sizes and types of wood needed. Too, a lot of people simply prefer the conventional style home, whether it is basic rectangle or a somewhat fancier A-frame, with or without a prow.

Most people today have at least a bare idea of how to work with 2 by 4s, 2 by 8s, and the other chunks of wood that form a conventional house. Too, there are many hangers and other devices that make nailing a simple matter, even for those among us who have a great deal of difficulty in not mashing our thumbs. Some companies put out nailing braces that mean we don't have to do even the simplest toenailing job at the base of wall studs. Though this adds minimally to the overall cost of a home, the savings in time and split wood should more than cover that.

On top of all this, modern framing styles allow us to hide water pipes, heat ducting, wiring, and insulation inside the house walls. In fact, with minor changes, it is possible to reach the optimum insulation values by switching construction from the older 2 by 4 framing to 2 by 6s. While the 2 by 4s are set on 16-inch centers, the larger studs can be moved out to 2 feet (24-inch centers), cutting down on the cost increase. Windows and doors are now available in sizes to fit these thicker walls, so it becomes a simple matter of nailing things up.

Design variations in frame homes are so great as to allow us to choose just about any style home we might wish to live in. Erection is relatively simple, and if problems do crop up experts are easy to locate in any area.

Exterior and interior finishes run a gamut that starts with the simplest board siding, moves through fancier boards, into aluminum, vinyl, and plywood sidings and slips from there into brick and stone veneers.

Too, there must be a million house designs available for the various intended uses. Almost every home magazine out on the newsstand offers floor plans, with builder's plans available at reasonable cost. These plans can be used as is, or easily adapted to your family's needs by a local architect in a few hours time. The need for having an architect in attendance is cut a lot.

If you can afford the cost, I would recommend that you have an architect design and oversee the building of your vacation home. But the cost is not low, so unless you're up in the income range where you can hire a contractor to build your house, you'll likely have to go without. If you do hire a contractor to build a home, my feeling is that an architect is even more essential to the process.

The wood frame house starts with the accurate location of the site for the home. General siting considerations apply as strongly here as anywhere else, as do the decisions for depth of excavation—frostline, the desire or need for a basement, etc.— type of foundation, and so on.

LOCATING HOUSE CORNERS

A check of local codes, if any, will assure you that you are not building too close to a road, someone else's home, or some other obstruction. After that, you can locate the first corner of your vacation home.

Drive a small stake at this point, then measure the distance along the plot to your next corner and drive another stake. This process is repeated for all four corners, with as great accuracy as possible in distance measurement. The stakes indicate the outside edge of the foundation walls. About 4 to 4½ feet outside the edge of these stakes, you'll set up stakes of greater size, three per corner, connected by batter boards. The first job, though, is to square the corners. Simply laying them out is not quite enough.

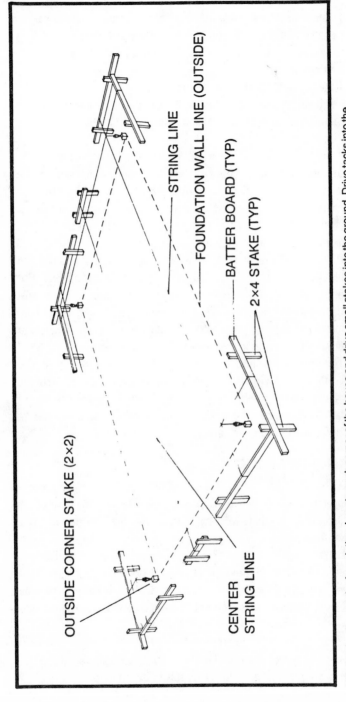

OUTSIDE CORNER STAKE (2×2)

CENTER STRING LINE

STRING LINE

FOUNDATION WALL LINE (OUTSIDE)

BATTER BOARD (TYP)

2×4 STAKE (TYP)

Fig. 4-1. Laying out the foundation. Locate each corner of the house and drive small stakes into the ground. Drive tacks into the tops of these stakes to indicate the outside line of the foundation wall (not footings). Check the squareness of the house by measuring the diagonals, corner to corner, to see that they are equal. Use the 3-4-5 triangle method to determine if the diagonals are correct. (Courtesy of American Plywood Association.)

Using your mason's cord, run a length down one wall-to-be at least a dozen feet long, and place it on another small stake driven at that point; drive shingling nails in the top of the stakes to hold the cord. Now move out on the adjacent line, (at 90 degrees to the first laid out line, and lay out 16 feet of cord, driving another stake with a nail in its top. With measurements of 12 and 16 feet, you need only measure the diagonal to determine whether the corner is square. If it is, your diagonal will measure 20 feet. You can use other lengths, as shown in Fig. 4-1, but the longer lengths provide greater accuracy. Do this for each corner, moving the stakes until each and every diagonal is at the exact measurement. This may require slight relocations of your first corner stakes.

These dimensions, 12, 16, and 20 feet, are simply an expansion of a basic 3-4-5 triangle. Remember high school geometry? All of the legs of this 3-4-5 triangle have been multiplied by a factor of four. You can use any multiple of the 3-4-5 triangle in your calculations.

Now the batter boards are installed, using 2 by 4s and 1 by 6s. Set up your outside foundation wall lines as shown in Fig. 4-1. Start by holding the line so that it falls directly over the stake, using a plumb bob to make certain of your alignment (Fig. 4-2). Cut a saw kerf or drive a small nail into the batter board, and pull the line taut. This is done on every batter board. The lines will cross directly over

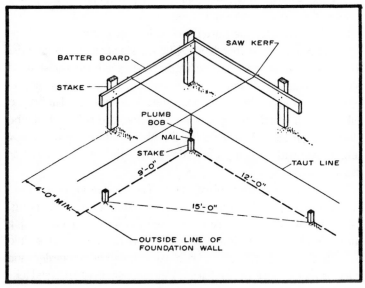

Fig. 4-2. Using a plumb bob to check alignment.

the stakes showing the outside corners of the foundation; this must be carefully checked.

If your floor plan requires something other than a rectangle, such as an L-shape or U-shape, then just divide the plan into rectangles of the correct size.

No matter what kind of underpinning your house will have, the excavations for piers, crawl space or full basement will now proceed and the stakes will disappear in the digging. Too, the foundation should be extended so that it is above the proposed finished grade so that the frame of the vacation home does not contact the ground. Ground contact makes termite infestation a problem and can cause rapid rot of the wood around sills. Provide for at least 8 inches of clearance.

If a crawl space or piers are to be used, then make sure there's plenty of room to actually crawl around under the house. You'll want to make some checks every so often so that you can keep up with any changes in the underside of your home; such changes could include floor drafts, termites, etc. The minimum clearance here is probably 2 feet, though 3 feet would be more comfortable.

Excavating for piers is simple, and if the frost line in your area is not too deep and the soil not too compacted or rocky, it can be done most easily by hand. Full excavations are a different story entirely.

Floor framing in a house consists of several parts: the posts, beams, sills, joists, and subflooring.

Sills and header joists are the outside edge portions of the floor system resting on the foundation. The sill lies flat and is held to the foundation with anchor bolts, while the joists and header joist stand on edge, spanning the foundation. Anchor bolts, by the way, should be not farther apart than 8 feet on center. A sealer is used under the sill, between it and the top of the foundation; the sealer should be glass wool at least 2 inches thick and should sit on top of a metal termite cap with the edges bent down over the foundation wall or piers.

Sills are, of course, placed first. The header joists are then placed on the sills where the other joists will butt up to them (Fig. 4-3). The two end joists are then nailed to the header joist, using three 16d (16 penny) nails at each end. Where the house span is wide enough, the joists will come in two parts, meeting at a girder, and must be joined there with at least a 4-inch minimum overlap and four 16d nails used to hold them.

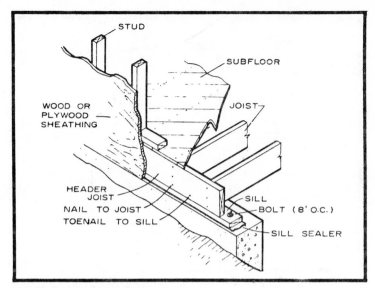

Fig. 4-3. Platform construction.

If the house has bearing partition walls, then the joists under these must be doubled for the greatest strength.

STAIR CUTOUTS

Floor openings present weak points in any floor framing system, so that reinforcement is essential. Joists and headers around the opening must be doubled, and no header designed to carry beam loadings may be over 10 feet long. The best practice, too, is to make sure that all stairwell openings are arranged so that the longest part of the opening runs parallel to the joists. Otherwise, that 10-foot length limit must apply, and tripled joists and headers are needed as well as some other forms of support (Fig. 4-4).

Naturally stair openings will not be the only openings in forming up a house. There will be openings needed in floors and roofs for such things as vent pipes (if larger than normal), chimneys, and so on. These too must be framed out much as stairs are framed out with doubled headers and joists, or as in the case of roofs, doubled headers and rafters.

SUBFLOORING

Once the joists are in and the floor openings framed out, you'll find a need for covering the floor in order to frame the walls and move

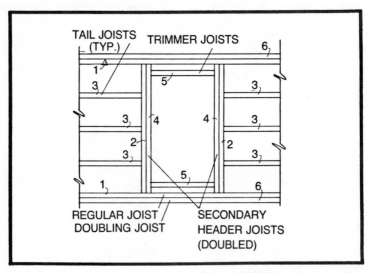

Fig. 4-4. Construction of floor openings. Circled numbers indicate order of placement. (Courtesy of American Plywood Association.)

on up the sides of the house. Subflooring of one kind or another takes care of this job. There are now many ways to subfloor a house, but by far the most used today is plywood subflooring. This is my recommendation for two basic reasons. First, it simplifies the entire job. Second, the cost between plywood and board subflooring is not all that great. Too, the great variation in plywood thicknesses allows you to space joists differently for differing house styles and construction styles with little or no effect on overall floor strength.

In most applications, the American Plywood Association recommends C-D interior grade plywood, with the C or smoother side placed to receive the finish flooring. For 16-inch on center construction, use 32/16 graded C-D; the 32 means that this is the allowable spacing on roofs, while the 16 is for floors. If you don't expect to get the house under cover rapidly, then you'll have to use C-D exterior to prevent delamination; this adds slightly to cost, but is well worth it. If your joists are 24 inches on center, you'll need to use plywood with a 24 in the second spec, usually 48/24.

Subflooring is started at the corner of the house where you started putting in the joists. Check with a tape measure, and by making a rough drawing, to see how the panels are going to lay out as you go along. This can not only save time in the long run, but can cut down heavily on wasted material. Once this is done, measure care fully and pop a chalk line across the entire length of the floor area exactly 4 feet in from the outside edge of the header.

That first row starts with a full 4 by 8 sheet of plywood set flush with the outside edge of the joist, using the chalk mark as an alignment guide. To allow for expansion and contraction, leave a space of about 1/16 inch between sheet ends. The end of the last panel is cut flush with the header if it doesn't fit exactly. Should the last panel be too short, you'll need to nail in a scab of 2 by 4 on the inside of the header joist and use a filler. This technique will come in handy, too, where sheet ends fall short of joists (Fig. 4-5).

The next row is staggered. Cut the first panel in half, 4 by 4 feet. The third row starts with a full panel, and the staggering continues until the entire floor area is covered. Panels laid in the second and succeeding rows must have twice the clearance as allowed for expansion at the ends, that is ⅛ inch.

Once the subflooring is in, you're ready to get on with the wall framing.

WALL FRAMING

Wall framing includes the erection of studs and the placing of the top and bottom plates forming the internal part of both exterior and interior walls. Too, this includes the rough framing for windows and doors. Where totally conventional 16-inch on center construction is

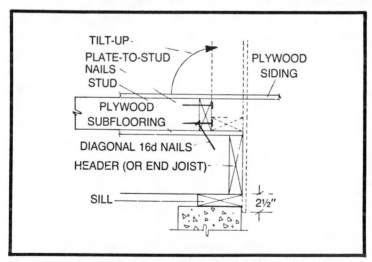

Fig. 4-5. Adding a scab to a floor joist to give support to panel subflooring. (Courtesy of American Plywood Association.)

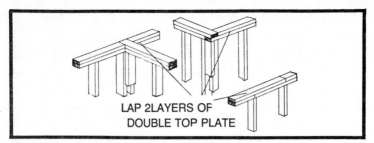

LAP 2 LAYERS OF
DOUBLE TOP PLATE

Fig. 4-6. Special framing methods used where walls intersect. (Courtesy of American Plywood Association.)

used, the studs and top and bottom plates will be 2 by 4s. The door and window headers may be 2 by 6s, 2 by 8s, or a couple of 2 by 4s nailed together. For more modern framing, the studs, top and bottom plates, and all headers should be 2 by 6s, which allows a 5½-inch insulation depth for energy conservation.

For the type of framing we're covering here, platform, the entire length of each wall framing section may be constructed directly on the subfloor, then tilted into place. Exterior and interior wall layout is marked on the subfloor in advance of framing. First, after the layout, temporarily, nail the bottom plates in place in the proper position. Start with the exterior wall bottom plates, and go from there to the interior wall plates. This is done in order to locate specific areas where walls intersect, for these are points where special framing methods will be needed (Fig. 4-6).

Mark the locations of all major openings in the walls, too, while the bottom plates are in place. After that, the job of framing will be considerably simplified if you also lay out lines for all studs; check which type of on center distance, 16 or 24 inches, you are using. Start measuring at one exterior corner, marking both sides of the stud location as you go. Don't be fooled by nominal sizes; 2 by 4 and 2 by 6 lumber is not that size. Measure your own first to get exact sizes. Mark the locations of extra studs to be installed at door openings and wall intersections.

At this time, you can remove the bottom plates. Use them as marking devices for a second set of plates. This set of plates, when cut, will serve as the bottom of the doubled top plates.

CUTTING WALL STUDS

Wall studs can either be bought as precuts, or can be cut to height using a single stud as a pattern. First, add at least 1 inch to the overall desired ceiling height to make up for finished flooring and ceiling material. To get an exact figure here, you'll want to measure the materials you plan to use for these jobs. Now knock off 4½ inches for the height of the three plates used. Lay this measurement out on your single stud, then cut.

Check the height again to make sure all is accurate; then count the number of these full size studs you'll need. Go ahead and use the pattern stud to mark them and cut.

This procedure, with careful measuring, marking, and cutting, insures a uniform stud height, which makes wall assembly a lot easier. Those ¼-inch variations add up and can cause many problems later on, so use as much care as possible.

Now check for size of jack studs, the shorter studs needed under window openings, over door openings, etc. Cut these to size, using one for a pattern when more than one stud is to be the same length.

ASSEMBLING THE WALLS

The longest exterior walls should be assembled first. Start by nailing on the bottom plate to the two end studs, then frame in from one end, checking on center distances, window placements, and door placement carefully as you go along.

Once the first wall assembly is framed, it is tilted into place. The bottom plate has now been nailed to the studs, as has the bottom of the top plate. Rough window openings are framed out as are door openings. All intersections are framed and ready for nailing to the next (Fig. 4-7).

The walls are braced using 1 by 6s after 16d nails are used to nail the bottom plate to the header joists (Fig. 4-8). After that, the top layer of the top plate is nailed in place. This step can be put off for a bit if single layer sliding is contemplated, but in most cases the tilt-up is completed before the siding is installed. Too, you can either tilt each section into place and brace it as it is made, or you can assemble several such sections and tilt them up at the same time, cutting down on the number of braces you'll need to use.

The interior walls are done in a similar manner.

Walls to be tilted up are limited in size by the number of workers on site. If only a couple of average size persons are to be around, then you should limit wall size to no more than 24 feet. If half a dozen

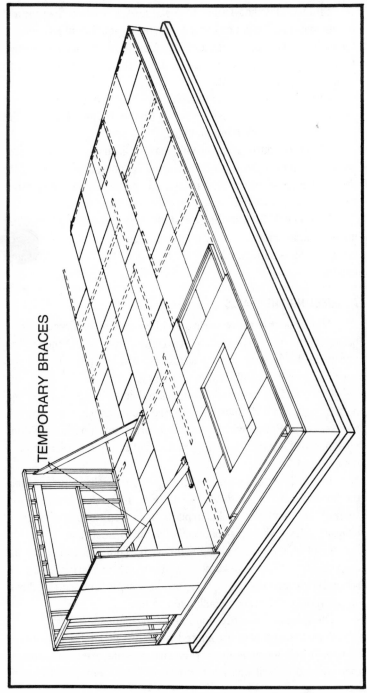

TEMPORARY BRACES

Fig. 4-7. Temporary braces used to hold walls after tilting them into place. (Courtesy of American Plywood Association.)

weightlifters are included in your crew, then you can use just about any wall size you wish.

WALL SYSTEMS

Probably the simplest and cheapest of wall construction types for frame houses is the American Plywood Association single wall system. As its name implies, this system requires nothing more than the installation of one of many kinds of top quality plywood panel siding (Fig. 4-9). It requires no diagonal bracing of the wall, covers quickly, and comes in lengths to fit most wall heights: 8, 9, and 10 feet long by 4 feet wide, with thicknesses ranging from ⅜ to ¾ inch, dependng on type and style. In most cases, the panels are installed vertically though for those who prefer a particular style carried horizontally, that too is easily done. Panels have the allowable on center distances for their design and thickness stamped on the back.

The APA recommends that you check your house plans carefully to ensure the panel thickness is the correct one. Plans that specify for instance, ⅜-inch thick paneling willl also specify windows to fit the wall thickness. Using ¾-inch paneling may seem like a good idea to increase strength, but can cause all kinds of foulups around windows, doors, and exterior molding pieces.

Use building paper where joints are not shiplapped or covered with battens.

Panel installation starts in the same spot as did your framing: the end of one of the long sides of the house. The nails used here are of great importance to the final and lasting appearance of your house. Only two types of 6d nails are suitable. Either hot dip galvanized or

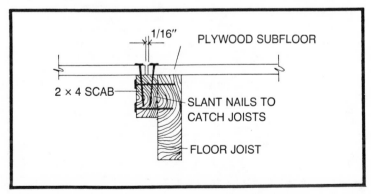

Fig. 4-8. Nailing the bottom plate to the subfloor will keep the wall from sliding off the floor deck when it is tilted up. (Courtesy of American Plywood Association.)

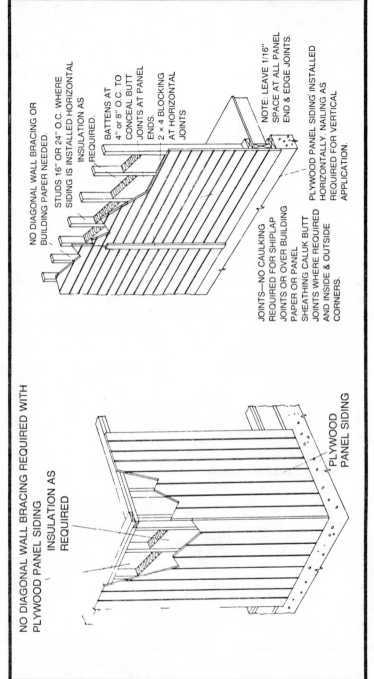

NO DIAGONAL WALL BRACING REQUIRED WITH PLYWOOD PANEL SIDING

INSULATION AS REQUIRED

PLYWOOD PANEL SIDING

NO DIAGONAL WALL BRACING OR BUILDING PAPER NEEDED.

STUDS 16" OR 24" O.C. WHERE SIDING IS INSTALLED HORIZONTAL INSULATION AS REQUIRED.

BATTENS AT 4" OR 8" O.C. TO CONCEAL BUTT JOINTS AT PANEL ENDS.

2 × 4 BLOCKING AT HORIZONTAL JOINTS

NOTE: LEAVE 1/16" SPACE AT ALL PANEL END & EDGE JOINTS.

PLYWOOD PANEL SIDING INSTALLED HORIZONTALLY. NAILING AS REQUIRED FOR VERTICAL APPLICATION.

JOINTS—NO CAULKING REQUIRED FOR SHIPLAP JOINTS OR OVER BUILDING PAPER OR PANEL SHEATHING CALUK BUTT JOINTS WHERE REQUIRED AND INSIDE & OUTSIDE CORNERS.

Fig. 4-9. The single wall system

aluminum. Any other kind will eventually rust and stain the siding. The panel edges must fall on studs or other solid uprights (if paneling is over ½-inch thick, use 8d nails). Figure 4-9B, shows the approximate allowance needed for overlap at top and bottom of the wall framing, but your best bet is to measure. All panel sides must have the standard 1/16-inch allowance for expansion and contraction, as shown in Fig. 4-10.

The final sheet of paneling goes up as indicated, with corner trim or without, as one chooses (Fig. 4-11).

STANDARD WALL CONSTRUCTION

Standard, or two layer, wall construction most of the time today still involves the use of plywood. Basic construction and framing of the wall is identical to that used in single wall construction, but ⅜-inch C-D exterior glue sheathing plywood is used as sheathing. You can also use nominal 1-inch board sheathing, but the job is more complex, time consuming, and not much less expensive because diagonal bracing is needed and a greater number of nails is required. The recommended application for sheathing is horizontal.

Again, sheathing is started at one end of a side wall and continued on across. As in any other work with plywood, a rough drawing so that you can determine the best method of laying out the panels is a large help. Use the drawing to make sure that you use the fewest number of panels, piecing in only where absolutely essential and making as few cuts as possible. An hour or two with graph paper can save quite a few dollars in materials and several hours of working time.

Sheathing will overlap just as the paneling does in single wall construction (Fig. 4-12). Spacing between sheets is the same, 1/16

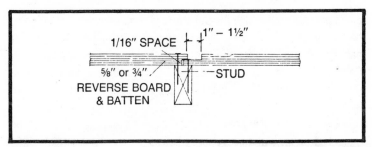

Fig. 4-10. Panels must have 1/16-inch gap between them to allow for expansion. This applies to panels of other thicknesses as well. (Courtesy of American Plywood Association.)

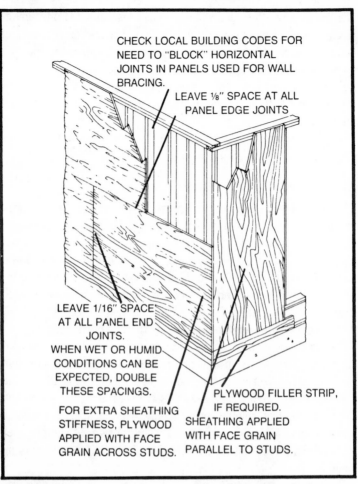

CHECK LOCAL BUILDING CODES FOR NEED TO "BLOCK" HORIZONTAL JOINTS IN PANELS USED FOR WALL BRACING.

LEAVE ⅛" SPACE AT ALL PANEL EDGE JOINTS

LEAVE 1/16" SPACE AT ALL PANEL END JOINTS. WHEN WET OR HUMID CONDITIONS CAN BE EXPECTED, DOUBLE THESE SPACINGS.

FOR EXTRA SHEATHING STIFFNESS, PLYWOOD APPLIED WITH FACE GRAIN ACROSS STUDS.

PLYWOOD FILLER STRIP, IF REQUIRED. SHEATHING APPLIED WITH FACE GRAIN PARALLEL TO STUDS.

Fig. 4-11. Siding over sheathing in a double wall system. (Courtesy of American Plywood Association.)

inch for sides and ⅛ inch for the ends. If conditions are expected to be exceptionally humid, double these spacings. When the exterior paneling is applied over the sheathing, you can use a lighter panel (less thick), thus saving a few dollars, or you can stay with the same thickness you would have used in single wall construction in order to increase strength. This is not necessary in most cases, but sometimes is a good idea in areas where tornadoes and high winds can be expected on any kind of frequent basis.

Overlap, nailing, and other details are the same as for single wall construction.

Generally, paneling applied over sheathing need not be more than 7/16 inch thick if the distance on center is 16 inches. The same thicknesses can be used if the face grain of the siding is applied horizontally across the studs. Siding under a ½ inch thick uses 6d nails, while siding over that thickness requires 8d; the nails are driven every 6 inches along the outer edges of the panel, with spacing moved out to every 12 inches for intermediate supports.

Second floor framing is very similar to first floor work when balloon framing is not used; it seldom is these days. Platform framing is just what its name implies, a series of platforms, one for each floor. The second floor platform starts with an edge or header joist laid on edge and flush with the outside edge of the top plate for the first story. Joist framing and stair cutouts follow the same pattern as for the first floor.

POST AND BEAM FRAMING

One other type of framing is of importance in vacation homes, post and beam or plank and beam framing (Fig. 4-13).

Like the log cabin, basic post and beam framing dates back quite a few years. It predates modern framing methods, and is coming

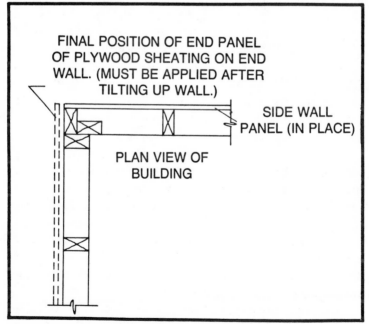

Fig. 4-12. Sheathing overlap. (Courtesy of American Plywood Association.)

Fig. 4-13. Post and beam framework uses massive timbers with much greater on center distances. With correct techniques the timbers are left showing on the interior. Few if any load bearing partitions are needed on the interior, allowing greater freedom of layout.

back to popularity in many types of prefabricated homes. The rustic look of exposed beams, plus a somewhat greater speed and simplicity of erection account for a great deal of this, but the effort of working with larger timbers tends to eliminate or cut down on some of the advantages, as does the need for finding ways to hide pipe runs, wiring, and some modern devices we all now consider essential.

Still, the wider spaced beams, the differences in the overall look of such houses, and the quicker construction do make at least a cursory look at this 8-foot on center framing a good idea.

To hide wiring, posts and beams can be spaced using cover plates to give the appearance of one heavy beam where two lighter ones are used. Pipe runs can be lost in the same types of beams, but careful design is necessary to make sure the beam or post and the pipe run are in the same area.

Generally, post and beam construction must be fully sheathed to provide shear strength in the exterior walls. Too, a lot of the newer post and beam homes use sandwich construction in the exterior walls so that insulation may be hidden.

Basically, the post and beam home is framed in the same manner, today, as is any other type of platform construction, except

type	recommended joist or beam size	steel gauge	dimensions A	B	C	D	E	nails (packed in each carton) header	joist	nail dia. equiv. to	wire gauge	length	recommended safe working values (1/4 ultimate)
24	2x4	18	3 1/4"	1 9/16"	2"	7/8"	7/8"	4	2	8d	11	1 1/4"	400 lbs.
A28	2x6 to 2x10	18	5"	1 9/16"	2"	1"	1"	6	4	10d	9	1 1/2"	900 lbs.
B28	2x10 to 2x14	18	8 1/2"	1 9/16"	2"	1"	1"	10	6	10d	9	1 1/2"	1200 lbs.
A36	3x6 to 3x10	16	5 1/4"	2 9/16"	2 3/4"	1 1/4"	1 1/2"	8	4	20d	6	2 1/8"	1700 lbs.
B36	3x10 to 3x14	16	8 1/2"	2 9/16"	2 3/4"	1 1/4"	1 1/2"	12	6	20d	6	2 1/8"	2800 lbs.
A46	4x6 to 4x10	16	5 1/4"	3 9/16"	2 3/4"	1 1/4"	1 1/2"	8	4	20d	6	2 1/8"	1700 lbs.
B46	4x10 to 4x14	16	8 1/2"	3 9/16"	2 3/4"	1 1/4"	1 1/2"	12	6	20d	6	2 1/8"	2800 lbs.
AD6	2-2x6 to 2-2x10	16	5 3/8"	3 1/16"	2 3/4"	1 1/4"	1 1/2"	8	4	20d	6	2 1/8"	1700 lbs.
BD6	2-2x10 to 2-2x14	16	8 5/8"	3 1/16"	2 3/4"	1 1/4"	1 1/2"	12	6	20d	6	2 1/8"	2800 lbs

If desired, most types of TECO-U-GRIPS are available in heavier gauge steel, although no increase in safe working values will result.

Recommended safe working values may be increased 1/3 (or as provided by local practice) for wind or earthquake loading.

Values for all types except Type 24, A28(26) and B28(26) can be increased 350 lbs. if two 3/8"x2 1/2" lag bolts are used (one each per header flange).

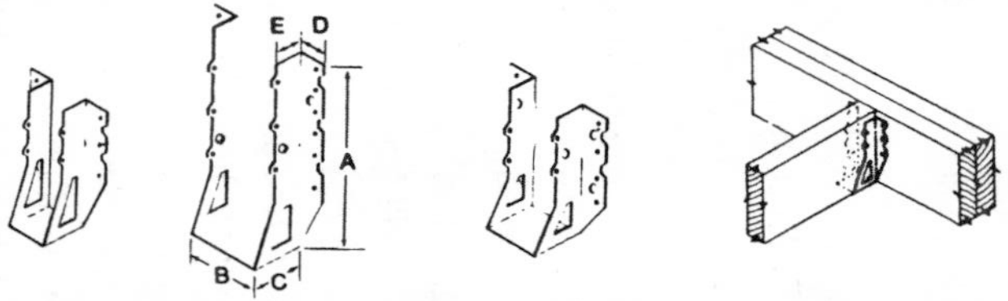

Fig. 4-14. Joist hangers can make joist nailing considerably easier and result in a stronger structure. (Courtesy of TECO.)

for the beam and post size and the on center spacing. Floor openings are framed conventionally inside the beam layout on the floor. Any heavy objects, where the load is not dispersed over wide areas, will require extra support from conventional joist style framing. Such items as bathtubs and refrigerators come to mind instantly.

The easiest method of framing out a post and beam home is to use hangers and connecting straps as made by companies such as TECO (Fig. 4-14). Other joint styles are possible, but require a great deal more time and work.

Floors and decking used with post and beam construction are a great deal heavier than are those used in standard framing. Generally both the flooring and the roofing will be at least 3 inches thick and 6 to 8 inches in width. They are face-nailed at their ends and often nailed to each other, though this sometimes requires drilling.

One big advantage is where windows and doors fall between posts, no headers are needed. This cuts materials costs as well as installation time.

Today, post and beam construction is seldom carried out totally in a house, so that the floor systems are most often standard joists, cutting out the need for special supports. Roof systems will depend on the extent of insulation considered essential. While solid types of insulation, such as styrofoam, can be used over the decking with the shingles laid directly on sheets of plastic 2 to 4 inches thick, some people will frame out a more or less conventional roof, either with standard rafters or truss systems, and provide the insulation needed for a particular area on the inside of the roof.

Once the walls are up, you have arrived at the time when total enclosure becomes necessary. The roof must be put on, starting with that nemesis of all amateur buildings, the framing out of the rafters and collar beams.

Actually, this should be no nemesis for anyone. Once the first rafter on a simple gable roof is laid out, it becomes the pattern for the rest of the rafters. The hard measuring and figuring need be done only once.

Chapter 5
Roof & Ceiling Framing

Roof framing, rafters and collar beams, can be installed in at least three different ways, depending on your desires, the type of vacation home you're erecting, and the availability of certain materials locally. In general, any ceiling framing that must be done is performed just before the rafters are installed so that the walls are set up to resist the outward push from a pitched roof; however, this is not always the case when trusses and other prefabricated forms of roof framing are used.

As usual, a check of any local codes specifying on center distance and rafter and ceiling joists is essential to getting an occupancy permit for any home. This may not apply in some rural areas, but most of the time you'll find a check with either the local office handling building codes or your building inspector will make the final moving into the home a great deal simpler.

CEILING FRAMING

As I've already said, one of the jobs of the ceiling joists is to support the walls, to prevent their being pushed out onto the ground when the pitched gable roof is in place. A second function of these joists is obvious; they support the materials you use for a finished roof. Should the home be a two story job, the ceiling joists for the first floor also provide a base for the second story floor, or if the house has an attic, for the attic floor. In addition, a framed and subfloored set of ceiling joists provides a stable and safe working platform for erecting the roof rafters.

Your house plans, when checked against local codes, will provide accurate sizing for the ceiling joists. The length of the span will determine the size of the joists because it will the size of your rafters. Ceiling joists and rafters are laid out on the top plates at the same time. This assuming you are building a single story house. For two story homes, the second floor platform is built with no reference to rafters at that time. Ceiling joints must meet and lap the rafters with at least three large nails used to secure the two together at the top plate portion of the roof. For simplicity, you should space the ceiling joists and the roof rafters using the same on center distance for both. This could require larger ceiling joists than you would need, for example, if ceiling joists were laid in at 16 inches on center. This is because rafters today are most often placed 24 inches on center, but the smaller number of joists needed makes up for the larger cost for the increased size of the members.

Generally, you can easily follow your house plans for joist and rafter location. If you are using, as I recommend, plywood sheathing and siding, there is no need at all for the joists or the rafters to line up over the wall studs, so the fact that you have decided to use 2 by 4s and go with 16-inch on center wall framing does not mean you have to do the same with the roofing. Twenty-four inches on center is ample unless expected snow loads are truly extreme, in which case, the 2-foot on center distance can be maintained, usually—check local codes—if the pitch of the roof is increased enough. Sometimes you'll need to increase the size of roof rafters to meet codes and maintain a 2-foot on center distance. As an example, using 2 by 8s in heavy snow load areas may not be allowed, but an increase to either 2 by 10s or 2 by 12s will not only mean you meet code requirements for roof loading safety, but will also allow you to install enough insulation to meet the most stringent modern requirements for energy savings in heating and cooling. Refer to Chapter 9 for the techniques and specifications associated with insulation now recommended. Overall, the increase in price may not seem justified immediately, but such extra heavy insulation usually pays for itself in something on the order of 3 years in more or less moderate climates, and more rapidly, often in a single year, in harsher weather conditions.

Where ceiling spans exceed the allowable limits for a particular size of wood, you have two choices. First, interior load bearing partitions can be used to support the joists at a point which cuts the span to allowable limits. Second, the size of the rafters may be

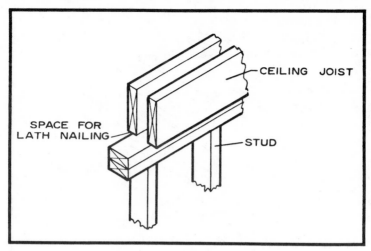

Fig. 5-1. Using a ceiling joist over a stud wall.

increased. In most cases, the use of a load bearing partition, as shown in Fig. 5-1, is a more likely choice since the usual vacation home will be divided into rooms when it is large enough to require such wide spans.

The Southern Forest Products Association provides a very handy series of charts giving allowable spans for various size pieces of timber with on center distances ranging from 1 foot to 2 feet. The change between 2 by 4 ceiling joists and 2 by 10 ceiling joists, 2 feet on center, is great. The smaller timbers can be spanned over no more than 7 feet 4 inches, with a 20 pound per square foot loading, for storage, no sleeping, to a 19 foot 5 inch span for the larger chunk of wood. That's with a plaster ceiling. Using drywall ceiling construction, which is more normal these days, the spans increase to 8 feet 5 inches and 22 feet 3 inches. Floor joists, two by twelve, can be spanned up to 20 feet 8 inches, allowing a 30 pounds per square foot live load and providing sleeping or storage space as wished. For heavy traffic rooms, you'll cut that 2 by 12 span to 18 feet 9 inches and have a 40 pounds per square foot live load rating for rooms used for something other than sleeping—heavy traffic loads, bathrooms, etc.

Ceiling joists laid out to lap the rafters on the top plate should be separated at the load bearing partition by filler blocks of wood cut to just extend over the partition top. Use six nails from each hoist into the filler block, or into the opposite joist if no filler blocks are used.

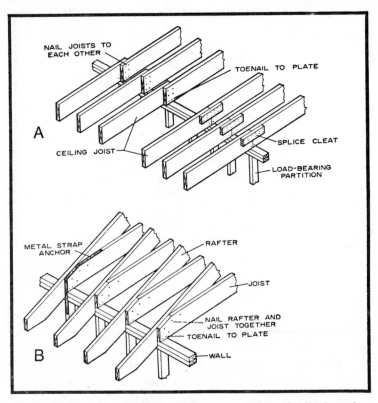

Fig. 5-2. Ceiling joist connections. (A) At center partition with joists lapped or butted. (B) An outside wall.

The filler blocks will keep you from having lap problems after the first set of rafters is lapped on the joists. End ceiling joists will not lap their rafters. The joists are placed flush with the end wall, as are the rafters (Fig. 5-2 and 5-3). You'll probably find it a lot easier to not bother placing this end joist until after the gable end of the house is framed out. Thus, the first ceiling joist to go in is placed to lap the first *interior* rafter, with its centerline exactly 24 inches from the face of the end wall.

Once all the ceiling joists are in place, you trim their ends to match the slope of the rafters. If a small amount of material is all that needs to be removed—and that's all that should need removing— you can leave this job until after the rafters are in place. Ceiling joists are cut to fit flush with the outer part of the wall, and to allow at least a 4-inch overlap over any loadbearing partitions where joists are joined.

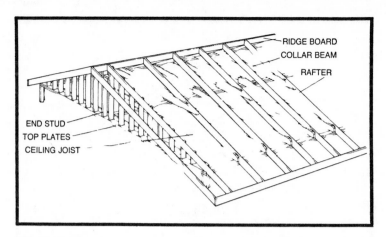

Fig. 5-3. Fascia rafters cover the end of the ridge board. (Courtesy of American Plywood Association.)

You can either toenail the ceiling joists, using two 10d nails per side, to the top plates of the exterior walls or use nailing anchors such as those made by TECO, which also allow the joists to be hung inside the top plates (Fig. 5-4) if you desire and have allowed for this extra height at the outset of framing.

Where the joists lap in the center, they are first nailed together or to the filler block, then toenailed to the top plate of the load bearing partition or beam. At least four 16d nails go into the filler block.

Nailing studs are now placed and nailed so that there will be sufficient nailing surface for the wallboard or other ceiling finish materials. Should the joists run parallel to a nonloadbearing wall, backing blocks are installed and toenailed (one 10d per side

Fig. 5-4 Installation of joist hangers. (Courtesy of TECO.)

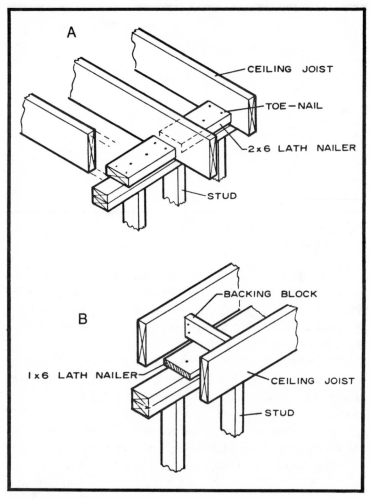

Fig. 5-5. Horizontal lath catchers at ceiling. (A) Lath nailer between ceiling joist. (B) Stud wall at right angle to joist.

minimum) to the top plate, as well as being end nailed to the joists (three 10d nails per joist). Then 1 by 6 or 2 by 6 nailers are installed for the ceiling finish materials shown in Fig. 5-5.

ROOF FRAMING

Roof framing is the part of building a house that scares off most amateur builders, for the use of the framing square seems extraordinarily difficult when one doesn't practice getting things correct. The basics of using the framing square were covered in Chapter 2, so we can assume you have that much down. We should remember, though, that while this part of the job is crucial, critical, and a bit hard to do, it need be done only a single time. One rafter is laid out as a pattern, cut, and checked for size and angle. If all is correct, you can now proceed to lay out and cut all remaining rafters to size using this first rafter as a pattern.

This, naturally, applies to simple gable roofs with equal runs; a *run* is half the *span*, and the *span* is the distance from one outside edge of the exterior wall to the outside edge of the opposite exterior wall.

For fancier work, things get correspondingly difficult, quite difficult in fact, as the job of laying out different size rafters, jack rafters, cripple jacks hip jacks, and such can puzzle even an experienced carpenter if the job is one that is done only infrequently. For that reason, I recommend any novice builder avoid such roofing styles. Even should the house demand a dormer, your simplest and easiest dormer style is the shed roof. Not only is the shed dormer easy to lay out and build, it offers more space than does any other design. Aesthetics aside, it is just about the only sensible way to go.

Too, gambrel roofs are quite attractive, especially in homes intended to look as if they had at one time been barns. But the extra complexity of figuring, cutting, and nailing main rafters, short rafters, and purlins take these, too, out of the reach of the average nonexperienced builder. Of course, if you're working with a home that has been prefabricated, any roof style is fine because the rafters and other pieces will already be cut for you, and usually will be marked with chalk or crayon indicating their locations.

Roof trusses are the next type of roof framing. In order to speed building and cut down on the size of the materials needed for the jobs, braced trusses, usually the W-style (Fig. 5-6) can be bought or made. No load bearing partitions are needed for a correctly designed and built roof, so great open spans are possible. For truss use, some engineering data is needed, with the most obvious figures being the total span and the pitch of the roof. Too, you must know just what size lumber and plywood bracing plates you'll need to keep the roof from collapsing on you when the house is finished and snow starts to fall, or the winds start to blow. While trusses, like rafters, can be formed to a pattern, cut, and constructed on the site, then lifted into place, most of us at one time or another have seen a truckload or two of these items moving down the road. The reason is

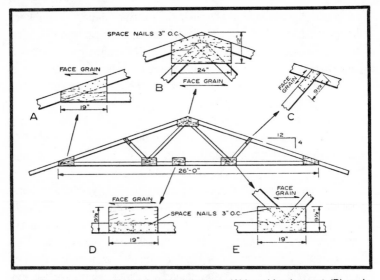

Fig. 5-6. Construction of a 26-foot W-style truss. (A) bevel-heel gusset. (B) peak gusset. (C) Upper chord intermediate gusset. (D) Splice of lower chord. (E) Lower chord intermediate gusset.

simple: the cost of having a properly equipped lumber supply yard build trusses is often offset by the ease of handling and lack of worries about getting all the angles and sizes correct.

In fact, many dealers will already have trusses built for your span and pitch. Simply go in, look, and order. They'll be delivered to the site; it is then an easy job to lift the trusses in place and either toenail or anchor plate nail them in place.

Trusses offer one major disadvantage: most of the attic space is lost. Other than that, they're suitable for use in any type of construction, though greatest ease is found in houses where the design is rectangular. Then only a single size of truss is needed, and no fancy cutting on site is required.

RAFTER LAYOUT

If you didn't do so when the ceiling joists were installed, it's now time to lay out the rafter positions along the top plates. The first and last rafter pairs are kept flush with the outside end walls. Your next interior rafter will be 2 feet from the end of the building to the center of the rafter, with each succeeding rafter being placed 24 inches from the center of that first interior rafter. Keep the rafters to the sides of the ceiling joist ends.

If a ridge board is used, first allow for specified gable over hang at each end; then move in and mark the positions of the first two rafters. Go from there back to your 24-inch on center measurements. If the ridge board requires splicing, as many will on larger houses, that should be saved for nearly last. The reason is simple. You can work more easily with 16-foot or so long boards than you can with those possibly 32-feet or more or longer. When splicing is needed, use a plywood splice brace, as shown in Fig. 5-7, on both sides of the joint.

Now, check your house plans for the specified roof slope. For pitched roof construction using asphalt or wood shingles, the rise cannot be less than 4 inches for every foot of run. See the left side of Fig. 5-8. A look at slope and pitch is a good idea about this time.

Slope shows the incline or slant of a roof as a ratio of the vertical rise (again see Fig. 5-8) to the horizontal run. Slope is described, always, as so many inches in 1 foot, for example, 4 inches in 12 inches.

Pitch shows the slant of the roof as a ratio of the vertical rise to the span. This is a fraction. Assuming a 5-foot rise in a 30-foot span, the pitch would be 1/6.

While we've already taken a bit more than a cursory look at the use of the framing square to lay out rafters, this is the time to cover the thing in more detail. That first pair of rafters is of great importance in getting the entire roof cut to the correct size and in place properly. As a start, go through the rafter material and select the straightest piece of material you can find. Set the pattern piece on your sawhorses, and place yourself on the side to become the top side of the rafter. Look at the rafter square. Your unit on the blade (the wide portion of the square) will be 12 inches. Select the proper rise for as many inches as your plans specify. Take your marking

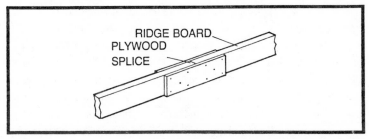

Fig. 5-7. Method of splicing ridge board. (Courtesy of American Plywood Association.)

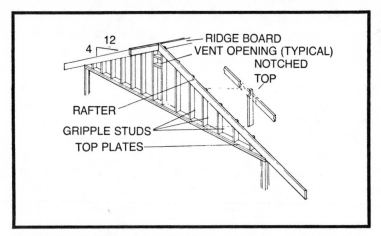

Fig. 5-8. Checking the roof slope. In this example the slope is 4 inches in 12 inches. (Courtesy of American Plywood Association.)

clips and set them so that these figures are exact. Starting at the ridge line, place the square on the stock, and mark the ridge line. With the square still in that same position, mark the length of the odd unit; it may be anything less than a foot. If the total run is, for example, 7 feet 9 inches, the odd unit marked first will be 9 inches. Move the square until the tongue, the narrow part, is along the 8-inch mark. Mark once more and continue on until you have the correct number of full units (seven here). The bottom line will be the portion that rests on the top plate.

Often, when an overhang is used, you will need to shape and cut a portion known as a bird's mouth. This is the part of the rafter that is actually toenailed to the top plate. Or it may be direct nailed if the stock is cut so that a nail will penetrate without splitting the material. If an overhang is used, that distance must also be added to the rafter's length, while a ridge board in use will require you to take half the thickness of the ridge board from the top, or ridge board end, of the rafter.

To form a bird's mouth cutout, draw a line to show the building line as the last full run is made. This is most easily done by flipping the square over. Bird's mouth sizes and shapes will vary depending on the style and amount of overhang. As shown in Fig. 5-9, the overhang can be laid out about the same time, using the flipped square to mark off the full unit and partial distance of the overhang.

Once this first pattern rafter is cut, you can go on to cut the rest of the necessary rafters. For a house 48 feet long, with rafters 2 feet

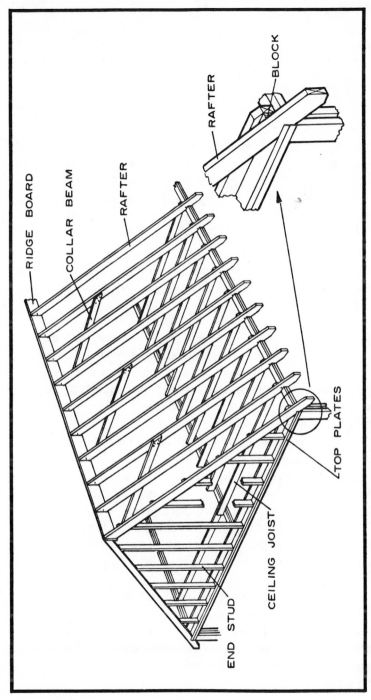

RIDGE BOARD

COLLAR BEAM

RAFTER

RAFTER

BLOCK

END STUD

CEILING JOIST

TOP PLATES

Fig. 5-9. Ceiling and roof framing with collar beams and overhang shown.

on center, you will need a total of 25 pairs of rafters. In every case, you'll need one extra set of rafters. A 24-foot cabin will require 13 pairs, etc.

In cutting rafters, it is best to use the straightest wood possible, but with today's lumber supplies being what they are chances are good that none will be too straight. When you run into a rafter stock piece that has a severe bow, it should be discarded, as should severely warped pieces. But with moderate bows the best method of conserving material is to cut the rafter to keep the bow up. As time passes, the weight of the roof will force the rafter to straighten.

Erecting the rafters can be a chore. In the first place, you'll need a "flotilla" of 1 by 4s and 1 by 6s as bracing, plus about eleven extra hands and a safety rope if you plan to do the job alone. First, make certain all the materials are ready to go, all rafters cut, and the ridge board ready. Incidentally, the ridge board should also be made from the straightest possible stock, but can be treated as are the rafters if slight bows are present. Next collect your nails, hammer, bracing, level, and plumb line.

Start by nailing some 2 by 4s at the gable ends in a position where they can easily be shifted over to support the end rafter pairs. These props must be long enough to reach from the top plate up to the bottom of the ridge board. Cut and double toenail to the top plates directly under the spot for the first rafter pair at the ridge board. Do the same at the opposite end of the building if the ridge board is to be a single piece unit. If it is to be spliced, set a second brace about a foot from where the short ridge board will end. The ridge board at the tops of these braces can be tacked with 10d nails only partially driven home. This will serve to hold them fairly well in place until you get a chance to raise at least one pair of rafters, though you may wish to set in diagonal braces to keep them near plumb. Exact plumb isn't essential here, but the entire job is a bit easier if they're more than fairly close when the rafters start to go up. It means less pushing and hauling once the rafters are nailed into place.

Lift the end rafter pairs (or the last short ridge board rafter pair and one end pair) onto your working surface along with the ridge board. If the ceiling is framed but not floored, it is a good idea to lay sheets of plywood down as a safety measure: stepping off a joist is guaranteed to at least cause a solid case of fright and can cause severe injury.

Now, erect the first set of end rafters. Move the ridge board into place, and erect a supporting set of rafters. (Fig. 5-10.) Toenail the first set of rafters to the ridge board at the correct marks. Use 8d nails, two to each side. Toenail the first set of rafters to the top plates, using 10d nails, then nail the rafters to the ceiling joists using at least four 16d nails per side. If the span is over 24 feet, or if you're building in an area of high winds, you can add a support strap here to increase security a great deal.

With the second set of rafters toenailed to the ridge board, check the ridge board for level, and drop a plumb line to make sure it is over the house center. Continue with the ridge board if it is in two pieces, setting in another pair of rafters at the inside end, and moving to the fianl set of gable end rafters. Check this section for level and centering over the house. Nail at ridge board, top plates, and ceiling joists. Once the full ridge board is in place, you can continue with placing and nailing the rafters, doing a pair at a time. Check level and centering about every third pair of rafters. If all cuts were made correctly, and the original pattern rafter was laid out properly, the roof will just about pull itself into alignment with no extra work from you.

While collar beams (Fig. 5-9) are not always essential (already in when roof trusses are used), they do add rigidity, cut the span width (effectively for support of live loads), and provide nailers for

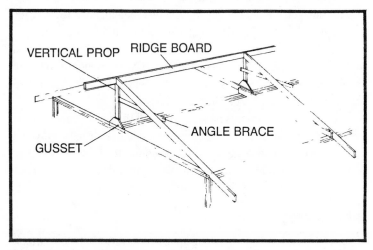

Fig. 5-10. Erecting the first set of rafters. (Courtesy of American Plywood Association.)

second floor or attic ceilings. One by sixes are most often used, placed on every other rafter. Personally, if use as nailers is intended, I would use them at every rafter. Collar beams should be kept in the upper third of the rafter length, with each end of the collar board getting four 8d nails.

Once the collar beams are in, the roof framing is done, so all temporary props can be taken down.

Gable ends require framing so that the siding can be continued on up. In the case of log cabins, you may have carried the logs up the end wall with their ends cut to the correct roof slant, but with frame housing the end gable walls need more work. Framing starts just to either side of the ridge board, with 2 by 4s notched to fit the particular angles (these are known as cripple studs (Fig. 5-8 shows the notched cripple studs).

As a start, drop a plumb line down from the center line of the ridge board, and mark on the top plate. Now square a line from this, and, if a vent is to be installed (if you don't properly vent the vacation home, you'll have constant moisture problems, so this is essential), measure it and divide that in half. Use half this measurement on each side of the line to show where the first two cripple studs will go. After those are measured, notched, and nailed, measure on 16-inch centers for the remainder, cutting and notching to fit as you go along.

If the overhang at the ends requires a floating rafter, this is the time to cut that. The floating rafter will nail to the end of the ridge board, thus you should not cut the half distance on each to allow for the ridge board, nor should you cut a bird's mouth. In all other ways it is just like any other rafter. The bottom of the floating rafter is nailed to the fastia board, which is installed first. The fascia board will be of stock the correct size to cover the rafter ends, and must be nailed with hot dip galvanized or aluminum nails.

Roof sheathing comes next, as does all the finish trim work on the roof. Once this is done, assuming the siding is already up, you'll be weatherproof and ready to continue no matter how the weather is. Because sheathing requires a fair amount of detail work, almost more than roof framing, it is the subject of Chapter 6.

SHED DORMERS

Before moving onto finishing up the roof, though, at least a look at the aforementioned shed dormer framing is a good idea. In order to add extra space to an attic story, the shed dormer is the most efficient style, while being the simplest and quickest to frame out.

Generally, the shed dormer runs from the ridge board right on out to the edge of the house. Double trimmer rafters are used at the outside edges of the dormer to carry any extra loadings, with nailer strips on each side for roof sheathing. The slope of the roof rafters on the dormer is controlled by the style of the original house and the expected loadings, as are the rafter sizes. Studs from the outside of the rafters drop down to the top plates of the floor below, with bottom plates, also in use with the dormer. It also has its own doubled top plate on which its rafters are nailed. Windows are framed out just as they are in other exterior walls, while the end walls of the dormer are framed with notched cripple studs in a manner very much like that used for gable end framing.

Flashing, as will be covered in Chapter 6, is needed around the bottom sides of the dormer to prevent water splashback and seepage.

Shed dormers need not be framed immediately, as they do not absolutely have to tie in at the ridge. The external roof and several rafters can be removed at a later date and a shed dormer inserted with the dormer rafters tied in to the gable rafters at a point just above the collar beams, but this requires internal support of the part of the dormer rafters (and the house rafters) on their ridge board side of the house. It is best, whenever possible, to make the tie-in directly to the ridge board and to add the shed dormer prior to original roof completion.

Chapter 6
Finish Roofing

Vacation homes vary so greatly in style and location that a wide range of roofing materials comes into play. In some ways the finish of a roof is more complex than the framing of a roof simply because the choice is so wide. Naturally a lot tends to depend on the roof style. Steep pitched roofs can use types of roofing, shingles and shakes, that flatter roofs cannot. About the minimum slope for the use of shingles or shakes is 4 in 12, with anything less than that requiring some form of roll roofing to prevent leaks from water being driven or seeping back between sections of roofing material.

Today tile and slate are much too expensive for all but the most affluent. In more general use are the mineral surface roll roofings, mineral surface strip shingles, wood shakes, wood shingles, aluminum sheets, fiberglass shingles, and fiberglass sheets. Almost any of these are suitable for vacation homes. In addition, you'll need to flash valleys, flash around dormers, and flash around vent pipes and chimneys, so aluminum roll flashing is also essential to most any roof.

The job is started with roof sheathing. As you will have noticed by now, I have recommended standard framing styles for almost all roofs whether on a log cabin or a conventionally framed home. This type of roof framing makes the sheathing job a great deal easier, but the final selection of sheathing material stills rests at least in part on the type of material to be used for the finish covering of the roof. For example, under most types of roll roofing, sheet metal roofing, and strip shingles, where there is a good roof pitch or slope, plywood of the correct type and thickness is the most economical when costed out in terms of time, durability, and actual price. But with wood shakes, and often with shingles, plywood sheathing can contribute to early failure of the roof by trapping moisture. This is most especially true in extremely humid areas. While the exterior grade plywood used for this job is most likely to be unaffected, moisture blown back under the wood shingles will proceed to rot the shingles in something under 10 or 15 years. The expected normal life of such a roof—assuming the use of cedar or redwood shingles—should be well over 30 years.

It was only last year that my wife's parents had to replace the roof on their main cabin on a lake in southern Quebec. The original roof was installed in July of 1898 when the summer camp was first built. This is something over 77 years of roof life in an area that is not only damp all year, but has extreme snow loads all winter. As far as I know, not any modern material can surpass that though a few may come close. Fiberglass shingles haven't been around long enough for us to know, but properly installed metal sheet roofs have endured for over 50 years on barns and homes in the area in which I now live, southwestern Virginia.

In areas where humidity isn't a problem less care need be taken with roof types, but consideration should always be given to wind speeds. Check for the expected maximums and build to meet them or exceed them in resistance. Your local building inspector will usually have this information, or the wind speed resistance will be specified in local codes. If your locale requires no building inspection check with the county extension agent. That's right, the local farmer's helping hand. They'll know.

ROOF SHEATHING

The sheathing you place on your roof does more than keep the rain and snow out while you get ready to put on the shingles. It ties the rafters together to add strength to the roof and the rest of the interrelated systems of the house, at the same time making the entire unit more rigid. For 2-foot spans, check the plywood for the APA grade marks, in this case 24/0. Such plywood sheets are available in ⅜-inch and ½-inch thicknesses. If snow loads in your area are exceptionally heavy and the roof has only a mild slope, 5 in 12 or less, select a ⅝-inch thickness. Look at your plans to see

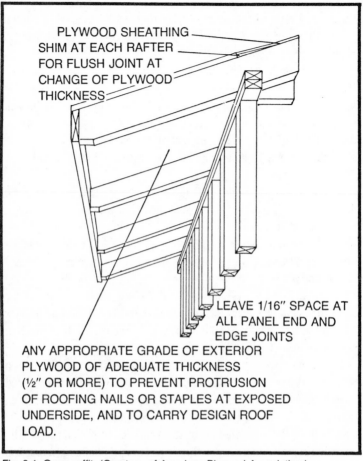

PLYWOOD SHEATHING
SHIM AT EACH RAFTER
FOR FLUSH JOINT AT
CHANGE OF PLYWOOD
THICKNESS

LEAVE 1/16" SPACE AT
ALL PANEL END AND
EDGE JOINTS

ANY APPROPRIATE GRADE OF EXTERIOR
PLYWOOD OF ADEQUATE THICKNESS
(½" OR MORE) TO PREVENT PROTRUSION
OF ROOFING NAILS OR STAPLES AT EXPOSED
UNDERSIDE, AND TO CARRY DESIGN ROOF
LOAD.

Fig. 6-1. Open soffit. (Courtesy of American Plywood Association.)

whether you have open or closed soffits; the soffit is the underside of your eave overhang. This will affect the selection of the plywood grade used along the house eaves, as closed soffits can be made with interior grade plywood, while open soffits, exposed continually to the weather, must use an exterior grade. In fact, for this area, the APA recommends that you choose one of the textured designs, one pleasant for you to look at, and install it with the textured side facing down, so that no finishing is then needed under the soffit and between the rafter overhangs (Fig. 6-1). This adds a bit to cost though, so you may wish to stick with exterior-grade plywood and add decorative touches at a later date. Sheathing for open soffits must be at least ½ inch thick, otherwise roofing nails will show through when the shingles are installed; ⅝ inch thick is better, but remember that this thickness must be carried on up the roof, and the thicker the plywood, the higher the cost.

From this point, you'll need to sketch the roof layout. Back to the graph paper. Make a rectangle representing half of the roof. Make a second for the other half. Now, locate on the drawings all chimneys, vent pipes, and so on. It is essential that these items be located before the roof is sheathed: the actual chimneys, vent pipes, and such need not be installed at this time, but you must know where they'll be, and have framed their openings in the roof. If this isn't done, a lot of extra work, including some rather sloppy cutting will be needed to get you through the finished roof.

If you have open soffits with the overhang being less than 2 feet, you can mark the drawings so that half-panels can be used all the way around the roof edges. If the soffits are the closed type, start with an entire 4 by 8 sheet of plywood at the bottom edge of the roof, working on up to the ridge from the eave. Panels used to sheath roofs are staggered just as are panels used to provide subflooring. The second row of sheets would be started with a 4 by 4 section of plywood (Fig. 6-2).

A tip: if you have a wide overhang and this forces you into a lot of cutting that adds up to a lot of waste, this is a good time to consider shortening the eave overhang. Get it down to 2 feet or less, so that the panels will work out evenly as they approach the ridge and you can save yourself much work with a saw, folding rule, and chalk line.

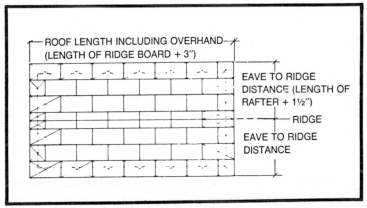

Fig. 6-2. Top view of roof for panel sheathing layout. For open soffits all panels marked Xs must be EXT-OFPA soffit panels. (Courtesy of American Plywood Association.)

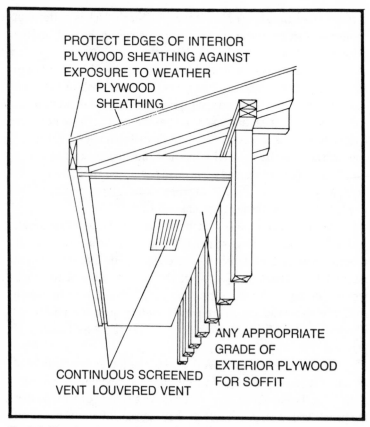

PROTECT EDGES OF INTERIOR
PLYWOOD SHEATHING AGAINST
EXPOSURE TO WEATHER

PLYWOOD
SHEATHING

ANY APPROPRIATE
GRADE OF
EXTERIOR PLYWOOD
FOR SOFFIT

CONTINUOUS SCREENED
VENT LOUVERED VENT

Fig. 6-3. Boxed or closed soffit. (Courtesy of American Plywood Association.)

Closed soffits can be either straight across or slanted on the rafter ends. A fascia board protects the ends of the rafters and the ends of the plywood where water might otherwise drive up and delaminate it. For flat surface closed soffits, a nailer board is necessary (Fig. 6-3).

Where panel cutting is needed, make the measurements and marks with great care and take precautions to make any corners square while cutting. For greatest ease of cutting along a 4-foot or longer mark, I would recommend you check with Sears for the *cutting guide* for plywood they sell.

It makes straight cuts over long distances a lot easier, and is long enough for use to cut angles along the length of an 8-foot sheet. These cut guides are probably available elsewhere, but Sears is the only company I've seen selling them to date.

Mark and make cutouts for around vents, etc. Start the nailing at any corner you wish, using 6d ring shank nails. This adds to holding power, cuts down on nail popping, and will cost less than $5 for the total house. Nail to the rafters, spacing the nails 6 inches apart along the outside edges of the panel, and 12 inches apart on the inner parts. When the second panel is laid, provide a 1/16-inch gap to allow for expansion. Double this for highly damp areas. When the second course or row of panels is started, and for each succeeding row, leave ⅛ inch for a gap at the edges. Again, double this figure where the area is high in humidity.

Sheathing need not be of plywood, and often won't be on post and beam homes no matter what the final type of roofing to be laid down. In the case of post and beam construction, the long distances on center planks with thicknesses of 2 to 3 inches and a minimum width of 4 inches (Fig. 6-4). These planks are laid lengthwise, not diagonally, but must be tongue and groove or spline and groove for greatest strength. In most cases, rigid plastic foam insulation will be applied over the roof sheathing, which will be covered with roofing paper and shingles.

For wood shingles or shakes, an open work style sheathing is often used. With proper layout of roofing paper, the open work wood slats, not really sheathing at all, allow any moisture absorbed by the wood roof to pass through instead of building up to cause rot. Still, the Red Cedar Shingle & Handsplit Shake Bureau recommends solid sheathing, either plywood or board, for areas in which there is a lot of snow. Even then, minimum pitch or slope figures must be adhered

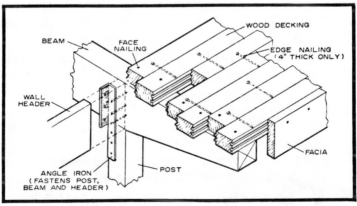

Fig. 6-4. Roof decking for post and beam construction.

to. Shakes and wood shingles have maximum recommended weather exposures, too. If more than the recommended portion of the wood is exposed to the weather, the life of the roof will be considerably diminished.

There are three standard lengths of shingles according to the Red Cedar Shingle & Handsplit Shake Bureau: 16-inch, 18-inch, and 24-inch lengths. If the roof pitch is 4 inches in 12 inches or steeper on a three ply roof, allow a 5-inch exposure for 16-inch shingles, a 5½-inch exposure for 18-inch shingles, and a 7 ½-nnch exposure for 24-inch shingles. If the roof pitch is less than 4 inches in 12 inches but not below 3 inches in 12 inches on a four ply roof, allow a 3 ¾-inch exposure for 16-inch shingles, a 4 ¼-inch exposure for 18-inch shingles, and a 5 ¾-inch exposure for 24-inch shingles. If the roof pitch is less than 3 inches in 12 inches, cedar shingles are not recommended.

With the roof sheathed and the application of asphalt shingles being the immediate choice (this installation, in most ways, also applies to other mineral covered shingle styles and fiberglass shingles), you will begin by installing the drip edging along the eaves of the house. This metal edging keeps water and ice from raising the shingle edges.

Next, roofing felt must be installed. Use 3-foot wide roofing felt of the heaviest quality you can find (usually 30-pound grade). Snap a chalk line 3 feet up from the edge of the roof and a second line 32 inches (4-inch difference) up from that. Lay the first underlayment strip, using roofing nails with large heads or using the flat tin washers made for this purpose. Nails used must be hot dip galvanized or aluminum. Each succeeding course of felt underlayment must have a 4-inch overlap on the preceding course, the reason for the 4-inch shorter measurement after the first course is laid. Continue to snap chalk lines to lay the roofing felt unless it has, as many kinds do, a line 4 inches in from the edge. Make sure the roofing felt lies absolutely flat or you'll later have trouble with the shingles.

You'll need a bundle or two of wood shingles, not shakes, to start your asphalt roofing. The shingles, 16 inches long, are laid first along the eave lines with two nails, hot dip galvanized, used per shingle. Then a course of asphalt shingles is laid down, reversed. Finally, you start the final trip. Most asphalt shingles in use today are 12 inches by 3 feet, and require six 1-inch roofing nails per shingle. Nailing is done about 1 inch up from the spot where the next row of shingles will cover the one going down. Exposure distance is usually about 5 inches, but may vary a bit depending on the brand and the weight of the shingle. Because roofing is one of the more tedious jobs and demands a great deal of concentration, it is best to use the absolute finest quality shingles you can buy. The minimum for most codes now is 235 pounds, but weights up to 300 pounds are easily found. The heavier it is the better.

In areas where there is a good chance of high winds, look for shingles that have sealing tabs on the lower edges (underside). These sealing tabs are simply blobs of roofing cement. The sun hits the shingle, the roofing cement gets sticky, and the cement adheres tightly to shingle underneath.

Use chalk lines to keep the courses of shingles straight. The first, reversed, course will hang about ½ inch over the wood shingle used as a starter course, with the finish course matching that edge distance, so the first chalk line is snapped about 11½ inches up from the eave. Succeeding course lines would be snapped at 6½-inch intervals if the exposure for the shingle is 5 inches. The ½-inch overhang is repeated at the gable ends of the roof (Figs. 6-5 and 6-6).

The ridge can be finished in any of several ways, though probably the most common type of cap in use today is called the Boston

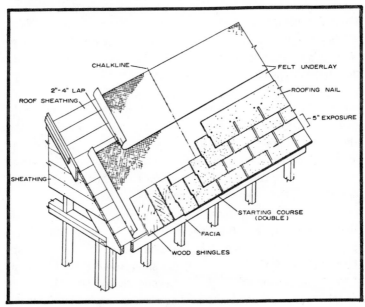

Fig. 6-5. Application of asphalt shingles.

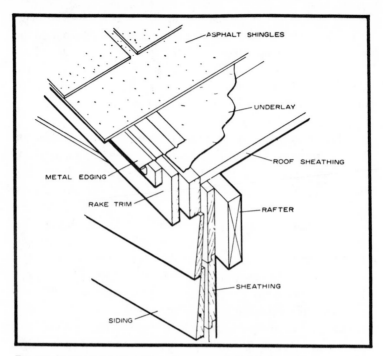

Fig. 6-6. Metal edging at gable end on an asphalt shingle roof.

ridge. Cut enough of the 12-inch by 3-foot shingles into thirds. Now, starting at one end, nail one of these 1-foot square pieces so that there is a 6-inch overlap on each side of the ridge (Fig. 6-7). The next ridge cap piece is nailed so that the first third of a shingle keeps about 6 inches of exposure. Nailing is done so that the nails are covered by the next piece to go down, known as blind nailing. In most cases, it is a good idea to cover the last 3 or 4 inches of the shingle with roofing cement to prevent water blowing in or the wind lifting the shingle. Make sure you don't slop the cement far enough out on the ridge cap to make it visible. That black glop can really detract from the looks of almost any roof.

If you don't wish to use this Boston style ridge, you can use metal ridge caps (Fig. 6-8) that are face nailed along their bottom edges. This kind of face nailing seldom causes leakage problems because most ridges are sufficiently steep to keep water buildup here to a minimum. Still, it would be a good idea to coat the underside of any metal ridge used with roofing cement. Again, careful that it doesn't slop over onto the finished roof.

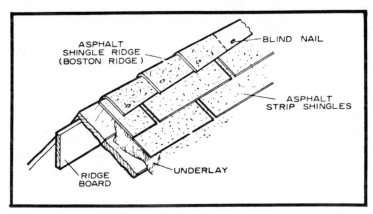

Fig. 6-7. Boston edge with asphalt shingles.

Wood shingles and shakes are similar in application to asphalt mineral coated materials, but there are enough variations to cause at least a few problems if you've never done this type of roofing before. Again, use only top quality material: number one grade heartwood, red or white cedar, shingles or shakes. You will need a shingling hatchet, too. This hatchet includes a movable guide to show the proper exposure length for your particular length of shake or shingle.

The particular process described here is for shakes. Generally wood shingles are little different in installation; a bit easier as they are smoother.

Figure 6-9, information supplied by the Red Cedar Shingle & Handsplit Shake Bureau, shows how quality is controlled and how

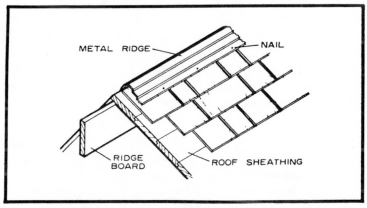

Fig. 6-8. Metal ridge can be used with either asphalt shingles or wood shingles.

109

many courses and square feet you can expect to get from a bundle of shakes in the various sizes to be found.

The variation in exposure can be a lot from one length of shake to another, with a maximum of 10 inches exposed for 2-foot shakes, while a 1½-foot shake can only have 7½ inches out in the weather. Shakes are spaced ½ inch apart when being installed, with the next course covering the gap left. Too, different shake thicknesses allow different exposures. That is, thinner ⅜-inch shakes 2 feet long are not recommended for more than 7½ inches of weather surface unless the roof pitch is at least 8 in 12, which is very steep.

APPLYING WOOD SHAKES

Select your roofing felt in at least a 30-pound weight, and apply it along the eave line over the sheathing boards. If open work lath or slats are used, they should be closed up along the eave line for at least the first three boards.

Start at the eave line with a double course of shakes, leaving the correct ½-inch distance between them and trimming the first gable end shake to get the correct overlap to cover that gap by at least 1 inch. The thicker end of the shake is the bottom edge exposed to the weather. This first course is not reversed as it would be with asphalt shingles, but if you prefer the way it looks you may go ahead and lay a triple line of shakes. The eave edges of the shakes should extend from a ½ inch to a full inch over the edge of the sheathing, and both courses should be even.

Now, you'll need to cut the 3-foot-wide roofing felt into 18-inch-wide strips. As you go up the roof, the 18-inch-wide strip of roofing felt is laid at a distance of twice the weather exposure up the shakes. For example, we'll assume you're using 18-inch shakes. The exposure should be 7½ inches. Roofing felt is laid on 15 inches up the shake, covering about 4 inches of that shake and extending back along the open work slats some 14 or 15 inches (Fig. 6-10). As I said, the shakes are spaced a ½ inch apart to allow for expansion. Of importance, too, is the overlap on those gaps. You must overlap at least 1½ inches to prevent water runthrough. The roofing paper, by the way, may be eliminated in areas which have neither driving rains nor heavy snowfall.

As you can see, this process of roofing actually gives you a triple roof over your sheathing or slatting. This is a good part of the reason

Shake Type, Length and Thickness	No. of Courses per Bundle	No. of Bundles per Square	Approximate coverage (in sq. ft.) of one square, when shakes are applied with ½" spacing, at following weather exposures (in inches):								
			5½	6½	7	7½	8½	10	11½	14	16
18" x ½" to ¾" Resawn	9/9 (a)	5 (b)	55 (c)	65	70	75 (d)	85 (e)	100 (f)			
18" x ¾" to 1¼" Resawn	9/9 (a)	5 (b)	55 (c)	65	70	75 (d)	85 (e)	100 (f)			
24" x ⅜" Handsplit	9/9 (a)	5		65	70	75 (g)	85	100 (h)	115 (i)		
24" x ½" to ¾" Resawn	9/9 (a)	5		65	70	75 (c)	85	100 (j)	115 (i)		
24" x ⅜" to 1¼" Resawn	9/9 (a)	5		65	70	75 (c)	85	100 (j)	115 (i)		
24" x ½" to ⅝" Tapersplit	9/9 (a)	5		65	70	75 (c)	85	100 (j)	115 (i)		
18" x ⅜" True-Edge Straight-Split	14 (k) Straight	4								100	112 (l)
18" x ⅜" Straight-Split	19 (k) Straight	5	65 (c)	75	80	90 (i)	100 (i)				
24" x ⅜" Straight-Split	16 (k) Straight	5		65	70	75 (c)	85	100 (i)	115(i)		
15" Starter-Finish Course	9/9 (a)	5	Use supplementary with shakes applied not over 10" weather exposure.								

(a) Packed in 18"-wide frames.

(b) 5 bundles will cover 100 sq. ft. roof area when used as starter-finish course at 10" weather exposure; 6 bundles will cover 100 sq. ft. wall area when used at 8½" weather exposure; 7 bundles will cover 100 sq. ft. roof area when used at 7½" weather exposure; see footnote (m).

(c) Maximum recommended weather exposure for three-ply roof construction.

(d) Maximum recommended weather exposure for two-ply roof construction; 7 bundles will cover 100 sq. ft. roof area when applied at 7½" weather exposure; see footnote (m).

(e) Maximum recommended weather exposure for sidewall construction; 6 bundles will cover 100 sq. ft. when applied at 8½" weather exposure; see footnote (m).

(f) Maximum recommended weather exposure for starter-finish course appli-cation; 5 bundles will cover 100 sq. ft. when applied at 10" weather exposure; see footnote (m).

(g) Maximum recommended weather exposure for application on roof pitches between 4-in-12 and 8-in-12.

(h) Maximum recommended weather exposure for application on roof pitches of 8-in-12 and steeper.

(i) Maximum recommended weather exposure for single-coursed wall construction.

(j) Maximum recommended weather exposure for two-ply roof construction.

(k) Packed in 20" wide frames.

(l) Maximum recommended weather exposure for double-coursed wall construction.

(m) All coverage based on ½" spacing between shakes.

Fig. 6-9. Red cedar shakes grading and packaging. (Courtesy of Red Cedar Shingle & Handsplit Shake Bureau.)

Fig. 6-10. Openwork roofing used under wood shingles. (Courtesy of Red Cedar Shingle & Handsplit Shake Bureau.)

that wood roofing lasts such a long time when combined with the rot resistant qualities of cedar.

With wood roofing you again have a double choice of ridge styles. Basically, the Boston style here is a simple variant of that used with asphalt shingles. Actually, since wood roofing existed long before asphalt, it would be more reasonable to say the asphalt Boston ridge is the variant.

Select the most uniform shakes you can. The smoother the better and the less taper the better. Apply a strip of roofing felt 8 to 10 inches wide over the ridge. Make sure each shake is close to the same width, about 6 inches for best results. Tack, very lightly, two wood straightedges the entire length of the ridge line, 5 inches down from the ridge peak, and one on each side.

Now, coat the roofing felt with a light dose of asphalt cement, and lay the first shake with one side butting the straightedge. Nail in place, with two nails back beyond the area that will be exposed to the weather. Place the second shake against the straightedge on the opposite side of the ridge and nail that in place. Leave about the same weather exposure as you did for the actual shake courses on the roof as you go along.

Once you reach the opposite end of the house, start a second course there and continue on back. The second course can be eliminated, but it provides a much better weather seal, especially as you now start the first shake butted against the straightedge on the opposite side of the roof from where you first started, which provides a joint overlap (Fig. 6-11).

LOW PITCH OR BUILTUP ROOFS

Low pitch roofing is more of a problem, but if your roof is only 4 in 12, it becomes magnified. Too, roll roofing can sometimes save a fair amount of time over asphalt shingles even with higher pitched roofs, and may be lower in overall cost, too. Builtup roofs are referred to in years: 10-, 15-, and 20-year applications are those most commonly used by the contractors who do this work. Like all other roofing jobs, it pays to use the best materials so that the job doesn't have to be repeated. If you're doing the work yourself, the materials add only a small amount to overall housing costs, while keeping you off ladders and scaffolds for many years. If you're hiring the job done, the materials cost is usually lower than the labor cost, so it doesn't even pay to think of getting a cheap job done only to have to have it repeated in a short time.

Builtup roofing starts with 45-pound roofing felt (for a 15-year roof, start with 30-pound felt), laid down dry, and nailed at 6-inch intervals along the edges. Use hot dip galvanized nails, 1 inch long and make sure they either have ⅜-inch heads or are driven through

Fig. 6-11. Ridge construction with wood shakes. (Courtesy of Red Cedar Shingle & Handsplit Shake Bureau.)

113

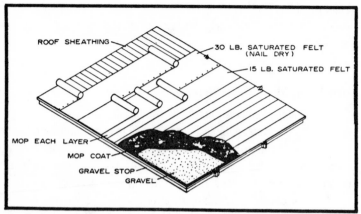

Fig. 6-12. Installation of a built up roof.

1-inch diameter tin caps. This dry sheet will keep later applications of hot tar from seeping through the roof joints and messing up your attic space. Overlap at least 1 foot.

Now, lay down a layer of 30-pound roofing felt, a strip at a time, again with at least a 1-foot overlap. Here the use of a 1½-foot overlap would be a good idea. Each strip is mopped with hot tar, and no nails are used. This application is repeated at least twice more to build up the roof.

When the final layer of tarred felt is laid down, it is covered with a coating of hot roofer's tar and you have a choice of finishes. Actually, it could be left this way, but such a roof is most suitable for industrial buildings as it is supremely ugly. While the final coat of tar is still hot, you can lay down a coating of roofing gravel, or lay down mineral covered roll roofing (Fig. 6-12).

Where you come up to cornice or eave lines with built up roofing special procedures are needed. First, metal edging is used, and a metal gravel strip must be used when the final covering is to be roofing gravel. The roofing gravel stop goes on last, just before the gravel, that is, and is tarred into the builtup roof in at least two strips, as shown in Fig. 6-13.

Should you have a dormer or some other building addition extending up above the roof, you must install a cant strip, a strip of wood cut at a 45-degree angle, along the base of the wall. Bring the roofing up over that and under the flashing from the side of the house addition. The cant strip serves to keep the roll roofing from tearing (Fig. 6-14).

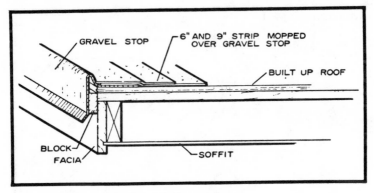

Fig. 6-13. Gravel stop used on a built up roof.

METAL ROOFING

While most of today's metal roofing application seems to be on farm buildings of one sort of another, a quick look around will show us that wasn't always so. There are distinct advantages in the use of metal roofing, whether it is of galvanized steel or aluminum. To start with, the weight of the roofing is low, making installation easy even in large sheets. Durability of the higher qualities of metal roofing rivals that of the most expensive wood roofing, with aluminum

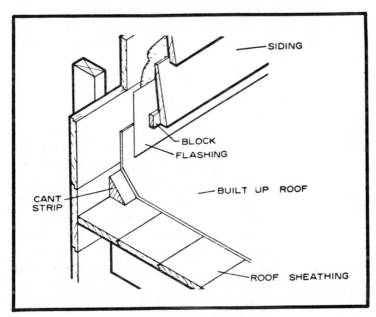

Fig. 6-14. Installation of flashing on a built up roof.

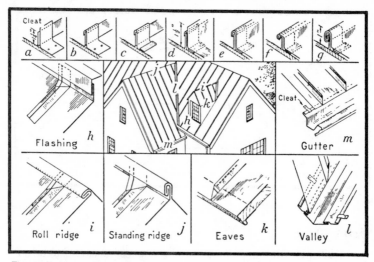

Fig. 6-15. Installation of tin, or terne metal, roofing. (A through G) Steps in forming a standing seam. (H through M) Joints at breaks in the roof.

roofing about the most expensive of the presently available styles, and the longest lasting.

The basic disadvantages are the unattractiveness of the unfinished metal, which is easily cured through an application of a high quality paint, and the noise the roof will make in heavy rainstorms, especially in hail and sleet storms. The noise, though, is rather easy to get used to when the cost and rapidity of installation are considered.

Metals still found are tin (actually called terne), galvanized steel, and aluminum. Tin roofing is a malleable steel coated with an alloy of lead and tin, and can be expected to last for about 50 years if properly installed and if painted every few years. Look for a lead coating (per 436 square feet just to make things odd) of at least 20 pounds, with preference going to the 40-pound coating. Two metal weights, IC and IX, are to be found; stick with IX as it is the heaviest. To install tin roofing, which comes in rolls 14, 20, 24, and 28 inches wide by 50 or 100 feet long, you'll need some metal working tools not usually in the homeowner's toolbox. Basically you'll need a metal brake for forming square corners, a couple of other metal forming tools for making joints, and a propane torch for soldering seams. You may wish to leave this type of roofing to a contractor, but most of the tools can be rented, and most of the techniques can be covered rather quickly right here, so just in case, we'll take a look at them.

Sheathing for metal roofing of all kinds is of the normal plywood or board types, covered with roofing felt. The biggest difference is the fact that the roofing felt should be rosin saturated instead of tar saturated. The roofing felt is not essential, but will do more than a little to dampen the noise of rain on the roof. Overlap roofing paper 2 to 4 inches at the seams.

For roof slopes under 3 in 12, a flat seam, which requires a solder seal, is used. A standing seam can be used on roofs with a slope greater than that. Figure 6-15 shows the basic techniques for laying a standing seam roof, including the steps taken to form the standing seam. One strip at a time is laid. A couple of special tools are needed to form the standing seam. Check with your tool rental agency for these metal bending tools.

The formation of a flat seam requires pretty much the same technique as the standing seam, but no second roll is taken in the seam (Fig. 6-16). A single roll is used, the seam is then flattened down its length. You can use a 2 by 4 and moderately heavy 28- to 32-ounce ball pien hammer for this job. You then take a 70/30 tin-lead solder and a propane torch and flow the solder along the open edge of the seam. I recommend the 70/30 solder simply because it is quite easy to work with, while still having enough tin in it to keep the melting point low enough to prevent fire problems. You may wish to use a soldering iron to cut those problems even more, but fast use of

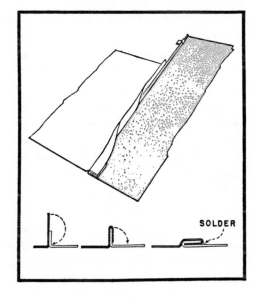

Fig. 6-16. Method of forming a flat seam.

a propane torch, or the use of a propane torch with a solid tip, should keep them down to almost nothing.

Simpler styles of metal roofing installation start with galvanized steel. Fewer special tools are needed: a hacksaw with the correct size blades, a pair of metal snips, and a rented power shear or a reciprocating saw with metal blades. Either of these last two will make long cuts a lot neater and more easily than will the metal snips.

Various designs are to be found in galvanized roofing. The metal may be formed into *V*s or *U*s, either of which has sufficient strength, if you use at a minimum 28-gauge thickness. Remember, too, that the lower the gauge of the metal, the heavier that metal is. Look for the type of galvanized roofing that has a coating of 2 ounces of zinc per square foot. This is the heaviest coating available and will help the roofing endure for many years.

V-crimp roofing comes in 2- and 2½-foot widths. The sheets are available in 6- and 12-foot lengths. Select the roofing with five crips.

Corrugated sheets are 26 inches wide if 1½-inch corrugations are used and 27½ inches wide where the corrugations are 2½ inches. Select either, as coverage is 2 feet in either case. Lengths range from 6 to 32 feet.

For residential use, galvanized roofing should be laid on tight sheathing, covered with heavyweight rosin impregnated roofing paper to cut down on rain noise.

For slopes of 4 in 12 or less, you must lap the sheet ends by 9 inches, while steeper roofs require a lap of no more than 6 inches.

Use screw shank nails, hot dipped galvanized. Do not use aluminum nails here as the two different metals in contact will corrode rapidly. Use neoprene washers under the nail heads, and make sure the nails are long enough to fully penetrate the sheathing when nailing is done from the tops of the corrugations or crimps. Never nail in the valleys as this can cause leakage.

All flashing must be of galvanized steel. In metal roofs, you must always match metals to prevent electrolytic corrosion from setting in.

After about a year of letting a galvanized steel roof weather, you should give it a good coat of primer and paint. Clean the entire roof thoroughly before priming, paying a lot of attention to any rust spots. Use a zinc base paint or you'll have peeling problems inside of 6 months.

Aluminum roofing is our final style of metal roofing. It reflects a bit more heat, usually, than does steel roofing, requires no painting, and corrodes only on the surface. Oxidation of aluminum is self-limiting as the resulting oxides form a barrier impenetrable to air. Aluminum roofing is available in V-crimp and corrugated styles, as is galvanized steel roofing. The 26-inch-wide size has five crips, while the 50-inch-wide style has eight, producing coverage of 2 feet and 4 feet when lap is allowed for. Finishes can vary from smooth to embossed, and thickness will vary from 0.019 inch to 0.024 inch. Select the heaviest for geatest durability. Lengths run from 6 to 32 feet.

Corrugated styles are similar in all ways, though corrugations may be 1¼ inches or 2½ inches.

Again, the roofing is laid over solid sheathing of either boards or plywood when used for residential purposes. Asphalt impregnated roofing felt is used underneath, in a 30-pound weight, to cut down on rain noise. Lap the roofing felt at least 3 inches, and, if steel nails are used to hold it, make sure those nails are prevented from touching the aluminum.

End laps for aluminum roofing must be at least 6 inches, and the edges at the eaves should extend over at least 1 inch, with 2 inches preferred. Nailing is done with aluminum ring shank nails, using neoprene washers. Only aluminum flashing can be used.

MATERIAL ESTIMATION

Figure 6-17 shows the most common roof styles, with the dimensions needed for estimating the correct amount of roofing materials. Generally the materials will be sold by the square; a square is 100 square feet. Once you know how many 100 square feet are in your roof, you'll have a good idea of how much to buy. Allow extra material for overhangs at eaves and gable ends, and allow 10 percent for waste. Subtract any materials not needed to cover spots where chimneys and vents come through the roof.

ROOF FLASHING

Even if your house is a simple rectangle with a gable roof, you will find spots that need flashing. Around vents and chimneys are the most common. If the roof you use is more complex, or there is an L-addition on the house, you'll need to flash the valleys. If this job is

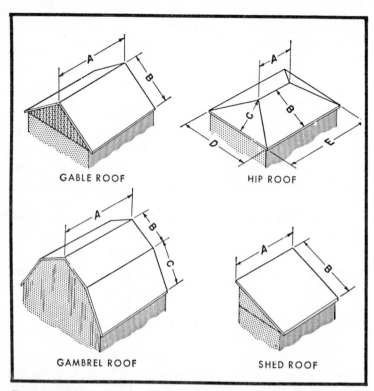

Fig. 6-17. Method of determining the area of a roof. Gable roof: multiply roof length A by rafter length B; multiply by two. Hip roof: add roof length A and eaves length E; divide by two; multiply by rafter length B; multiply by two. Multiply longest rafter length C by eaves length D. Add figures obtained. Gambrel roof: add rafter lengths B and C; multiply by roof length A; multiply by two. Shed roof: multiply roof length A by rafter length B.

not done, or is done incorrectly, you'll spend all the time searching for water leaks that may prove nearly impossible to locate.

Usually today the flashing material used with almost all shingle roofs is aluminum sheeting. Copper used to be used, and is still quite effective, but it is also murder on the wallet. Where galvanized roofing is used, you must also use galvanized flashing.

Valley flashing uses flashing strips no less than 20 inches wide, whether the valley is open or closed. For open valleys, that is, valleys where the shingles do not come close to meeting in the V, the top should open out to no less than 4 inches, with a widening taper to the bottom of about ⅛ inch per foot of roof length. If one side of the roof is of much greater size, or has a steeper slope, than the other, place a V-crimp down the center of the flashing. This is done so that the greater volume of water flowing off the larger roof section or steeper slope cannot wash across the valley and up under the shingles on the other side.

Figure 6-18 shows the flashing held down under the shingles with cleats. This is only one method. Shingle nails (hot dip galvanized for steel, and aluminum for aluminum) with neoprene seals are used more often. Every shingle, by the way, should have two extra shingle nails to hold the shingle in place just *outside* the edge of the flashing.

Flashing in closed valleys (Fig. 6-19) should be coated with roofer's cement or mastic. Shingles still require the extra nails. Use ring shank nails.

Flashing around a chimney varies according to its site. In fact, chimney flashing also applies to any vertical style of flashing. It is two piece, with one piece attached to the vertical portion and one piece on the roof. The two pieces are not tied rigidly together. With a solid tie in, expansion and contraction forces in the house will eventually force the flashing to work itself free. The flashing extends up the vertical surface a minimum of 6 inches and back under the shingles about 2 inches further (Fig. 6-20). Cap flashing is set into the mortar of the chimney and comes down *over* the under flashing. If vent pipes

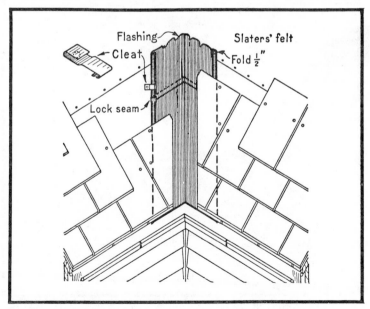

Fig. 6-18. Flashing in an open valley.

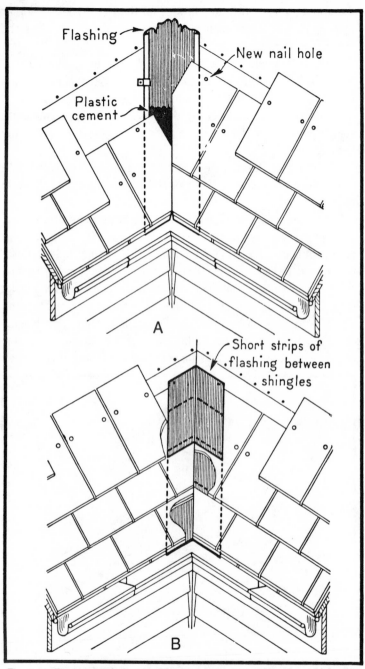

Fig. 6-19. Flashing in a closed valley. (A) Long metal strip under shingles. (B) Short pieces of metal intermembered with shingles.

are not designed with grooves for cap flashing, you have two choices: you can eeither layer the cap flashing on with roofer's cement very heavily, or run a solder bead around the vent pipe to hold the flashing and seal it. I would recommend in almost every instance that you go with the roofer's mastic. While this type of solder joint is long lasting it is also not all that easy to make if you haven't got better than fair skills with a soldering torch. Here, too, allowance must be made for expansion and contraction, which adds to soldering problems.

Cap flashing should reach down at least 4 inches over the base flashing.

GUTTERS AND DOWNSPOUTS

Many homes are erected without guttering, letting nature take care of the run off from the roof in any kind of rainfall. While 1 or 2 years of this may not be a problem, over time the falling water tends to cut away at the ground around the house, even when gravel drip lines are put in. Sooner or later, the water starts to erode around the foundation, with the result being either a weakening of the foundation wall or water seepage into the basement or crawl space. Often both will happen.

Formed metal gutters of almost any metal imaginable are still to be found, but today's emphasis seems to be on aluminum. Copper, again, has priced itself out of the market, while steel tends to corrode much too easily and quickly. Thus either anodized aluminum

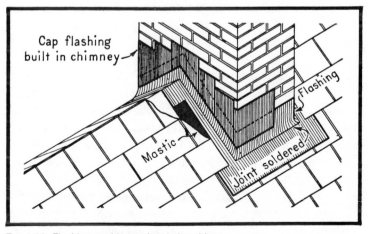

Fig. 6-20. Flashing at chimney located at ridge.

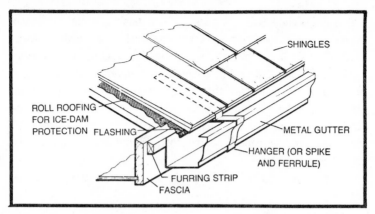

Fig. 6-21. Installation of formed metal gutter.

in its natural color or any of a variety of factory enameled aluminums are most often used. Wooden gutters can still be found, but with their short lifetime there seems little real point in bothering with them.

The most difficult part of the installation job with gutters and downspouts seems to be the location, size, and number of downspouts. Basically, the simplest and usually the best location for downspouts is at the corners of the house. The size is reasonably simple to determine also, according to a family member who makes a living working with residential aluminum siding, windows, and such. Use 1 square inch of downspout for every 100 square feet of roof. Keep gutter areas the same as downspout areas if the gutters are no more than 40 feet apart and you should have no problems—until the time comes to clean leaves out. When longer gutter runs between downspouts need to be used, simply increase the size of the gutter width.

Select a gutter that has a starting drain size larger than the area of the downspout entrance for smoothest water flow in heavy rains.

Gutter hangers should be spaced about 4 feet apart if galvanized steel gutters are used. As Fig. 6-21 shows, the strap goes back up between the first course and the finish course of shingles so some planning is needed. Aluminum gutter straps should be no more than 30 inches apart. The gutter is also nailed to a furring strip laid along the fascia. This furring strip should receive at least two prime coats and three finish coats of paint for greatest longevity. For even more durability, go for the extra cost of redwood here.

Gutter shape is a factor, but mostly it is decided by availability and personal taste, as a fair number of styles can be found (Fig. 6-22).

Downspouts are fastened to the walls using straps and hooks (Fig. 6-23). Too, the downspout should have an elbow on its lower end and a splash block of concrete, slate, or some other hard material under its end. This splash block can be eliminated if the downspouts are led into shallow dry wells; simply a hole loosely filled with gravel and covered over. Or they can feed into the unfolding type of seepage hose seen in many catalogs, although I've never seen one actually on a house.

Gutter slope or slant is of great importance, too. Each gutter should slant at a rate of 1/16 inch per foot towards the downspout entrance. Use a wire guard over the downspout entrance to keep leaves from clogging what can be a hard to reach area.

Gutters are joined by fitting the lower section outside the upper section (higher as for slant). Joints should be sealed, though soldering is seldom used anymore. Use a mastic cement designed for gutters. These should be applied carefully if color matching isn't possible.

SNOW GUARDS

Your need for snow guards, of course, depends on the area in which you live. Not of use to many Floridians, snow guards can, in

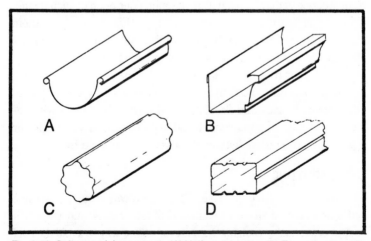

Fig. 6-22. Gutters and downspouts. (A) Half-round gutter. (B) Formed gutter. (C) Round downspout. (D) Rectangular downspout.

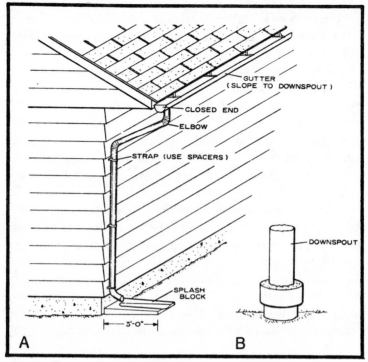

Fig. 6-23. Downspout installation. (A) Downspout with splash block. (B) Drain to storm sewer.

other areas, prevent damage to gutters and even people who may be walking out of a door when the whole pile of white mud starts to go. Roof steepness may also have an effect on your need of such things. If snow guards are used, no matter the type (Fig. 6-24), space them about 8 inches apart along the edge of the roof, and use three rows about 1 foot apart, or a bit more, for greatest safety.

Once your roofing is installed as recommended, a check every few years, assuming no damage from falling limbs, will allow you to keep loose shingles and flashing nailed down and coated with cement. Any kind of good roof should last at least 30 years. Better types may not start to leak until 50 years have gone by.

SHAKE SPLITTING

Wood roofing is expensive. There is no way around it. While a cedar or redwood shake or shingle roof may outlast most of us, it costs a great deal of cash for the materials. One way to avoid the cost is to make your own shakes.

Our ancestors did it. And the job is relatively simple. Too, if you're willing to replace the roof in a shorter time, the use of woods such as cedar (construction cedar is not cedar, it is arbor vitae, but what the devil), when yellow pine and other woods can be substituted.

Your first chore, and it may be a chore, is to locate a tool known as a froe. Check any handicrafts areas in your locale. The odds are excellent your local hardware clerk never even heard of the thing.

A froe is simply a thick balded knife with a handle at right angles to the blade. You'll also need a mallet.

Once the tools are in hand, you need to look for an item known as bolts. Bolts are nothing more than sections of pine, cedar, or some other wood with the bark removed at the mill. You can also mill them roughly with a chainsaw. They should be in lengths appropriate

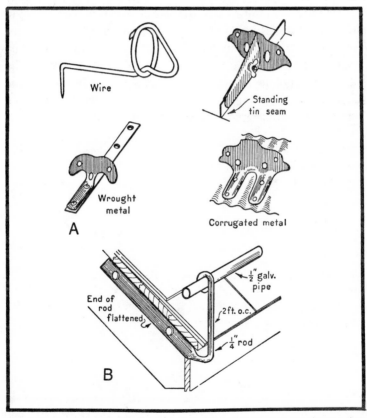

Fig. 6-24. Snow guards. (A) Common types installed at the same time as the roofing. (B) Homemade type.

to the size (length) of the shakes you want. Look for wood that has had few, if any, branches, thus is knot-free or close to it.

Find a large stump, or heavy workbench. Place the first bolt on the stump, set the froe in at the width you wish to start your shake. Hit the end of the froe with the mallet.

If the wood is straight grained, as are most pines, cedar, etc., it will take just a few seconds to get your first handmade shake. Believe it or not, with minor variations, this is still the way its done commercially today. You can lay out lines on the bolt to where the froe should sit for each split for greatest consistency, but after about 2 hours you'll probably find eye judgement the easiest.

While the process sounds time-consuming, and is when you first start out, it rapidly becomes an automatic thing, with the finished shakes piling up rapidly. Even for a large house, a normally coordinated person of average strength or less should be able to do a roof full of shakes inside of 3 days. Stronger people with greater endurance, and a capacity for organizing friends to tote and set up bolts, will do the same job in a single day. Just remember, the thinnest part of the shake, and the smoothest, will be the side you start the split on. If you reverse the bolt each time you split off a shake, greater uniformity will be the result.

Chapter 7
Foundations & Other Masonry

Once the house corners and lines are laid out, you must start the excavation. Most of us putting in a full basement, a crawl space, or building on a slab will hire a contractor to make the excavations. That's an awful lot of digging to handle with a shovel!

A cabin or vacation home going up on piers, though, is easier to excavate for, especially in areas where frost depth is not more than 2 feet below the surface.

Foundation design is of great importance to the overall home structure. If the foundation is understrength in any way, the house cannot be expected to last without extensive repairs and, usually, a lot of expensive work on the underpinnings in the years to come. In addition, a poorly constructed foundation is unsafe.

No matter the type of foundation, there are several design factors that must always be followed. Footings must be used on all foundation walls and on all piers. These footings should never be less than 6 inches thick, while a footing thickness of 8 inches to 1 foot is much preferable. Footings must project past the foundation wall, or pier, at least half the thickness of the wall. So for an 8-inch foundation wall, your footings would be double that width, or 16 inches, while 1-foot-thick foundation wall would require 2-foot-wide footings. Local codes and soil conditions may modify those needs, but the modification will almost never be on the down side.

Excavations should be as close to the exact depth needed as is possible, and the bottom of the excavation cleared of loose dirt and

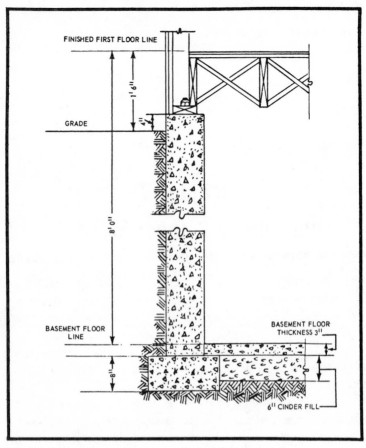

FINISHED FIRST FLOOR LINE

GRADE

BASEMENT FLOOR LINE

BASEMENT FLOOR THICKNESS 3"

6" CINDER FILL

1' 6"

8' 0"

8"

Fig. 7-1. Wall section showing excavation depth data.

rock. This area, incidentally, is not tamped or otherwise fooled with regardless of what a few people say. Should the excavation be carried too far down, it is *never* filled with earth or rock. Simply build the footing forms at the correct depth and allow concrete to flow out and fill the extra depth.

In most areas the soil being removed will not cut away sharply enough to be used as a form for footings or foundation walls, so wooden forms will be needed. In fact, for foundation walls, whether of concrete block or poured concrete, most plans will require you to excavate to at least 2 feet outside the wall plane. This allows work to be carried on around the outside of the foundation wall, and provides the space for drain tiles at the base of the wall, when they're required.

Most often the excavation for full basements will be carried at least 9 inches below the plane of the finished floor, allowing you to place a 6-inch depth of gravel fill under a 3-inch finished concrete.

Your plans will contain a drawing much like Fig. 7-1, which will allow you to rather easily determine the depth of excavation. As this drawing shows, the foundation wall depth is 8 feet from the first floor plane, while that plane is 1½ feet above the surface. This drawing allows only a 4-inch clearance between the top of the masonry and start of the wood structure: 8 inches is better.

With a total floor thickness of 9 inches (including fill) in the basement, your main excavation would be 7 feet 3 inches deep. But the edges, or footing excavation, will be deeper, dropping at least 2 inches lower than the main excavation so that the top of the footing is level with the 6 inches of fill as shown.

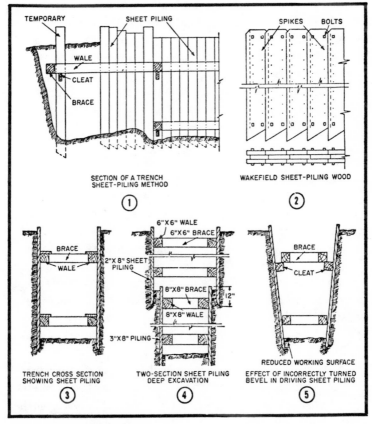

Fig. 7-2. Wooden sheet piling.

Concrete poured forms are essential for footings and any poured walls. Footings for piers can usually be poured directly in their holes if the ground is reasonably firm and the edges of the hole are cut carefully.

By the way, if the excavation is over 4 feet deep, it is a good safety measure to brace the sides of the trench to prevent any possibility of cave ins (Fig. 7-2). While most adults who will be working in and around foundation walls are well over 4 feet tall, burial to the chest level can restrict breathing badly enough to cause suffocation in a matter of just a few minutes.

Other safety precautions involve removing any large rocks and trees which could create hazards. No heavy equipment should be brought within 2 feet of the edge of the excavation, and when it is brought at all close, anyone working in the hole should get out.

Once the excavation is made and shored up, you can make forms for the footings, piers, and walls. Figure 7-3 shows the correct construction for a form when the wall is to be of poured concrete. A simple reduction in dimensions will give you the proper forms for footings and piers.

When the forms are in, it's time to start considering the cement, sand, gravel, and water that will go into the concrete needed to complete the job.

CONCRETE

Unless the four ingredients named above are used, you will not be working with concrete. Leaving out the large aggregate (gravel) means you have mixed up mortar. Concrete hardens by a process known as hydration, not by evaporation of the water in the mix. In fact, for the first stages of hardening, the wetter you're able to keep the concrete the better for the hardening process. Hydration is a chemical process and concrete must be cured while it goes on in order for it to reach its greatest strength. Curing is essentially nothing more than making sure the water content of the concrete stays high enough for a long enough time to allow hydration to continue.

Concrete reaches different strength levels at different times during the curing process, with most of today's work being centered around 7-day strength, though some types of concrete will reach the correct cure in 3 days.

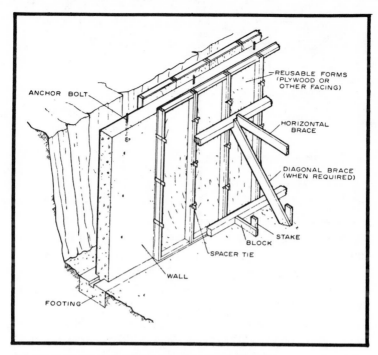

Fig. 7-3. Typical form needed for pouring concrete walls.

Type I, or regular portland cement, is used for general sidewalk and other construction, while Type II is a type that has a lower heat of hydration. Type III is a high early strength modified portland cement and is often used in cold weather as it requires less protection against cold. Type III also reaches 28-day strength levels for types I and II in 7 days, and reaches their 7-day levels in 3 days. Types IV and V are of less interest. Type IV is a very low heat style, sets up slowly, and is most used in dam construction, while Type V is for use when the resulting structure will be exposed to soils with a high alkali content.

Cement to be used and mixed on site will come in 94-pound bags, about 1 cubic foot of cement. Storage is simple. Stack the sacks as tightly as possible, and keep them totally dry. Do not use the cement if it doesn't flow freely or if it contains lumps.

AGGREGATES

For home construction, we'll be using both fine aggregates, sand, and coarse, gravel. Depending on your particular mix, the

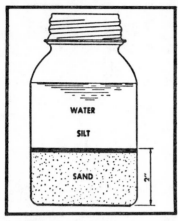

Fig. 7-4. Quart jar method of determining silt content of sand.

aggregates will form between two-thirds and nearly four-fifths of the total of the concrete, so it is important to get the best quality available. Both sand and gravel too often contain silt, clay, various salts, and organic matter, which can either interfere with the hydration process or with final strength.

The sand can be easily tested for suitability, either where it is purchased or on site after delivery. Simply take a quart jar, pour in about 2 inches of sand and bring the jar up to about three-quarters full with clean water. Shake it hard for about a minute, then set it aside for about an hour. When the hour is up, take your folding rule and place it alongside the jar. If the settled sand has more than ⅛ inch of silt on top of it, you'll have to wash the sand before making concrete (Fig. 7-4).

While washing sand may sound like a silly job, you are now working with the base of your vacation home, and that base is a support for everything else. Build a washer about 4½ feet high at the top end, 10 feet long, 1½ or 2 feet wide. The last or bottom 2½ feet should be left open, and covered with a sixteen mesh screen. Fill the washer top with sand, and turn on the garden hose (Fig. 7-5).

Coarse aggregate is generally rather easy to check with just a look. Pick up several handfuls around and through the pile and look for easily pulverized material, laminates such as shale, and large amounts of dirt, sticks, and so forth. All are to be avoided.

WATER

Water serves two purposes in mixing concrete. It allows the start of the hydration process, and also allows the mix to be made

134

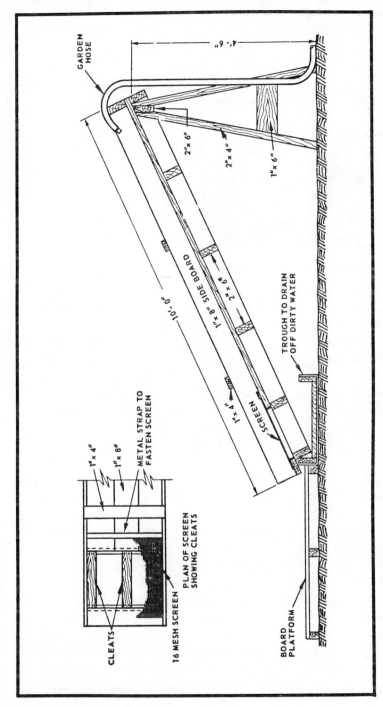

Fig. 7-5. Field constructed for washing aggregate.

135

Fig. 7-6. Slump test.

workable enough to use. Water used to mix concrete should be free of alkali, decayed organic matter, acids, and oil. Usually if the water is fit to drink, it is suitable for making concrete.

While more water must be added to the mix than is really needed to start and carry out the hydration process (otherwise the mix would be too stiff to use), too much water will actually weaken the concrete, and will also impair its watertightness. Use just enough water to get a concrete mix that will flow into the forms and no more.

To test a batch of concrete for consistency, you will need to make a metal cone with a base 8 inches in diameter and a top 4 inches in diameter. The cone is 12 inches tall. Both base and top are open. You'll also need a smooth rod, ⅝ inches thick and about 2 feet long with a pointed end.

The cone is placed on a moist, flat surface of nonabsorbant material. It is then dampened, and a sample of the concrete batch taken. The cone is filled in three layers, a shovel at a time, with each layer being about a third of the cone's capacity. Each layer is rodded in. That is, the pointed rod is used to poke through the concrete. Generally, it is recommended that each layer receive twenty-five pokes, spread uniformly around the cone's interior. When the cone is a bit more than full, use a piece of scrap board to strike the top surface off flat. The cone is now removed and the slump measured, as shown in Fig. 7-6. Your plans should specify the amount of slump considered proper, but if they don't you can work with a 3-inch slump for concrete that is to be poured. For more general uses, less slump may be desirable.

The slump pile gives you a chance to check some other qualities of your concrete mix. A well-proportioned mix, when gently tapped on its side, should only slump a bit lower. No falling apart or separation of the aggregates should be visible. Should the mix crumble apart, there is too much sand in it. If it segregates, there is too little sand.

Water is never added to get the degree of slump needed, unless additional mixing also includes differing amounts of aggregates and cement. Most adjustments are made by adjusting the amount of the aggregates. The table in Fig. 7-7 will provide starting places for most mixes.

Most of us tend to shy away from estimating the amount of concrete we'll need to do any given job, hoping we can con some local expert into doing at least that part of the job for us. Actually, the estimation is quite simple. Start with the footing forms. Measure width, height, and depth, then multiply these three figures. You should do this in feet, by the way. As an example, let's assume a total perimeter for the house of 140 feet, a 40-foot by 30-foot rectangle. The footings are to be 24 inches, or 2 feet, wide. Depth is 1 foot. So, grabbing the old pocket calculator, we come up with a total of 280 cubic feet. A cubic yard, the standard concrete volume, contains 27 cubic feet, but to make things easier, we can go ahead and use 25. This gives an automatic allowance for waste just a bit under the standard 10 percent recommended for most building materials. Total needs for this job are 11.2 cubic yards.

BUYING CONCRETE

Once the forms are in, the amount of concrete estimated, you have to decide on which way you want to buy your cement. You can buy it by the bag and do all the mixing by hand, or in a small power driven mixer, but for anything other than the smallest jobs, that's totally impractical. In most cases, we'll want to use some form of ready mixed concrete delivered by truck. Small batches can be hand mixed where transport is a problem; if you're far enough back in the boonies with your vacation home, you'll want to rent a small power mixer to trail in there and do the job.

*Increase or decrease water per cu. yd. of concrete by 3% for each increase or decrease of 1 in. in slump recalculate quantities of cement and aggregate to maintain the quality of concrete. For stone sand, increase percentage of sand by 3 and water by 15 lb. per cu. yd. of concrete. For less workable concrete, as in pavements, decrease percentage of sand by 3 and water by 8 lb. per cu. yd. of concrete.

Maximum size of aggregate, inches	Water, gallon per sack of cement	Water, gallon per cu yd of concrete	Cement, sacks per cu yd of concrete	With Fine Sand—Fineness Modulus 2.20-2.40						With Medium Sand—Fineness Modulus 2.60-2.90						With Coarse Sand—Fineness Modulus 2.90-3.20					
				Fine aggregate—per cent of total aggregate	Fine aggre—lb per sack of cement	Coarse aggre—lb per sack of cement	Fine aggregate—lb per cu yd of concrete	Coarse aggregate—lb per cu yd of concrete	Yield, cu ft concrete per sack of cement	Fine aggregate—per cent of total aggregate	Fine aggre—lb per sack of cement	Coarse aggre—lb per sack of cement	Fine aggregate—lb per cu yd of concrete	Coarse aggregate—lb per cu yd of concrete	Yield, cu ft concrete per sack of cement	Fine aggregate—per cent of total aggregate	Fine aggre—lb per sack of cement	Coarse aggre—lb per sack of cement	Fine aggregate—lb per cu yd of concrete	Coarse aggregate—lb per cu yd of concrete	Yield, cu ft concrete per sack of cement
¾	5	38	7.6	43	170	230	1290	1750	3.56	45	180	220	1370	1670	3.56	47	185	210	1370	1595	3.56
1	5	37	7.4	38	160	255	1185	1890	3.65	40	165	250	1220	1850	3.65	42	175	240	1295	1775	3.65
1½	5	35	7.0	34	150	300	1050	2100	3.86	36	160	290	1120	2030	3.86	38	170	280	1190	1960	3.86
2	5	33	6.6	31	157	335	990	2210	4.09	33	160	325	1055	2140	4.09	35	170	315	1120	2080	4.09
¾	5½	38	6.9	44	195	250	1345	1725	3.91	46	205	240	1415	1655	3.91	48	215	230	1480	1585	3.91
1	5½	37	6.7	39	180	285	1205	1910	4.03	41	190	275	1270	1840	4.03	43	200	265	1340	1775	4.03
1½	5½	35	6.4	35	175	320	1120	2050	4.22	37	185	315	1185	2015	4.22	39	195	305	1250	1950	4.22
2	5½	33	6.0	32	175	370	1050	2220	4.50	34	185	360	1110	2160	4.50	36	195	350	1170	2100	4.50
¾	6	38	6.3	45	225	275	1420	1730	4.29	47	235	265	1480	1670	4.29	49	245	255	1540	1610	4.29
1	6	37	6.2	40	205	305	1270	1890	4.36	42	215	295	1335	1830	4.36	44	225	285	1395	1770	4.36
1½	6	35	5.8	36	200	355	1160	2060	4.66	38	210	345	1220	2000	4.66	40	225	310	1305	1945	4.66
2	6	33	5.5	33	200	400	1100	2060	4.91	35	210	390	1155	2145	4.91	37	225	355	1210	2090	4.91
¾	6½	38	5.9	46	245	288	1445	1700	4.58	48	255	280	1505	1650	4.58	50	220	265	1560	1560	4.58
1	6½	37	5.7	41	230	330	1310	1880	4.74	43	240	320	1370	1825	4.74	45	250	310	1425	1765	4.74
1½	6½	35	5.4	37	225	380	1215	2050	5.00	39	235	370	1270	2000	5.00	41	250	355	1350	1920	5.00
2	6½	33	5.1	34	225	430	1150	2195	5.30	36	235	415	1200	2120	5.30	38	250	405	1275	2065	5.30
¾	7	38	5.4	47	280	315	1510	1700	5.00	49	290	305	1565	1650	5.00	51	300	290	1620	1565	5.00
1	7	37	5.3	42	255	355	1350	1880	5.10	44	270	340	1430	1800	5.10	46	280	330	1485	1750	5.10
1½	7	35	5.0	38	250	410	1250	2050	5.40	40	265	395	1325	1975	5.40	42	270	385	1350	1925	5.40
2	7	33	4.7	35	250	465	1210	2185	5.75	37	265	450	1245	2120	5.75	44	280	435	1315	2045	5.75
¾	7½	38	5.1	48	300	330	1530	1680	5.30	50	315	315	1605	1605	5.30	52	330	300	1685	1530	5.30
1	7½	37	4.9	43	285	380	1400	1860	5.51	45	300	365	1470	1790	5.51	47	310	355	1520	1740	5.51
1½	7½	35	4.7	39	275	430	1290	2020	5.75	41	290	415	1365	1950	5.75	43	305	400	1435	1880	5.75
2	7½	33	4.4	36	275	495	1210	2180	6.14	38	290	480	1275	2110	6.14	40	305	465	1340	2045	6.14
¾	8	38	4.8	49	330	345	1585	1655	5.63	51	345	330	1660	1585	5.63	53	360	315	1730	1510	5.63
1	8	37	4.6	44	315	400	1450	1840	5.87	46	330	385	1520	1770	5.87	48	345	370	1590	1700	5.87
1½	8	35	4.4	40	305	455	1340	2000	6.14	42	320	440	1410	1935	6.14	44	335	425	1475	1870	6.14
2	8	33	4.1	37	310	525	1270	2150	6.59	39	325	510	1330	2090	6.59	41	340	490	1395	2010	6.59

Fig. 7-7. Suggested trial mixers for concrete of medium consistency with a 3-inch slump.

A transit mix truck, though, is the best way to go for most home builders. This truck picks up the ingredients dry, and the driver pumps in water as he drives, while the turning tank does a thorough job of mixing the contents. By the time he arrives on your vacation home site, everything is ready to be transferred to your forms. Ready mix trucks pick up the wet mix at the plant and cart it to your site under continued agitation.

It is imperative that the forms and all needed bracing to support the truck as it approaches those forms be ready when the trucks arrive on the job. Tools for striking off and finishing should be laid out and ready to go, and you should have enough workers on hand to do the finishing jobs as quickly as you can.

Footing forms for piers, shown in Figs. 7-8 and 7-9, are easily constructed. Plywood can be used instead of boards as illustrated. Wall footing forms are no more difficult, but take more time, while forms for poured foundation walls are a bit more complex. Figures 7-10, 7-11, 7-12, 7-13 show different methods of constructing and bracing these types of forms. Figures 7-14 and 7-15 give some construction details for tying things together in midwall and at corners.

Forms must be coated to prevent the concrete from sticking badly. If the resulting footing, wall, or floor is not to be painted, coat the forms with a light grade of motor oil of the cheapest type you can

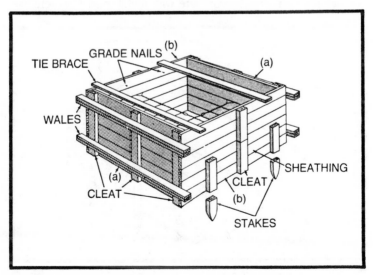

Fig. 7-8. Typical large footing form.

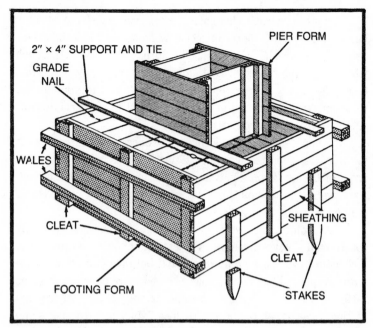

Fig. 7-9. Typical footing and peir form.

locate. If paint is to be used, a lacquer coating on the forms will prevent sticking, though you could also use a good, oil base paint.

If a floor is being poured, or in many cases a foundation wall, you will need to reinforce the concrete with metal rods. Concrete has

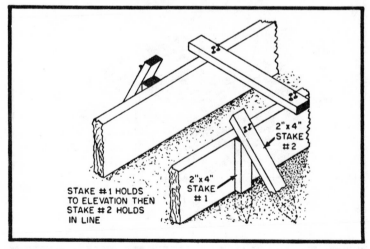

Fig. 7-10. Typical wall footing form.

140

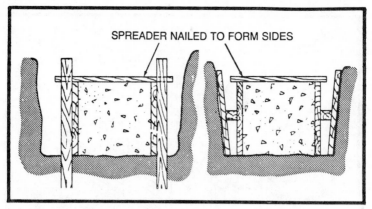

SPREADER NAILED TO FORM SIDES

Fig. 7-11. Methods of bracing footing forms.

immense compressive strength, but is not very strong under tension, so steel is imbedded in the concrete to add to tensile strength. Reinforcing bars are placed after forms are in place and oiled so that the bars remain oil-free. Rust, scale, and grease should be wire-brushed off the bars shortly before the concrete is poured. The bars need not have a bright, shiny surface, but all heavy rust and scale, and all grease and oil, must be cleaned off them.

Reinforcing bars are tied together with tie wire, and lap joints are triple tied (Fig. 7-16). Bars for the floor are laid as shown in Fig.

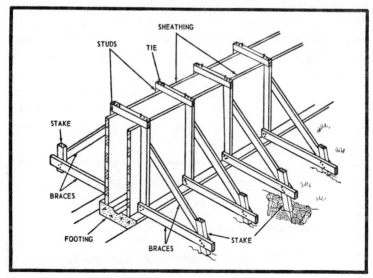

SHEATHING
STUDS
TIE
STAKE
BRACES
FOOTING
BRACES
STAKE

Fig. 7-12. Wall form without wales.

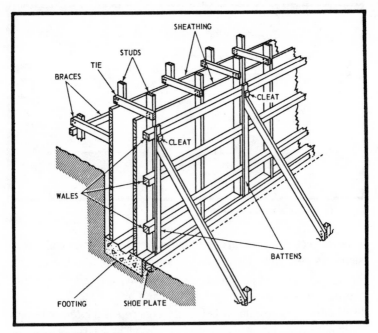

Fig. 7-13. Wall form with wales.

7-17, while those that go in a wall must be supported with wood blocks as in Fig. 7-18.

Once the pour starts, you want the job to go right on through to its finish, which is why accurate estimates are needed. Should the pour run out before completion, the second load may not bond properly to the first part of the pour, thus causing a lot of difficulty. Concrete is poured in layers from 6 to 12 inches deep, and a spading tool is used to consolidate these layers (Fig. 7-19). This consolidation with a spading tool works out large air bubbles and makes sure that any intricacies in and around the forms and reinforcement bars are completely filled.

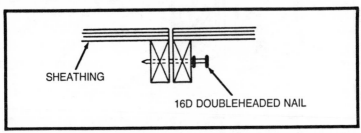

Fig. 7-14. Joining wall form panels together in line.

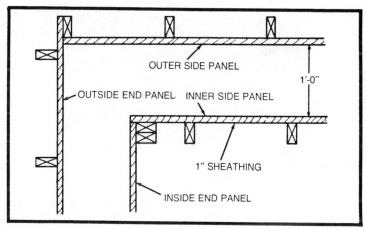

Fig. 7-15. Method of joining wall form panels at corner.

FINISHING THE CONCRETE

Different structures require different kinds of finishing. While footings don't require much more than striking off with a screed (simply a straight board used as a strike-off tool), floors, walls, driveways, and walks require more work if the surface is to be best suited to the purpose.

The tops of walls and foots, then, are simply struck off level with the top of the footing or wall forms. These forms must, naturally, have level tops.

After that, we start the finishing work on a slab or floor in a different manner. A longer strike off screed is needed for this work and it is sawed back and forth across the floor so that concrete is carried into any depressions resulting from the pour, and there'll be plenty. The pour should stay well ahead of the screed, and you should make sure there is plenty of concrete to cover in front of the screed. If more is needed—as it may be when you start seeing air under the screed—a few shovelsful should be tossed on the low spot.

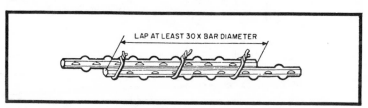

Fig. 7-16. Bars spliced by lapping.

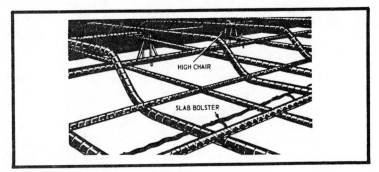

Fig. 7-17. Reinforcing steel for floor slab.

Screeding gives a moderately rough surface, basically doing little more than leveling the floor or slab. If the slab is to be floored over, as in a house built on a slab, the process usually stops here. For floors or driveways needing a slightly smoother finish, a wooden float is used. The person doing the floating kneels, with a short float, using flat boards under knees and toes to keep from sinking into the surface, and uses two floats to work the surface smooth. This floating operation does just what its name indicates: it floats mortar to the surface, and provides, thus, a smoother surface than does screeding. Too much floating work while the concrete is very plastic

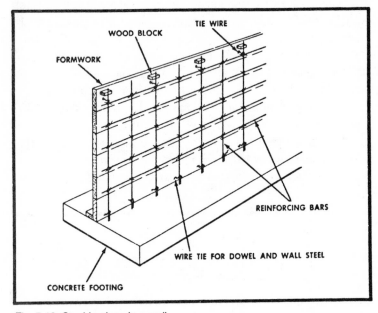

Fig. 7-18. Steel in place in a wall.

can cause a thin layer of water and mortar to form on the surface. This is not desirable, as within a short time this thin, weak surface will break up and flake off. For greater smoothness, a steel float can be used (Fig. 7-20).

Steel floats are not used until after the water sheen disappears from the surface of the concrete.

For extremely large slabs, 4-foot or wider floats with long, braced handles can be used to avoid having to do so much work in a kneeling position (Fig. 7-21).

If a moderately rough surface is desired for a walk or a drive, the wood float can be applied a second time after the surface obtained with the first floating has partially hardened. This type of surface is of greatest value on sidewalks and driveways.

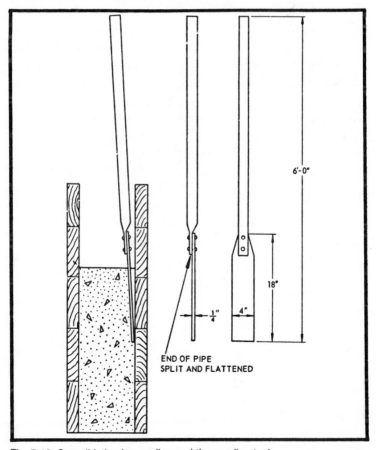

Fig. 7-19. Consolidation by spading and the spading tool.

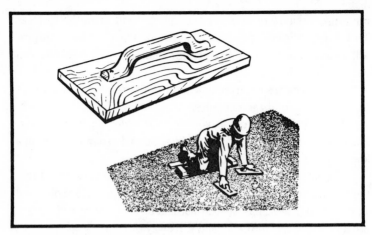

Fig. 7-20. Wood float and floating operation.

For the greatest smoothness and great density, the floating operation is followed by steel troweling. Usually a steel troweled floor is best for basements where the floor may be painted later on.

Troweling is carried out after the moisture film has gone from the surface of the slab or floor. The concrete must have hardened sufficiently to prevent the troweling operation from bringing fine material and water to the surface, or the result will be the same sort of weak surface layer as is produced by too much floating. But if you wait too long, the surface will be hard or impossible to work properly. Keep a careful eye on the concrete, and start troweling as soon as the sheen disappears. Then, if water and fine material seem to be coming to the surface, back off and wait a few more minutes. Should

Fig. 7-21. Long handle wood float and floating operation.

a wet spot occur anywhere on a surface being troweled, you should take a break until it goes away. For a fine texture on the surface, move the trowel in a circular motion immediately after the first troweling (done in wide arcs), keeping the trowel flat on the surface. Use about a 5-degree tilt for the first troweling.

If a supersmooth finish is desired, the final troweling won't take place until the surface is so dry no mortar adheres to the trowel. Test the surface to see that a ringing sound comes from it as the trowel passes over. For this type of hard, smooth finish, the trowel is tilted at a very slight angle and the person doing the work bears down heavily in order to compact the surface as much as possible (Fig. 7-22).

For a nonskid surface in areas where rain slickness might be a problem, brooming is the best way to work things. After the floating operations are finished, take a heavy pushbroom and run it over the surface, with the scoring cut by the broom cut into the slab at right angles to planned traffic wherever possible. Brooming leaves quite heavy score lines if a commercial pushbroom is used. For less heavy cuts, you can use lighter brooms of most any style.

CURING CONCRETE

Once the surface is finished, we have to pay attention to completion of hydration, or more simply the curing of the concrete.

Fig. 7-22. Steel finishing tools and troweling operation.

If the suraface of freshly poured and worked concrete is allowed to dry out too rapidly, the process of hydration will stop or slow down so much as to interfere with final strength. Most residential concrete will cure sufficiently within 7 days. Wood forms can be left in place to retard drying out. The surface can be covered with burlap, sand, straw or any other material that can be made to stay in place and prevent evaporation. Such coverings should be thick enough to prevent direct sunlight from passing much heat to the curing concrete for at least the first 3 days of the curing process. The surface covering should be kept damp or wet during the entire 7 day period, and any forms left in place should be well flooded with water at least daily, with the water penetrating between the forms and the concrete.

Polyethelene or other plastic sheeting can also be used to cover slabs being cured. Generally, assuming moderate sun and temperatures, using such a nonpermeable membrane means you won't have to fool with twice daily watering of the curing surface. But if watering does become necessary, the sheeting will need to be rolled back. In sunny weather, only light colored plastic sheeting should be used, as the heavy black material tends to absorb too much heat, which is then transferred to the concrete, interfering with proper curing.

Hay or straw used as a damping medium should be no less than 6 inches thick over the entire surface.

MASONRY

Three types of masonry construction are of interest to the vacation home builder: concrete block, brick, and stone. Each has a specific purpose and look, and in many cases one can be substituted for another with no loss of structural strength, and, sometimes, a savings in materials costs that may be quite large.

Masonry tools include a trowel, used for mixing, placing, and spreading the mortar; a mason's hammer for bedding masonry units in the mortar, chipping, and rough cutting; the bolster or brick chisel is used for fine cutting; and the jointer, which is used to finish the joints. These are available in a variety of designs (Fig. 7-23).

The first step, and one of the most critical, is the estimation of the amount of material needed to do the job. Wrong estimates, on the low side, waste a lot of time. Mistakes on the high side of actual needs waste a lot of money, for neither concrete block nor bricks are at all cheap these days. First, do your best, with concrete block, to

Fig. 7-23. Mason's trowels, holster, hammer, and jointer.

lay the wall out in modular units. That is, allowing for joint sizes, try
to make foundation or other wall lengths fit the sizes of available
blocks so that cutting is not needed. Nominal sizes of concrete
blocks allow for joint thicknesses, so that with 8-inch block you are
working with 8- by 4- by 16-inch dimensions. Plan length units in
multiples equal to half of the block length; length is 16 inches, so the
multiples would be 8 inches here. Vertical dimensions are planned to
the full height, or 4 inches. Figure 7-24 shows the actual size of most
of the commonly available concrete blocks, while the charts in Figs.
7-25 and 7-26 will give assistance in determining wall lengths and
heights.

Most above grade construction will use blocks 8 inches by 8
inches by 16 inches; actual size is 7⅝ by 7⅝ by 15⅝ to allow for
⅜-inch mortar joints. Below grade foundation walls may require
12-inch-wide block. Check local codes before starting.

In addition to the tools already described, you'll need three
other things. First, obtain a 2- to 4-foot level of top quality. Next, get
a straightedge at least 10 feet long (Fig. 7-27). Then have on hand a
mortar board on which the mortar can be placed while being used; it
can also be used to mix the mortar, though usually a rough mortar
box is constructed for that purpose (Figs. 7-28 and 7-29).

Portland cement lime mortar is the material of choice for setting
the concrete blocks. Plain lime mortar is more or less used only for
temporary construction. The addition of lime to the mix of portland

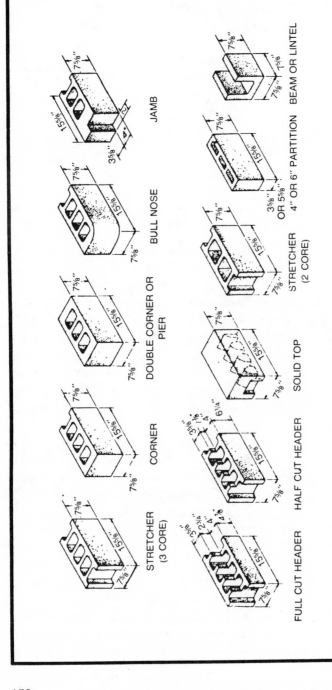

JAMB

BULL NOSE

DOUBLE CORNER OR PIER

CORNER

STRETCHER (3 CORE)

BEAM OR LINTEL

4" OR 6" PARTITION

STRETCHER (2 CORE)

SOLID TOP

HALF CUT HEADER

FULL CUT HEADER

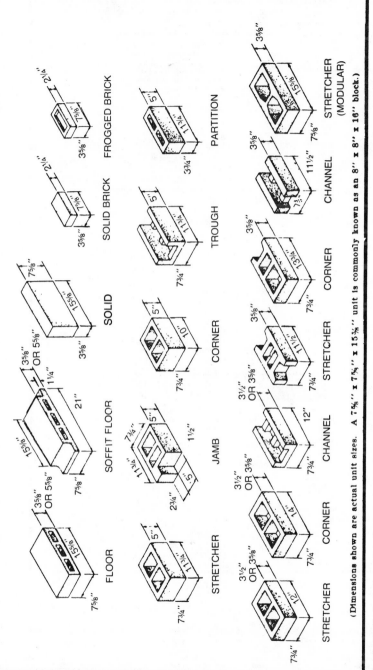

Fig. 7-24. Typical sizes and shapes of concrete masonry units.

(Dimensions shown are actual unit sizes. A 7⅝" x 7⅝" x 15⅝" unit is commonly known as an 8" x 8" x 16" block.)

151

(Actual length of wall is measured from outside edge to outside edge of units and is equal to the nominal length minus ⅜" (one mortar joint).)

No. of stretchers	Nominal length of concrete masonry walls	
	Units 15⅝" long and half units 7⅝" long with ⅜" thick head joints.	Units 11⅝" long and half units 5⅝" long with ⅜" thick head joints.
1	1' 4".	1' 0".
1½	2' 0".	1' 6".
2	2' 8".	2' 0".
2½	3' 4".	2' 6".
3	4' 0".	3' 0".
3½	4' 8".	3' 6".
4	5' 4".	4' 0".
4½	6' 0".	4' 6".
5	6' 8".	5' 0".
5½	7' 4".	5' 6".
6	8' 0".	6' 0".
6½	8' 8".	6' 6".
7	9' 4".	7' 0".
7½	10' 0".	7' 6".
8	10' 8".	8' 0".
8½	11' 4".	8' 6".
9	12' 0".	9' 0".
9½	12' 8".	9' 6".
10	13' 4".	10' 0".
10½	14' 0".	10' 6".
11	14' 8".	11' 0".
11½	15' 4".	11' 6".
12	16' 0".	12' 0".
12½	16' 8".	12' 6".
13	17' 4".	13' 0".
13½	18' 0".	13' 6".
14	18' 8".	14' 0".
14½	19' 4".	14' 6".
15	20' 0".	15' 0".
20	26' 8".	20' 0".

Fig. 7-25. Nominal length of concrete masonry walls by stretchers.

cement, sand and water aids workability. Start with a sack of cement, add 3 cubic feet of sand; then weigh out 13 pounds of hydrated lime and you will have the strongest mortar possible. Dry mix first, then add water only to the portion you will use in about 45 minutes to

(For concrete masonry units 7⅝" and 3⅝" in height laid with ⅜" mortar joints. Height is measured from center to center of mortar joints.)

No. of courses	Nominal height of concrete masonry walls	
	Units 7⅝" high and ⅜" thick bed joint	Units 3⅝" high and ⅜" thick bed joint
1	8"	4".
2	1' 4"	8".
3	2' 0"	1' 0".
4	2' 8"	1' 4".
5	3' 4"	1' 8".
6	4' 0"	2' 0".
7	4' 8"	2' 4".
8	5' 4"	2' 8".
9	6' 0"	3' 0".
10	6' 8"	3' 4".
15	10' 0"	5' 0".
20	13' 4"	6' 8".
25	16' 8"	8' 4".
30	20' 0"	10' 0".
35	23' 4"	11' 8".
40	26' 8"	13' 4".
45	30' 0"	15' 0".
50	33' 4"	16' 8".

Fig. 7-26. Nominal height of concrete masonry walls by courses.

1 hour. After that point, the wet mortar will have set up a bit and become unusable.

Dry mixing should be very thorough, with an energetic mixer able to do the job in 3 minutes or so. Water is added to form the correct consistency: mortar is mixed more stiffly than is concrete to be poured, as it must be "buttered" onto the ends of bricks and concrete blocks. Check by buttering a few blocks to make sure it

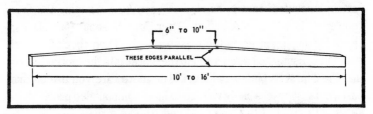

Fig. 7-27. Mason's straightedge.

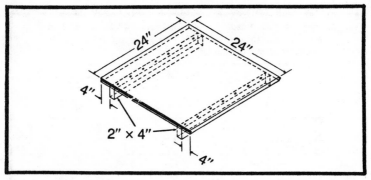

Fig. 7-28. Mortar board.

doesn't slump off while being applied. If it does, simply add a bit more of the already mixed dry ingredients.

WALL LAYOUT

For a concrete block foundation wall to be laid on already poured footings, the first step is the snapping of a chalk line at the proper spot on the footings. The first course of blocks is then laid out along the footings, gapped at ⅜ inch with no mortar used. This will provide an accurate check of the layout, and show spots where difficulties might arise, requiring either half blocks or cut blocks. Avoid cutting the blocks whenever possible. Now, the blocks on one corner are removed and a full bed—the width of the block—is laid down. This mortar bed is furrowed with the trowel edge so that it is concentrated a bit towards the edges of the block. The corner block is now laid in its mortar bed, with attention paid to careful positioning right on the chalk line. Lay all block with the thicker end of the face shell up as this gives a better amount of area for mortar bedding. Apply mortar to the ends of the face shells—those two spots that stick out from the block—and butt some more of the row of blocks to the corner block, using a downward push into the mortar bed and against the previously laid block. Obviously when the wall is first started a certain amount of care is needed to keep from scooting the first couple of blocks out of position. After you lay about four blocks, check for alignment using the mason's level. Then check for level and plumb, using the hammer to tap the blocks into the mortar bed so that the course is plumb and level. The more care you use on this base course, the less likely you are to have compounded problems in keeping the rest of the wall level and true as it rises.

As the wall goes up, each course should be checked for level and plumb, and the job is best done after no more than four blocks are laid along a wall. A constant check will catch any errors at a time when they are easily corrected. If you try to put off the checks until the entire course is up, you may be in a lot of trouble if things aren't lined up correctly.

After the first course is down, the concrete blocks are buttered with mortar only along the horizontal face shells for the vertical joint. Each joint is ⅜ inch thick, and each course is stepped back half a block from the corner so that joints are staggered up the face of the wall. Corner alignment is checked by placing the level diagonally across both corner blocks.

The courses will go up with more speed if mason's cord is stretched from the top of one corner block to the top of the next, and each block is lined up with this marker line. Such a line helps keep both vertical and horizontal alignment accurate, usually making only small adjustments necessary.

As you go along, cut off any excess mortar from the face of the blocks with the trowel. Throw this mortar back on the mortar board. It can be used again after it has been worked back into the fresh mortar. Don't pick up so-called dead mortar from the scaffolding or the floor.

The jointer is now used to tool the joints. Such tooling compresses the mortar in the joints into a pleasing, uniform shape. It also aids watertightness of the joints as it compresses the mortar. Tooling is started after a sector of the wall has set up so that the mortar is difficult to impress a thumbprint in. Joints are tooled to a concave U-shape or to a V-shape. Make your start at this tooling along the horizontal joints, finishing up with the vertical joints.

Wood sills are to be set in the tops of the foundation walls. These are bolted to the walls using anchor bolts which are set at a

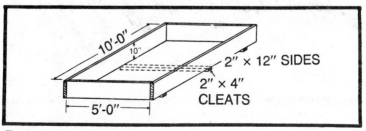

Fig. 7-29. Mortar box.

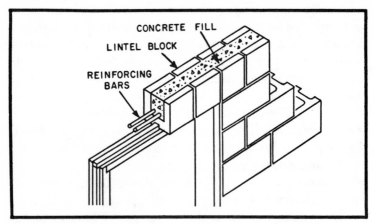

Fig. 7-30. Lintel made from blocks.

distance apart of about 8 feet. This may vary according to local codes. Anchor bolts are 1½ feet long and ½ inch in diameter. They must extend down at least two block course through the block cores, which are then filled with mortar. Allow enough of the threaded end of the anchor bolt to extend above the foundation wall. Provide plenty of bolt extending through the sill plate with room to add the washer and nut.

Precast concrete lintels are generally used today to provide door openings in concrete block walls (also for window openings). It is possible to use steel rod to reinforce lintel blocks by building your own lintels (Fig. 7-30).

Most concrete block walls used in residences are not reinforced, or if so, are only lightly reinforced. For vertical reinforcement, place steel rods, at the needed spacing, down the centers of the block cores and fill those reinforced cores with concrete, having at least 3 inches of slump. Generally, such reinforcement bars are placed 32 inches on center.

Horizontal joint reinforcement is taken care of with two longitudinal number 9 cold drawn steel wires, using truss style cross wires at least an ⅛ inch in diameter. (Fig. 7-31.) Such horizontal bracing does a lot to control joint cracking as overall wall flexibility is greatly reduced.

BRICK MASONRY

Bricks are made of baked clay or shale in many sizes and styles. The size and style used in any one wall are usually uniform, though

156

this is not essential. It does make the job quite a lot simpler for the novice, though. Standard United States building bricks are 2½ by 3¾ by 8 inches, though there is at least a slight variation from brick to brick because even very slightly different clay compositions and densities will react, thus shrink, a bit differently when baked. Most common brick is red, though other colors are easily available. Common brick is made of what is known as pit-run clay with no effort made to control the color of the brick, and no special glazing of the surface.

Face brick is a higher quality brick, with more uniform color, and may have a special surface glaze.

Brick grades indicate their uses in special circumstances. These classifications indicate special climate conditions for which the bricks are suited. SW grade bricks are made to withstand constant exposure to moist below freezing conditions such as those found in the Northern United States and through most of Canada. Bricks graded MW are suitable for use in areas where below freezing temperatures are common in winter, but where the surroundings are not as moist. NW brick is suitable for interior or back-up brick use, though it can be used on the exterior where no frost action is present if annual rainfall is also under 15 inches.

Bricks are also classified as to type. Building or common brick we've already described. Face brick is a finer quality for use as a final finish brick, commonly available in red, gray, yellow, and white, and in several different shapes. Glazed brick has one surface with a glaze

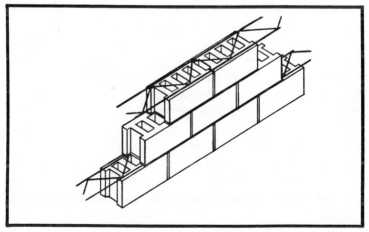

Fig. 7-31. Masonry wall horizontal joint reinforcement.

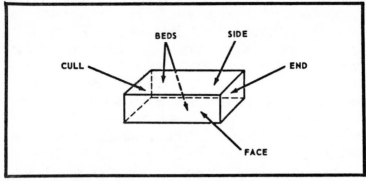

Fig. 7-32. Nomenclature of common shapes of cut brick.

in a color such as white. This type of smooth surface brick makes cleaning the wall surface a great deal easier. Cored bricks have double rows of five holes each extending through their beds. This coring reduces their weight but provides no significant change in strength when used in a wall.

Fire brick is made with a special clay and is used to line fireplaces and woodstove fireboxes, or in other spots where the brick will be constantly subjected to very high temperatures. Fire brick is usually a bit larger than standard brick, with the standard modern firebrick being 9 inches long, 4½ inches deep, and 2½ inches thick.

There are several other types of brick available, but they are of little or no importance in residential construction.

Figure 7-32 shows the nomenclature of a brick, while Fig. 7-33 provides the names of the common shapes of cut brick. These terms become helpful when you start to run a brick wall.

The mortar used for brick masonry is of great importance because a properly mortared joint will resist water penetration to a high degree. Because water penetration at the joints is about the only form of weathering that has any kind of effect on brick walls, keeping the joints as water resistant as possible cuts way down on wall wear. Water tightness of the joints is a result of solidly filling the joints. This cannot be done by adding mortar after the bricks have been laid, or at least not nearly as thoroughly. This is accomplished by tooling the joints to a concave shape before the mortar has a chance to set up. Tooling the joint properly requires that you use enough force to press the mortar tightly against the bricks on both sides of the joint.

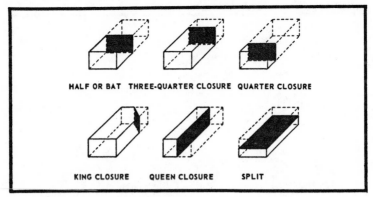

Fig. 7-33. Common shapes of cut brick.

The strongest mortar, and the most weather resistant, for brick wall use when the wall is extended below grade, is Type S, requiring one part portland cement, half a part of hydrated lime, and four and a half parts sand (by volume). For exterior walls above grade and subject to severe weather exposure use one part of portland cement, one part of hydrated lime, and six parts of sand.

BRICK BONDS

There are three different kinds of bonds referred to in brick masonry. The structural bond is the method used to tie the individual bricks into a single structural unit. This is accomplished by overlapping or interlocking the masonry units, or by the use of metal ties imbedded in the connecting joints (Fig. 7-34). A third method uses the adhesion provided by grouting to adjacent wythes (Fig. 7-35). The mortar bond is the adhesion of the joint mortar to the bricks or to reinforcing steel ties. The pattern bond may result from the structural bond used, or may simply be decorative. Five of the bond patterns shown in Fig. 7-36 are those in most general use today:

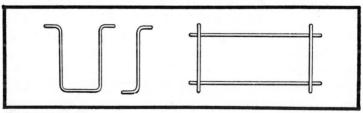

Fig. 7-34. Metal ties.

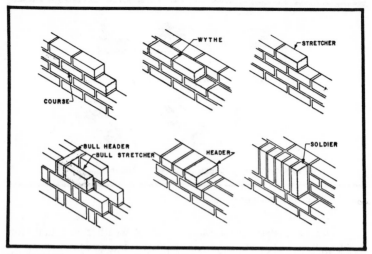

Fig. 7-35. Masonry units and mortar joints.

running bond, common bond, Flemish bond, English bond, and stack bond.

The running bond is the simplest, using only stretchers, and is most suitable for use on veneer brick walls.

The common bond is a variation on the running bond using courses of full length headers at regular intervals, which add to structural strength as well as appearance. The header courses will appear at every fifth, sixth, or seventh course, and will be dictated by your plans, as the location affects the strength of the wall. Corners must be started properly for common bonds, with a ¾ brick used to start every header course at the corner.

Flemish bond uses alternating headers and stretchers where the headers in alternate courses are centered over the stretchers in their intervening courses. Corners are started with ¾ bricks, and ¼ brick closures are used to fill in and space out.

English bond is also made up of alternate rows of headers and stretchers, but the headers are centered on the joints between the stretchers, as well as on the stretchers.

Stack bond is ornamental only and must be tied into the backing wall with rigid metal ties. All vertical joints are aligned and there is no overlapping.

As you can see, there are variations possible using features from several of the different kinds of pattern bonds. As you gain experience, you may wish to use one of these, but most often the

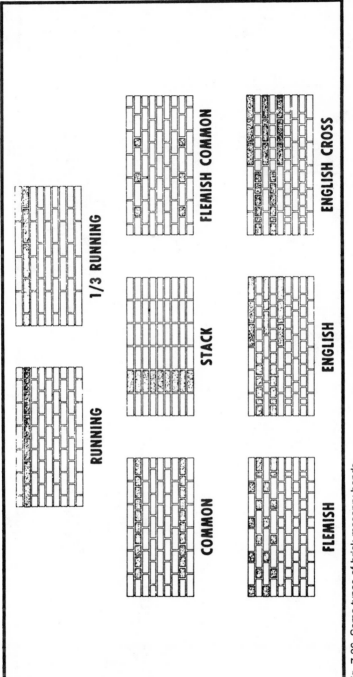

RUNNING

1/3 RUNNING

COMMON

STACK

FLEMISH COMMON

FLEMISH

ENGLISH

ENGLISH CROSS

Fig. 7-36. Some types of brick masonry bonds.

161

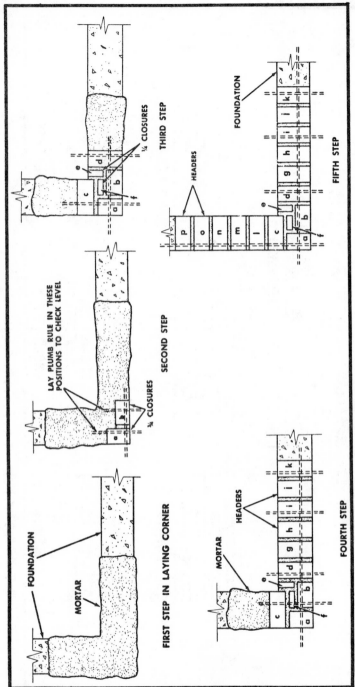

Fig. 7-37. First course of corner lead for 8-inch common bond brick wall.

162

novice is best advised to stick to the common bond for structural units and the running or stack bond for nonstructural units.

Brick courses are laid out in the same manner as are concrete block courses, with the first row of bricks laid down without mortar to check sizing and alignment. Because brick are smaller and have less inertia, the mason's cord used to line up the courses should be placed on a pole at the corner, and each corner should be built up for at least half a dozen courses before the walls are filled in.

LAYING BRICK

Once the wall design is decided, the bricks are on hand, and the mortar ready to go, you will have done the above and are ready to start laying the brick. Mortar is placed on the foundation, and the type of closure brick needed is laid in its mortar bed. The bricks are laid in the order shown in Fig. 7-37 for a common bond wall. The corner is built up course by course, with the mason's level used across the corner diagonals at each course (Fig. 7-38). Once the

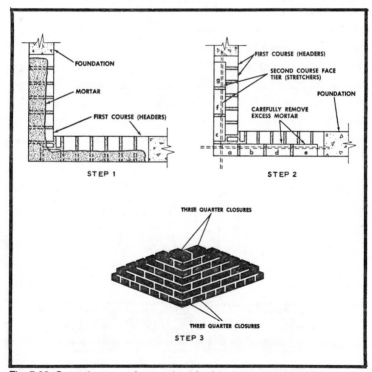

Fig. 7-38. Second course of corner lead for 8-inch common bond brick wall.

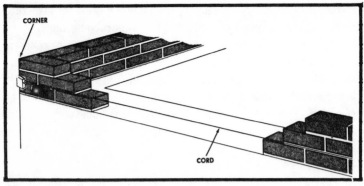

Fig. 7-39. Use of the line.

corner has reached three courses, you can start an opposing corner, then stretch your mason's cord so that the wall bricks can be easily lined up as they are laid (Fig. 7-39).

Before starting to lay bricks in mortar, wet the brick down. Wetting the brick provides a clean surface for better mortar adhesion, and the wet surface allows the mortar to spread more evenly. Too, the brick will not absorb water from the mortar as quickly as will a dry brick, which means hydration will continue at a correct rate and not be stopped by dryness.

There is a technique for holding the trowel, and a correct way to pick up mortar with it (Figs. 7-40 and 7-41). Certainly both can be done in other ways, but experience over the years show these to be about the best and most efficient methods.

Fig. 7-40. One way to hold a trowel.

164

Fig. 7-41. Proper way to pick up mortar.

As the center of the wall goes up, the mortar is thrown down on the brick course top as shown in Fig. 7-42. The mortar is then spread over a distance of about five bricks and furrowed with the trowel to form a bed joint for the brick to be laid. The end of the brick is buttered (Fig. 7-43) and then laid into the wall and aligned with mason's string used as a marker (Fig. 7-44). The brick is pushed into place with enough force to squeeze mortar out at the head joint and along the wall sides. The head joint must be well filled with mortar, so when you butter your bricks place as much mortar on them as they will hold. Any excess will be forced out, and can be cut off the wall with the trowel.

JOINT FINISHING

As we've said, the joint finish is of great importance to the durability of a brick wall. Joint styles vary (Fig. 7-45), but no matter which style is used it must be firmly packed. Excess mortar is first cut off with the trowel, then the jointing tool is used to form the joint. All exterior walls should have concave joints as these are more water resistant than all others, with the possible exception of the weather joint.

MISCELLANEOUS

Judging the number of courses and the size of a wall is simpler when using a chart than otherwise (Fig. 7-46). The actual wall height

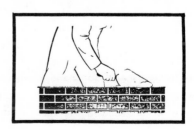

Fig. 7-42. Mortar thrown on brick.

Fig. 7-43. Proper way to hold a brick.

is determined in part by the size of the joint, so three charts (Fig. 7-46A, 46B, and 46C) for those different sizes are included.

Sooner or later, you'll have to cut a brick to fit in a tight spot. The bolster or brick chisel makes the cleanest cuts, and must be used if appearance is of importance (Fig. 7-47). This also allows cutting along an exact line. Often the mason's hammer must be used to cut away a part of the brick, while the chisel is used to finish up.

To make the more normal cuts, a line is tapped around the brick, using the head of the hammer to form a cutting line. Once the cutting line is formed, the hammer is reversed and the chipper edge used to strike a sharp blow just to the waste side of the cutting line (Fig. 7-48). The blade end can then be used to trim off the high spots left.

STONE MASONRY

With so many vacation home builders preferring log cabins, stone masonry along the foundation walls is of great importance because it continues the overall rustic look. Two basic types of stone masonry exist. The crudest, random rubble masonry, simply has stones placed in any manner in which they might fit. Rubble masonry may also be done in courses to form a neater looking wall. Ashlar stone masonry requires that any stones placed in surface spots have

Fig. 7-44. Bed joint and furrow.

those surfaces squared, so that a plane surface results. The two types of rubble masonry are more suitable for our work.

When selecting stone for use in any kind of wall, it is best to choose sizes that can be handled with relative ease by no more than two people. Make sure you get a variety of sizes, for there will be

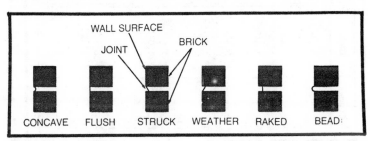

Fig. 7-45. Joint finishes.

Courses	Height	Courses	Height	Courses	Height	Courses	Height	Courses	Height
1	0' 2⅝"	21	4' 7⅛"	41	8' 11⅝"	61	13' 4⅛"	81	17' 8⅝"
2	0' 5¼"	22	4' 9¾"	42	9' 2¼"	62	13' 6¾"	82	17' 11¼"
3	0' 7⅞"	23	5' 0⅜"	43	9' 4⅞"	63	13' 9⅜"	83	18' 1⅞"
4	0' 10½"	24	5' 3"	44	9' 7½"	64	14' 0"	84	18' 4½"
5	1' 1⅛"	25	5' 5⅝"	45	9' 10⅛"	65	14' 2⅝"	85	18' 7⅛"
6	1' 3¾"	26	5' 8¼"	46	10' 0¾"	66	14' 5¼"	86	18' 9¾"
7	1' 6⅜"	27	5' 10⅞"	47	10' 3⅜"	67	14' 7⅞"	87	19' 0⅜"
8	1' 9"	28	6' 1½"	48	10' 6"	68	14' 10½"	88	19' 3"
9	1' 11⅝"	29	6' 4⅛"	49	10' 8⅝"	69	15' 1⅛"	89	19' 5⅝"
10	2' 2¼"	30	6' 6¾"	50	10' 11¼"	70	15' 3¾"	90	19' 8¼"
11	2' 4⅞"	31	6' 9⅜"	51	11' 1⅞"	71	15' 6⅜"	91	19' 10⅞"
12	2' 7½"	32	7' 0"	52	11' 4½"	72	15' 9"	92	20' 1½"
13	2' 10⅛"	33	7' 2⅝"	53	11' 7⅛"	73	15' 11⅝"	93	20' 4⅛"
14	3' 0¾"	34	7' 5¼"	54	11' 9¾"	74	16' 2¼"	94	20' 6¾"
15	3' 3⅜"	35	7' 7⅞"	55	12' 0⅜"	75	16' 4⅞"	95	20' 9⅜"
16	3' 6"	36	7' 10½"	56	12' 3"	76	16' 7½"	96	21' 0"
17	3' 8⅝"	37	8' 1⅛"	57	12' 5⅝"	77	16' 10⅛"	97	21' 2⅝"
18	3' 11¼"	38	8' 3¾"	58	12' 8¼"	78	17' 0¾"	98	21' 5¼"
19	4' 1⅞"	39	8' 6⅜"	59	12' 10⅞"	79	17' 3⅜"	99	21' 7⅞"
20	4' 4½"	40	8' 9"	60	13' 1½"	80	17' 6"	100	21' 10½"

Fig. 7-46A. Height of courses with 2¼-inch brick and ⅜-inch joints.

Courses	Height	Courses	Height	Courses	Height	Courses	Height	Courses	Height
1	0' 2¾"	21	4' 9¾"	41	9' 4¾"	61	13' 11¾"	81	18' 6¾"
2	0' 5½"	22	5' 0½"	42	9' 7½"	62	14' 2½"	82	18' 9½"
3	0' 8¼"	23	5' 3¼"	43	9' 10¼"	63	14' 5¼"	83	19' 0¼"
4	0' 11"	24	5' 6"	44	10' 1"	64	14' 8"	84	19' 3"
5	1' 1¾"	25	5' 8¾"	45	10' 3¾"	65	14' 10¾"	85	19' 5¾"
6	1' 4½"	26	5' 11½"	46	10' 6½"	66	15' 1½"	86	19' 8½"
7	1' 7¼"	27	6' 2¼"	47	10' 9¼"	67	15' 4¼"	87	19' 11¼"
8	1' 10"	28	6' 5"	48	11' 0"	68	15' 7"	88	20' 2"
9	2' 0¾"	29	6' 7¾"	49	11' 2¾"	69	15' 9¾"	89	20' 4¾"
10	2' 3½"	30	6' 10½"	50	11' 5½"	70	16' 0½"	90	20' 7½"
11	2' 6¼"	31	7' 1¼"	51	11' 8¼"	71	16' 3¼"	91	20' 10¼"
12	2' 9"	32	7' 4"	52	11' 11"	72	16' 6"	92	21' 1"
13	2' 11¾"	33	7' 6¾"	53	12' 1¾"	73	16' 8¾"	93	21' 3¾"
14	3' 2½"	34	7' 9½"	54	12' 4½"	74	16' 11½"	94	21' 6½"
15	3' 5¼"	35	8' 0¼"	55	12' 7¼"	75	17' 2¼"	95	21' 9¼"
16	3' 8"	36	8' 3"	56	12' 10"	76	17' 5"	96	22' 0"
17	3' 10¾"	37	8' 5¾"	57	13' 0¾"	77	17' 7¾"	97	22' 2¾"
18	4' 1½"	38	8' 8½"	58	13' 3½"	78	17' 10½"	98	22' 5½"
19	4' 4¼"	39	8' 11¼"	59	13' 6¼"	79	18' 1¼"	99	22' 8¼"
20	4' 7"	40	9' 2"	60	13' 9"	80	18' 4"	100	22' 11"

Fig. 7-46B. Height of courses with 2¼-inch brick and ½-inch joints.

Courses	Height	Courses	Height	Courses	Height	Courses	Height	Courses	Height
1	0' 2⅞"	21	5' 0⅜"	41	9' 9⅞"	61	14' 7⅜"	81	19' 4⅞"
2	0' 5¾"	22	5' 3¼"	42	10' 0¾"	62	14' 10¼"	82	19' 7¾"
3	0' 8⅝"	23	5' 6⅛"	43	10' 3⅝"	63	15' 1⅛"	83	19' 10⅝"
4	0' 11½"	24	5' 9"	44	10' 6½"	64	15' 4"	84	20' 1½"
5	1' 2⅜"	25	5' 11⅞"	45	10' 9⅜"	65	15' 6⅞"	85	20' 4⅜"
6	1' 5¼"	26	6' 2¾"	46	11' 0¼"	66	15' 9¾"	86	20' 7¼"
7	1' 8⅛"	27	6' 5⅝"	47	11' 3⅛"	67	16' 0⅝"	87	20' 10⅛"
8	1' 11"	28	6' 8½"	48	11' 6"	68	16' 3½"	88	21' 1"
9	2' 1⅞"	29	6' 11⅜"	49	11' 8⅞"	69	16' 6⅜"	89	21' 3⅞"
10	2' 4¾"	30	7' 2¼"	50	11' 11¾"	70	16' 9¼"	90	21' 6¾"
11	2' 7⅝"	31	7' 5⅛"	51	12' 2⅝"	71	17' 0⅛"	91	21' 9⅝"
12	2' 10½"	32	7' 8"	52	12' 5½"	72	17' 3"	92	22' 0½"
13	3' 1⅜"	33	7' 10⅞"	53	12' 8⅜"	73	17' 5⅞"	93	22' 3⅜"
14	3' 4¼"	34	8' 1¾"	54	12' 11¼"	74	17' 8¾"	94	22' 6¼"
15	3' 7⅛"	35	8' 4⅝"	55	13' 2⅛"	75	17' 11⅝"	95	22' 9⅛"
16	3' 10"	36	8' 7½"	56	13' 5"	76	18' 2½"	96	23' 0"
17	4' 0⅞"	37	8' 10⅜"	57	13' 7⅞"	77	18' 5⅜"	97	23' 2⅞"
18	4' 3¾"	38	9' 1¼"	58	13' 10¾"	78	18' 8¼"	98	23' 5¾"
19	4' 6⅝"	39	9' 4⅛"	59	14' 1⅝"	79	18' 11⅛"	99	23' 8⅝"
20	4' 9½"	40	9' 7"	60	14' 4½"	80	19' 2"	100	23' 11½"

Fig. 7-46C. Height of courses with 2¼-inch brick and ⅝-inch joints.

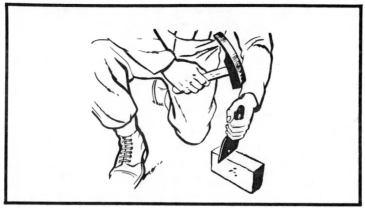

Fig. 7-47. Cutting brick with a bolster.

many spots where fill-ins are needed. Different areas will provide different kinds of stone for use in the walls, with varieties including bluestone, limestone, sandstone, and granite. Lime mortar like that used for concrete block is used here, too.

Stone masonry can save you the effort of pouring footings for your walls, but you will still have to dig down below frost depth and lay a footing. If you prefer to use stone for the footings, select the largest you have and lay each stone on its widest face.

If the stone you are using is an absorbent type (such as sandstone), it should be thoroughly wetted before the mortar is applied. Mortar should be thick enough to fill all spaces between stones. You can cut down on mortar use more than a little by having a supply of smaller stones on hand to fill a part of those interstices).

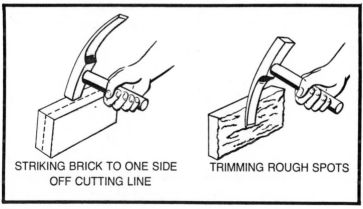

STRIKING BRICK TO ONE SIDE
OFF CUTTING LINE

TRIMMING ROUGH SPOTS

Fig. 7-48. Cutting brick with a hammer.

For foundation wall purposes, your wall will go up more easily and look better if you use the largest stones at the base and let them diminish in size as you go up the wall.

For greatest strength, locate stones wide enough to serve as bond header stones, and use them every four to five courses of stone. Make the header joint by slushing mortar and, if needed, inserting small stones between the bond stones. You can lay three to four stones on mortar beds before you need to fill in the header joints.

For greatest strength, locate stones wide enough to serve as bond header stones, and use them every four to five courses of stone. Make the header joint by slushing mortar and, if needed, inserting small stones between the bond stones. You can lay three to four stones on mortar beds before you need to fill in the header joints.

If you are running a rubble wall that doesn't allow for a full course of bond stones, lay bond stone headers about every 6 square feet of wall.

MORTAR JOINTS

There are only two types of joints in stone masonry: the bed joint is the horizontal and the header joint is the vertical. No constancy is possible in rubble masonry, so the joint is as wide as is needed to fill the gaps between stones with smaller stones imbedded in the mortar where needed to fill space.

Pointing of rubble masonry is not usually done. If you wish to finish a joint, simply cut it off as close to the surface of the stone as possible using the trowel. You can then either use the trowel to compress the joint, or use a burlap bag or other such textured device to change the joint appearance.

Chapter 8
Plumbing & Heating Systems

While a few vacation homes will keep to the outhouse and spring method of plumbing, and some will not be heated at all, most modern homes, whether for first or second home use, will also use modern plumbing and heating systems at least to a degree. You'll find more than a little emphasis in this chapter on using about the oldest kind of heating system around, a wood fire.

Home plumbing breaks down into three separate systems, starting with the water supply system, going next to the fixtures which the first system supplies, and moving to the drainage system which gets rid of the wastes produced.

A vacation home will usually have a water supply system fed by a well, though in some areas deep springs and even lakes can be used. If this is done, the water must be checked for purity at frequent intervals, while a deep well needs to be checked only infrequently. The intervals will depend on local conditions and requirements.

Well siting is of great importance in maintaining a supply of pure water. No matter the kind of well, it must be located at the highest practical spot, and must never be located downhill from the septic tank and field (Fig. 8-1).

Different areas will need different well making styles. Should the soil be hard or rocky, a machine drilled well is going to be needed. In any case, if water table depth is more than 50 feet, machine drilling

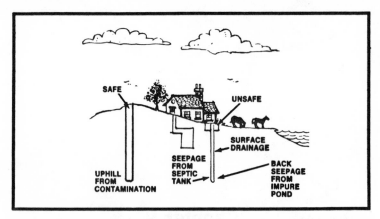

Fig. 8-1. To avoid contamination, a well should be located on the highest point which is practical. It should be placed a considerable distance from sources of possible contamination, such as septic tanks and farm barnyards. The well casing should terminate above ground and should be capped with a pitless adapter or a sanitary well seal. (Courtesy of Water System Council.)

will be needed (Fig. 8-2). A few of the luckier people around will site their vacation homes in areas with a high water table and soft soil. Such locales may be able to get by with a driven well, in which a well point screen attached to lengths of pipe is driven into the earth until water seepage through the screen starts. Depth limits for driven wells stay low. About 30 feet is the deepest practical. Too, the

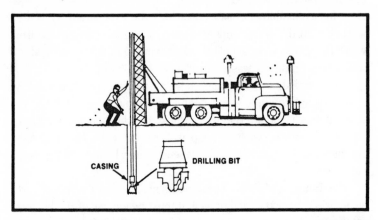

Fig. 8-2. Machine drilled wells are used where it is over 50 feet to water and where a high volume of water is needed. In percussion drilling, a drilling tool is lifted and dropped repeatedly in the bore hole until water is reached. In rotary drilling, a drilling bit is rotated to form the well. In both types of wells, a steel casing is placed in the bore hole to prevent cave-ins and pollution. A well screen is normally attached to the bottom of the casing to keep out sand and gravel while permitting the flow of water. (Courtesy of Water Systems Council.)

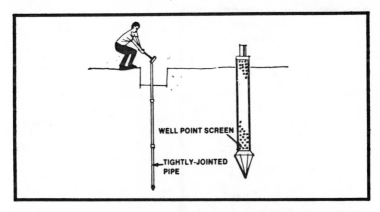

Fig. 8-3. Driven wells are used in areas where the soil is soft. This type of well is constructed by attaching a well point screen to the end of several lengths of pipe. After the pipe is driven down to the water table, water flows into the well through the screen. Driven wells are narrow in diameter, are seldom over 30 feet deep, and usually provide only limited quantities of water. (Courtesy of Water Systems Council.)

amount of water produced by a driven well is usually much lower than what you would get from a drilled well (Fig. 8-3).

A third type of well digging or making is still in use, though it suffers from a depth limitation of about 40 feet, and is subject to seepage from surface and near surface waters. This type of seepage can provide a health hazard, so tile lined bored wells are not often used today (Fig. 8-4).

Two types of pumps are used on today's well systems. The jet pump is a centrifugal pump (water enters the pump at the center of

Fig. 8-4. Bored wells are created manually with an earth auger. Machine bored wells are up to 14 inches in diameter and no more than 40 feet deep. This type of well is lined with vitrified drain tile. Because they absorb surface water, bored wells can often be health hazards. (Courtesy of Water Systems Council.)

175

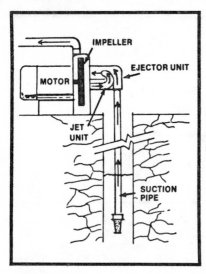

Fig. 8-5. A jet pump for shallow well use. For deep well applications the jet unit must be located in the well itself. (Courtesy of Water Systems Council.)

the impeller and is tossed into the supply system by the impeller rim (Fig. 8-5). The basic jet pump can lift water only about 15 feet, so the jet ejector is used to increase water lift. Shallow well jet pumps work well to depths of about 25 feet, but by moving the jet ejector into the well depth capacities can reach down to 180 feet.

The submersible pump (Fig. 8-6) is also a centrifugal style, but it is built in one slender piece, motor and pump, and positioned below water level inside the well casing. Submersibles are the quietest style because the motor is located down in the well. No maintenance is normally required, but if repairs are needed to the pump, hauling a couple of hundred feet of plastic pipe up to reach the pump can get expensive. Doing it yourself is a backbreaking job.

The well system also requires a pressure tank to store water discharged from the pump. Basically, the storage or pressure tank keeps a supply of fresh water constantly ready. In most cases, a 42-gallon storage tank is plenty for a family of four or five people (Fig. 8-7).

For the most economical plumbing installation in new homes plumbing should be planned in stacks if the house is of more than one story, or to back up (from one room to another) if the house is to be a single floor with several bathrooms. Planning keeps pipe runs down to a minimum, which helps cut materials costs a great deal. Right now plastic pipe is allowed by most codes and is appreciably cheaper than is copper, but we can't even begin to guess the upcoming costs ot such petroleum products as plastics in coming years. Correct planning for short pipe runs is of ever greater importance each year.

In single story construction, make an attempt to design, or have designed, so that bathrooms back up to the plumbing wall in the kitchen. If the utility room for the washer and dryer are also able to be hooked into the same grouping, all the better. In multistory homes, place bathrooms directly over each other, and back the kitchen up to the downstairs unit. This allows stacking of all plumbing. In fact, a few companies will sell the basic pipe runs of different kinds of pipe all ready to install to standard between floor measurements for this sort of stack, which saves a bit of cutting and measuring time. Figure 8-8 shows part of a single story floor plan with the kitchen and bathroom water use walls back to back. In such an arrangement, all pipe runs are hidden in this single wall. Even the hot water heater is kept close to the pipe runs, which does two things: first, pipe is saved, and second, the loss of hot water because of excess travel distance through uninsulated pipe is cut to a minimum.

Water pipe has to be made of materials that don't fall apart from the action of the water, both chemical—corrosive—and mechanical. At the same time some materials impart their own flavors to the water. This is not desirable. Today either copper tubing or copper pipe is popular, and sometimes required by local codes. It is easily worked, with the correct tools, and has an almost no limit lifetime.

Sweat soldering at joints seems to throw many people, though it shouldn't. Sweat soldering is actually very simple if a few easy steps are followed. First, use a very fine steel wool to clean the inside and outside portions to be joined, but don't remove a great

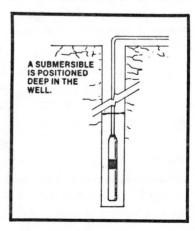

A SUBMERSIBLE IS POSITIONED DEEP IN THE WELL.

Fig. 8-6. A submersible pump used in deep wells. (Courtesy of Water Systems Council.)

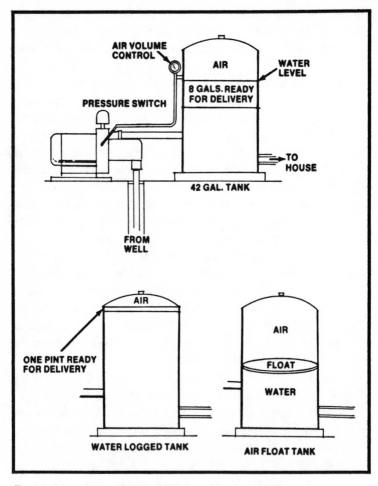

Fig. 8-7. A complete water system consists of the pump itself, a pressure storage tank, and control devices to insure automatic operation. (Courtesy of Water Systems Council.)

deal of metal. Next, apply a good soldering flux to the areas where you must have solder adhere. Now assemble the joint. Apply heat with either a large soldering copper or a propane torch. As soon as the flux bubbles, touch the solder to the side opposite that on which you are applying heat right at the joint line. Keep moving the torch around the fitting and move the solder along the joint until you see that the joint has filled with solder. Remove heat and solder. That's it. You've got a sealed joint. It doesn't matter whether you are applying solder in a position where it must flow up, down, or side-

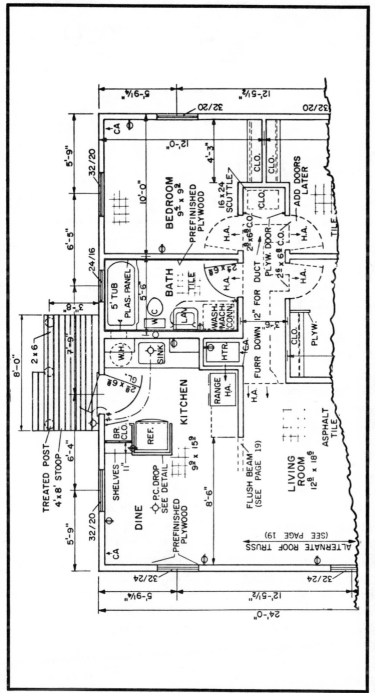

Fig. 8-8. Portion of a single story house plan showing back to back water use walls for the kitchen and bathroom.

179

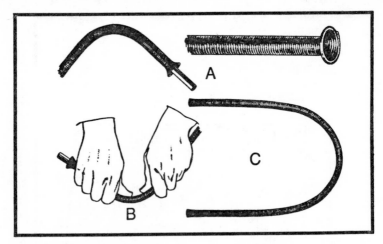

Fig. 8-9. Spring type tube bender.

ways as the capillary attraction caused as the solder becomes liquid will cause the solder to flow *to* the heat source. Make sure you flux only the area where solder must adhere, by the way. It will stick to all fluxed surfaces, so for a neat job, apply flux carefully.

Actually, bending the copper tubing in a pipe run is often more difficult than the sweat soldering. If the tubing is bent with no special tools, you're almost sure to crimp the stuff. An ingenious set of tools, that cost very little, can be used with thinwall copper tubing. These spring style tubing benders are slid over the tubing (they come in a variety of sizes), and gentle hand pressure applied as shown in Fig. 8-9.

Tubing can be cut with a hacksaw, but a neater job usually results when a tubing cutter and reamer is used. The cutting wheel is turned down lightly onto the tubing, and the cutter is then rotated as you slowly turn in the cutting screw adjuster. (Figure 8-10.) When the tubing separates, the reamer is used to remove burrs on the interior of the tubing section to be used (Fig. 8-11).

Plastic pipe is in the process of being accepted in most areas, but a few still have codes that don't allow its use. Where it can be used, I would recommend it, as the cost so far is still low and the stuff is very easy to work with. It is simply cut and glued together to form permanent, watertight joints. The particular type of plastic pipe for a use varies. Polyethelene is often used in wells, while polyvinyl chloride is used for cold water systems. Chlorinated polyvinyl chloride is needed for hot water systems.

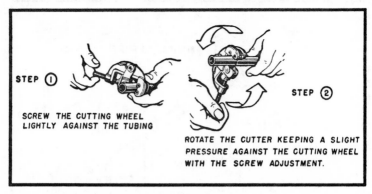

STEP ①

SCREW THE CUTTING WHEEL
LIGHTLY AGAINST THE TUBING

STEP ②

ROTATE THE CUTTER KEEPING A SLIGHT
PRESSURE AGAINST THE CUTTING WHEEL
WITH THE SCREW ADJUSTMENT.

Fig. 8-10. Steps for cutting tubing with a tube cutter.

Drainage system piping is much larger than is that used in the supply system. The reason is simple: the supply system is fed under pressure, but the drainage system is entirely a gravity flow one (with minor exceptions). Drainage systems must have a trap at each fixture to prevent the flow of sewer gas back into the house. Too, a vent stack is needed to equalize air pressure in the drainage system and to help protect the water seal in the traps. Next come the drainage lines to carry the actual waste material.

Local codes may modify materials use, but in general you can use cast iron, ABS, or PVC plastic or fiber pipe to connect to a sewage system. For underground pipe in the house you'll need to use cast iron. Aboveground in-house pipe can be made of cast iron, galvanized steel, copper, or ABS or PVC plastic. Any exposed piping will normally be chrome plated brass.

All these pipes must pass through joists and into walls, so some framing modifications are needed to keep pipe runs hidden while keeping the house from falling down from falling down from too much slicing away at structural members. Holes drilled through joists must fall in the first or last third of the member, never in the center third. Too, drilled holes cannot exceed 2 inches in diameter unless extra

Fig. 8-11. Reaming the burrs from a piece of tubing.

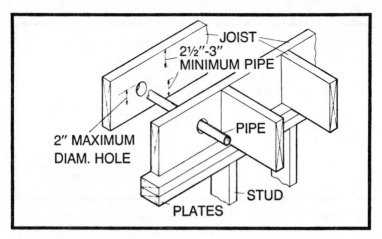

Fig. 8-12. Drilled holes in joists.

support is added to the joist. Notches may be made at the top and bottom of joists when needed, but should be held to a total of one-sixth the depth of the member. Closet bends for the toilet will sometimes require extra framing as more material has to be cut away. Frame with headers and tail beams as a sort of miniature reproduction of framing stair openings (Fig. 8-12).

Where pipe runs extend between floors, scabs are used to retain top plate strength. Studding, in the case of the heavier soil stacks, may need to be modified to allow room (Fig. 8-13).

Where the bathtub rests a doubled joist is a good idea. Any joist that might interfere with a space for the drain should be designed over a bit, with necessary movement seldom over 3 or 4 inches (Fig. 8-14).

Selection of plumbing fixtures for use throughout the vacation home can be confusing, but is essential to a good job. The present variety of bathtubs, shower units, stalls, kitchen sinks, hot water heaters, bathroom lavatories, toilets, and the fittings that go on them is truly bewildering. A large part of the problem is herewith turned back on you. Personal taste and finances will do a great degree to determine just what style of fixtures you end up with.

Some points, though, are worth considering. First, get the best quality your finances allow. Over the years, buying top, or close to top, quality plumbing fixtures can only result in a money savings as fewer repairs are needed, and replacement may be several decades further down the road than would happen with cheap fixtures.

Kitchen sinks come in stainless steel and various porcelainized finishes. Chipping is less of a problem with a sink of stainless steel, but porcelainized sinks provide decorative accents that many people prefer, available in different size double and single basins, with or without spray rinses. Get the one that suits the style of dishwashing and cleanup for your family. Get the absolute best washerless fittings you can find. You don't have to spring for fancy finishes, but make sure the internals are top grade.

Bathtubs are large items and tend to cost a lot. Cast iron with a porcelain enameled finish has for years been the accepted top quality standard, and still is. Sizes vary from 4½ feet, to the more or less standard 5 feet, on up past 6 feet in some decorator lines. Do not buy a steel tub unless you are getting extremely short of money, as they don't wear as well as cast iron, and tend to sound much like a boiler factory when filling.

You may wish to try one of the molded fiberglass models. Tub/shower units and shower units alone are now on the market. While greater care is needed to keep from scratching these fixtures,

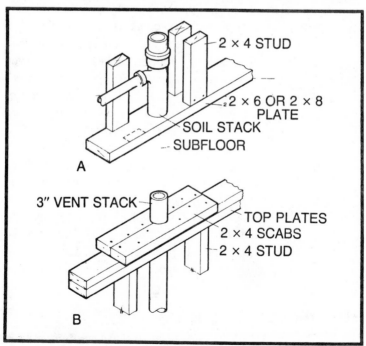

Fig. 8-13. Plumbing stacks. (A) Four-inch cast iron stack. (B) Three-inch pipe for vent.

183

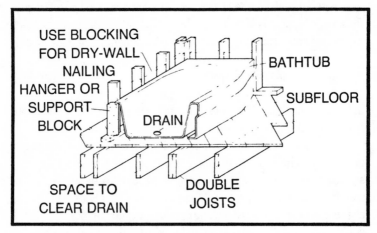

Fig. 8-14. Framing for a bathtub.

there are advantages. First, they're lighter than cast iron, thus easier to install. Second, they can be bought in single piece units (place the thing before you finish framing, or you've got problems), or in three and five piece units that save on tile setting. Third, they retain more of the heat of the room so that when you sit down in a partially filled tub or lean against the wall of the shower you don't catch a bad case of the shudders. Again, get the best quality taps you can.

Lavatories may be made of vitreous china with a glazed surface, enameled cast iron or enameled steel. The vitreous china lavatory top is considered the best quality and is the one I would select. Size and design to fit your family. Again, select top quality taps.

Toilets come in three basic styles. All for home use will have vitreous china bowls, with the top of the line models using a siphon jet action to clear the bowl. Top models will have the bowl and tank cast in one piece. Close coupled models have separate tanks and bowls, but the tank will rest on the rear of the bowl. These may be had with siphon jet or reverse trap flushing action. Exposed flush pipe toilets are the lowest in price, and a bit more difficult to install as the tank must be hung on the wall.

SEPTIC TANKS & DRAIN FIELDS

All the waste products that flow from the above fixtures must go somewhere. Disposal of human waste is a centuries old problem and one that gets harder to solve with each passing year. Restric-

184

tions on the use of waste disposal systems are getting tighter, necessarily, though in many cases the local building codes simply don't keep up with developments. For that reason, about the only practical form of private sewage disposal today is the septic field and tank system. A properly designed system is accepted by every community that doesn't have a city sewage system. Newer aerobic systems are still fighting the battle, but to date we most always have to go with the anaerobic systems (in other words, the bacteria that operate on the waste do not need oxygen).

Basically, the waste flows from the house to the septic tank, which is buried in the ground at a suitable point. You must make sure that effluent from this tank, and the drain field, cannot reach your well. The locale should be checked for rock structure that might allow passage of the effluents. Do all of this before drilling the well or installing the field, as replacing either is very expensive.

Septic tanks can be made of concrete, metal, or fired clay, and must be watertight. The inlet will be at a higher level than will the drain field outlet, though both are up near the top edge of the tank. Most septic tanks are baffled so that waste remains in the tank for no less than 16 hours. During that time, the bacteria dissolve most of the solids, and any remaining solid material settles in the bottom of the tank.

The liquid material then flows out of the tank and into the drain field where further decomposition makes it harmless.

It is best to have a professional design your septic system, for the requirements of each family differ greatly, as do local codes.

HEATING

Covering the subject of home heating today is a troublesome exercise. Prices of heating fuels continue to rise, solar energy gets a lot of publicity in experimental forms, wood stoves sell by the trainload, and new developments are just about sure to make any book on the subject out of date 6 weeks before the publisher's presses and bindery are through getting it ready for sale.

Until about 5 years ago, three basic home heating types were to be found. Oil fueled systems. Gas fueled systems. Electrical systems. Now we can add both wood and solar energy as either major home heating fuels or up and coming ones. Actually, with the newer wood stoves and multifuel furnaces, it is probably the most practical

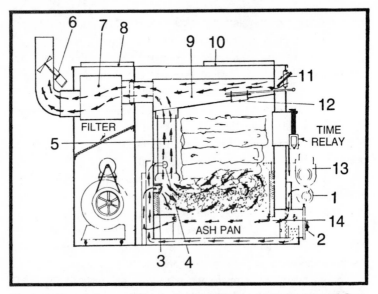

Fig. 8-15. Riteway furnace. (1) Ash pit blower. (2) Secondary air intake. (3) Cast iron air ports. (4) Cast iron secondary air ducts. (5) Cast iron gas combustion flue. (6) Draft inducer. (7) Return air heat exchanger. (8) Opening for return air plenum. (9) Bypass air flue. (10) Opening for warm air plenum. (11) Barometric damper. (12) Direct draft damper. (13) Optional oil or gas burner. (14) Grate bars. (Courtesy of Riteway Manufacturing Company.)

of all home heating types today for anyone with access to wood at low or modest cost. Solar energy is still very expensive to install, and must have a conventional system for back up in most parts of the country. Electric heat is no longer practical for the average person.

Gas is a fast disappearing resource. Though I'm not quite sure what various officials mean by 11-year supplies, as that figure has been about for about 4 years now and has suffered no reduction. It tends to make me wonder which is doing the better job of yanking the fabric over our eyes, the various state and federal agencies, or the producing companies.

In any case, for conventional heat today, oil seems to be the fuel of choice. It offers several forms, from gravity air to two pipe water systems, and is still reasonable in price. Though it is no longer cheap as prices in most areas reach 50 cents per gallon and get ready to go beyond the next time some oil producing country decides its leaders need a few more fancy cars or plush homes.

Solar energy, if you are able to locate components and find a competent solar engineer, is an alternative, though one that is presently too expensive for most people, even on a do-it-yourself basis.

For the more rustic second homes, wood stoves are a good answer, while for other types the multifuel furnace could be a fine way to cover problems associated with wood heat. Several companies produce what are basically two furnaces in one. The diagrams here show both Riteway's furnace and boiler (Figs. 8-15 and 8-16). These systems are primarily immense wood stoves, with wood capacities ranging from 20 cubic feet (Riteway's LF30) up to 45 cubic feet (LF70). Btu per hour output of the LF30 is 160,000, which should be enough to keep most any home warm, whatever the outside temperature.

The furnaces are designed to burn a long time with a load of wood, with a second thermostat set a few degrees lower than that for the wood, automatically kicking in the oil or gas burner when the wood fire runs out of fuel. One of the major problems with wood as a

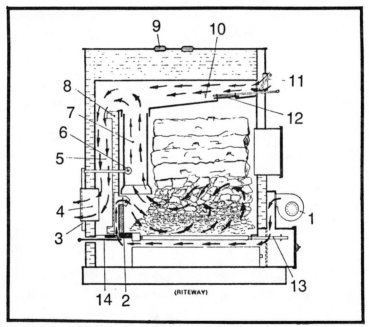

Fig. 8-16. Riteway boiler. (1) Ash pit blower. (2) Cast iron air ports. (3) Secondary air duct. (4) Smoke pipe collar. (5) Heat chamber. (6) Cast iron air distributor for secondary air. (7) Cast iron gas combustion flue. (8) Water circulating tubes. (9) Flow tappings. (10) Bypass air heating flue. (11) Barometric damper. (12) Direct draft damper. (13) Grate bards. (14) Fuel selector damper. (Courtesy of Riteway Manufacturing Company.)

fuel over the years has been the need for constant tending. These multifuel furnaces cure that just about totally. No worries about frozen pipes if you have to be away overnight. No constant feeding of the fire; one loading every day or two will usually suffice in all but the very coldest weather. According to Riteway, too, the ashes need be shaken through the grates only about once every week or 10 days, and the large ash pan needs to be emptied only once a month. This will vary according to type of wood used, climate, and so on, but it is a huge change from old wood stoves that required constant care and ash emptying.

Whenever wood heat of any type is contemplated for a home, you'll have to check local codes carefully. Few, if any, wood furnaces are presently approved by testing organizations such as Under-writer's Laboratories, and most codes require this, or some other, form of testing and acceptance before a heating system can be installed. This applies to central heating, of course, but problems can arise even installing wood stoves, though seldom with local codes if the basis of safe intallation is followed. The problem here could come from your insurance company. Some companies are now beginning to worry a great deal abut wood heaters in homes, and are either canceling homeowner policies or raising premiums to unheard of levels, which, with our yearly inflation, is a more or less normal affair even without the wood heaters. My own insurance costs have tripled in the past 5 or 6 years.

Forced warm air remains the most popular, using either a gas or oil burner to do the heating. Installation costs are low and the ducting for a correctly installed system should never require any maintenance (Fig. 8-17). Select a furnace that is of a size to fit your home. Too small a furnace can overheat, and is inefficient, while too large a furnace will also be inefficient, as it does not work at recommended efficient operating levels. Modern furnaces come in a variety of styles, and may have cooling coils for air conditioning. Forced warm air furnaces should be purchased with electronic air filtration in most cases, as this will help cut down on dust levels in the home (Fig. 8-18).

If oil is the fuel of choice, you will find a further selection necessary. Some of the selection of burner type will depend on the ease of availability of heating fuel oil types in your locale. Number 1 fuel oil is a lighter, slightly more expensive form of heating oil and is used in vaporizing pot style oil burners, which are the least expen-

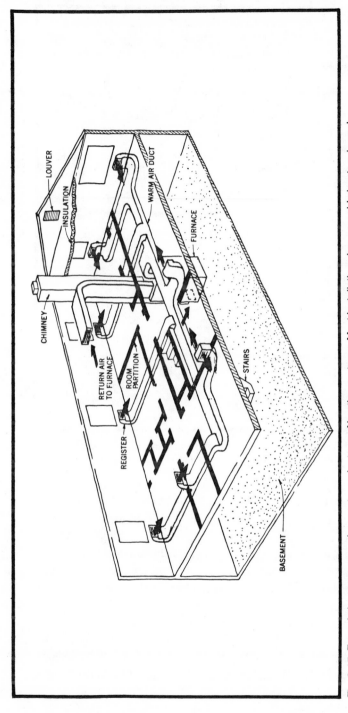

Fig. 8-17. Forced air systems are the most popular type of heating systems. Most installations have a cold air return in each room (except the kitchen and bathroom). If the basement is heated, additional ducts should deliver hot air near the basement floor along the outside walls. In cold climates, a separate perimeter loop heating system may be the best way to heat the basement.

189

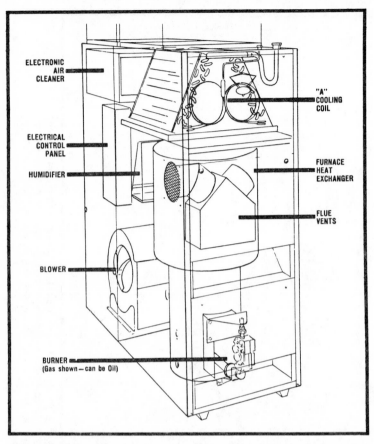

Fig. 8-18. Modern forced air furnaces may have an electronic air cleaner for better air filtration and cooling coils for summer air conditioning. This unit is a gas furnace.

sive types of oil burners. Number 2 fuel has a slightly higher heat value per gallon than does number 1, and is suitable for use in gun and rotary style oil burners. The gun style pressure burner is the most popular for home use. Basically, these two burners differ in that the vaporizing pot style burner uses a pot full of fuel, where the oil is vaporized by heat (Fig. 8-19), then burned, while the gun style (Fig. 8-20) uses a pump to force oil through an atomizing nozzle after which an electric igniter is used to fire the mixture.

While forced warm air heating systems are generally the most popular for homes, there are other types of systems to be found in many homes. Gravity hot water systems are not often used these

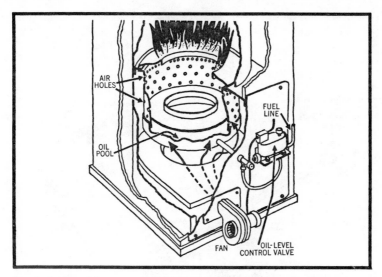

Fig. 8-19. Vaporizing or pot type oil burners are the least expensive units.

days, but single and two pipe forced hot water systems are. Expense here is higher than for forced hot air, and convectors or radiators are installed in heated rooms. A single pipe system requires special sizing of the convectors, as the single pipe used allows mixing of hot

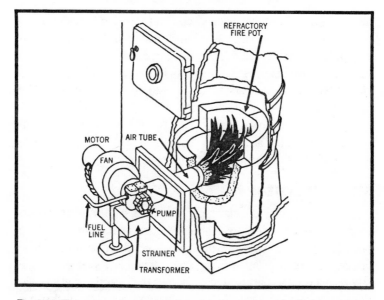

Fig. 8-20. The gun or pressure type burner is the most popular for home central heating systems.

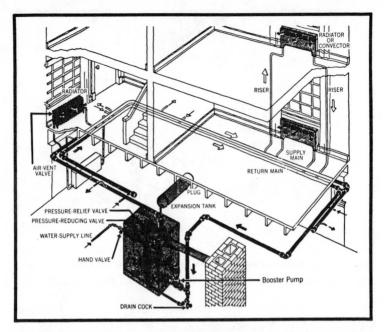

Fig. 8-21. Two pipe forced hot water systems have two supply pipes or mains. One supplies the hot water to the room heating units and the other returns the cooled water to the boiler.

and cold water at each convector so that the water temperature is reduced quite a lot on long runs. The radiators or convectors furthest down the line may need to be much larger than those closer to the furnace. A two pipe system prevents this commingling of hot and cold water, as one pipe carries hot water to the convectors while the other returns cooled water to the furnace. (Figure 8-21.)

Both styles of hot water systems are considerably more expensive than forced hot air systems, but provide more draft free heating, usually with slightly greater efficiency.

SOLAR HEAT SYSTEMS

The complexity of solar heat systems is high. As is the cost, today. Sooner or later, though, some governments are bound to provide tax breaks in the form of credits that will cut the present high original cost of installation. This could happen in 1 year or it could take as many as 5 years, but when it does the selection and installation of solar heating devices will increase even more quickly than it is doing right now.

Most home installations involve flat plate collectors which capture the sun's energy and pass it on for present or later use (Fig. 8-22). This collector has three main parts: a transparent cover, the collector or absorber plate, and channels in the collector plate. Figure 8-23 gives an idea of how a flat plate collector works.

The actual angle at which your collectors would need to be set will vary depending on your latitude. As Fig. 8-24 shows, the best way to judge is to take your actual latitude and add 10 to 15 degrees, with the collector always facing south.

Because the sun hides on us throughout the night, we need to have some form of storage for the heat collected during the day. Solar systems should be designed with a 3- to 5-day capacity, so that when the sun doesn't make an appearance through a heavy overcast for several days, you won't run out of heat. Several storage media are used, often depending on the type of collector system and the final system of providing heat to the house. You can use, as with oil and gas burners, hot air or hot water to transfer the heat to the home. Water is best if you're using a hot water system, while rocks

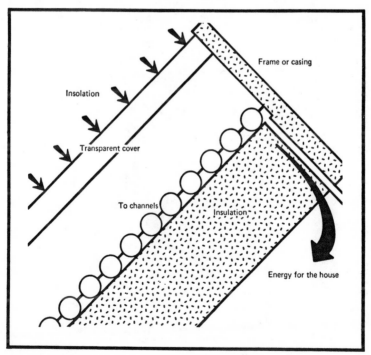

Fig. 8-22. Flat plate collector of a solar heating system.

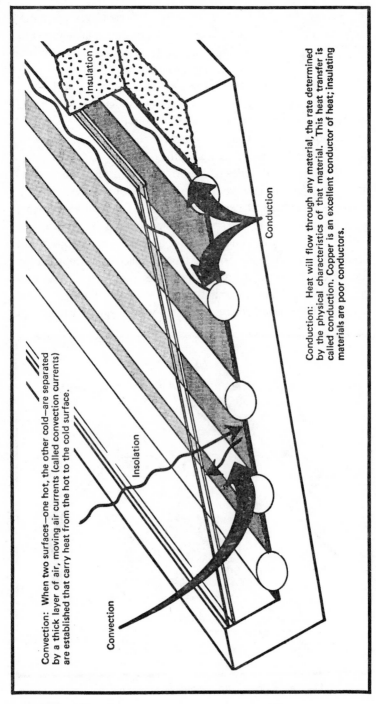

Convection: When two surfaces—one hot, the other cold—are separated by a thick layer of air, moving air currents (called convection currents) are established that carry heat from the hot to the cold surface.

Convection

Insolation

Insulation

Conduction: Heat will flow through any material, the rate determined by the physical characteristics of that material. This heat transfer is called conduction. Copper is an excellent conductor of heat; insulating materials are poor conductors.

Conduction

Fig. 8-23. How a flat plate collector works.

provide an economical form of storage, though one with much greater space requirements than water. Water is heavy, though, so any system using water as a medium of heat storage must be engineered to support that weight. For example, assume 2000 gallons are needed. That will weigh in at just about 9 tons. Too, water eventually corrodes most steels, so this must be taken into account during design stages (Fig. 8-25).

As you can see in Fig. 8-26, some sort of conventional heating system is needed as a backup with present day solar heating systems. This adds greatly to overall cost of installation, but is essential in certain areas of the country to prevent problems when the sun doesn't provide enough heat over a period of time beyond the storage   cap cities of your rock bin or water tank. In fact, most solar heat systems installed today are designed to provide no more than 60 to 80 percent of a home's heat needs, with the rest provided by the conventional system. The reason for this is simple. Adding the storage capacity and the collector plate area to bring the solar system up to 100-

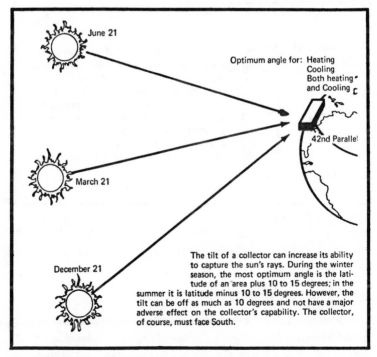

Optimum angle for: Heating
Cooling
Both heating and Cooling

42nd Parallel

The tilt of a collector can increase its ability to capture the sun's rays. During the winter season, the most optimum angle is the latitude of an area plus 10 to 15 degrees; in the summer it is latitude minus 10 to 15 degrees. However, the tilt can be off as much as 10 degrees and not have a major adverse effect on the collector's capability. The collector, of course, must face South.

Fig. 8-24. Position of the flat plate collector in relation to the sun.

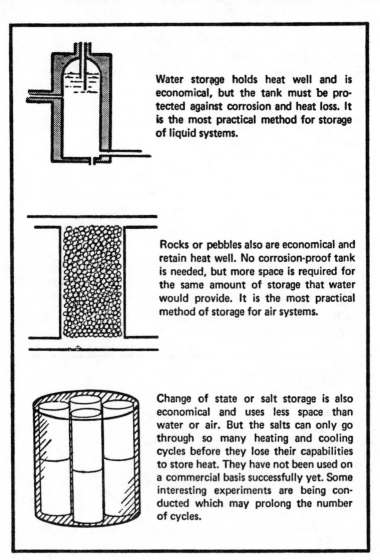

Water storage holds heat well and is economical, but the tank must be protected against corrosion and heat loss. It is the most practical method for storage of liquid systems.

Rocks or pebbles also are economical and retain heat well. No corrosion-proof tank is needed, but more space is required for the same amount of storage that water would provide. It is the most practical method of storage for air systems.

Change of state or salt storage is also economical and uses less space than water or air. But the salts can only go through so many heating and cooling cycles before they lose their capabilities to store heat. They have not been used on a commercial basis successfully yet. Some interesting experiments are being conducted which may prolong the number of cycles.

Fig. 8-25. Types of storage.

percent capacity is extremely expensive, inasmuch as you still need some sort of conventional heat backup.

WOOD STOVES & FIREPLACES

If you prefer, a wood stove installation can serve as a backup for a solar system, or it can serve in place of any other type of heating if you're willing to expend the energy to cut, transport, and stack wood, in addition to feeding the fire with some constancy. Such heat is best used in areas where there are plentiful supplies of hardwoods for fuel, but can be used in almost all areas of the United States and Canada. Fireplaces are for supplemental heat and romance, as the usual fireplace design is a possible contributor to total heat *loss* in a

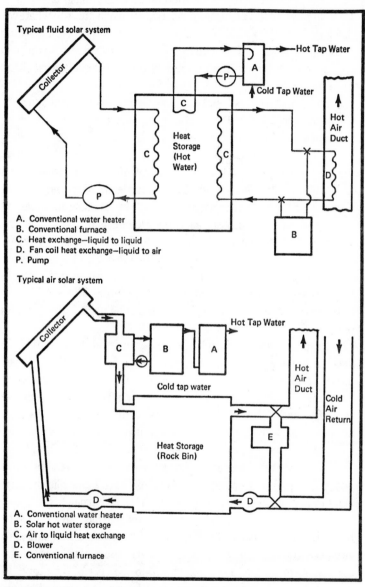

Fig. 8-26. Solar space heating and domestic hot water.

home. With vented designs, heating efficiency increases, but is unlikely the best fireplace in the world will be much more than 15 or 20 percent efficient, while even just about the worst made wood stove should give an efficiency of about 25 percent.

If your cabin or other vacation home is to remain unoccupied through much of the winter, a good modern wood stove in whatever design you prefer is a fine way to provide heat on chilly fall and spring evenings and nights. The wood stove market has grown so much in the past couple of years it is now nearly impossible to even list all the makers.

Half a dozen years ago, I don't think you would have had to go to a second hand to count the number of manufacturers, but, counting smaller local firms, today there have to be several hundred making stoves of virtually any design you can imagine from the old pot belly on up to modern variants of the Franklin design, such as that shown in Fig. 8-27. The illustrated stove is made by Vermont Casting Company of the highest grade of gray cast iron available and comes in two sizes, with the larger called the Defiant and the smaller the Vigilant. Cost is relatively high, though not as expensive as some other stove models. The flame path for the Defiant model is extremely long, the interior is baffled, and there is a secondary combustion chamber in which volatile gasses burn. The stove is an airtight when the doors are closed, but can be used with the doors open, too.

In general, there are today four types of wood stove from which you can make a selection, though the variations within the types mount into the dozens. These are all airtights, with the nonairtight sheet metal and cast iron models forming a generally less desirable category. In these older style cast iron models, take care, for a lot are being made overseas of cast iron much too thin for stove use. Cracking of the stove becomes a real problem after only a short time.

Category 1 is the basic airtight stove, exemplified by the Riteway (Fig. 8-28) and Ashley models. Most have bimetallic thermostats to help control air intake and the rate of burning.

Category 2 includes many of the Scandanavian stoves, such as Jøtul. These are cigar or front end burners, with internal baffles to direct and control air flow, forcing the wood to burn at the front of the stove first, moving at a controlled rate to the rear of the stove. In general these stoves provide excellent heating sources with sea-

Fig. 8-27. Defiant parlor stove. (Courtesy of Vermont Castings, Inc.)

soned wood, but do not burn green wood as well as some other models.

Category 3 is the downdraft stove where the wood load rests on grates and the volatile gasses driven off by the fire are forced back through the fuel supply and the grates. In this manner the gasses are more likely to be burned efficiently. The more of the volatile gasses driven off the wood that manage to get burned, the greater a stove's overall efficiency and heat output.

Category 4 is the convertible, such as the Defiant. Using both baffles and thermostats, as well as secondary air chambers and inlets, these stoves rival downdraft stoves for efficiency ratings.

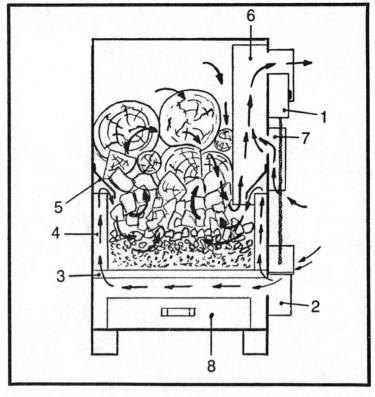

Fig. 8-28. Model 2000 wood heater by Riteway Manufacturing Company. (1) Temperature regulator. (2) Magnetic damper. (3) Grate. (4) Liners. (5) Liner retainers. (6) Gas combustion flue. (7) Secondary air duct. (8) Ash pan.

Efficiency ratings for wood stoves are extremely variable because of the uneven nature of wood as a fuel. Different woods have different heat values, while any woodpile will have split and unsplit pieces and gnarled and straight pieces. All these factors have an effect on the efficiency of any wood stove or furnace or fireplace.

STOVE SELECTION

Most airtight wood stoves will provide efficiency on the order of 50 percent in extracting heat from wood. A few may do 5 percent better, and some 5 percent worse. Your personal taste, the overall stove quality, its price, and its availability will probably prove as good in making a selection as would a comparison of claimed efficiencies. Manufacturer's claim efficiency ratings up to as much as 75 percent, but such rates are not provided by independent testing, though they may well be possible with a perfect installation, fed a wood such as air dried hickory or oak cut to uniform size and shape. In normal use, don't expect the wood stove to produce more than my above figures unless you wish to be disappointed.

The variety of steel and iron types of stoves is wide. If the stove is to be of plate steel or cast iron, select for durability. In the case of mild steel plate, look for thickness and carefully welded joints. In the case of cast iron, look for castings that are uniform in thickness. Too, look for surface porosity in the cast iron. The less porous, the better the quality generally. Of course, with stoves of enameled cast iron, such as those made in Scandanavia, you won't be able to tell a great deal about porosity, but most of these brands have been in existence for nearly 40 years, an indication that they must be doing something right as these are among the most expensive wood stoves you can buy anyway.

If the stove is made all, or partly, of sheet metal you will have a lower original cost, but will have to replace the stove at some point not too far in the future, though the airtights made by Ashley, Riteway, Shenandoah, and others have firebrick lined fireboxes which greatly increases probable life.

Loading the wood stove can be a pain. The smaller the stove, the more often it will need to be loaded. Stoves with top loading features are usually the easiest to load, but tend to throw some smoke into the interior of the home while loading is carried out. Look for a door large enough to take a fair size log unless you want to spend all your time splitting wood to fit the thing. End and side loading stoves feed less smoke back into the house on loading, but may require a lot of bending with lower models. In some cases, a stove will provide two types of loading.

WOOD STOVE INSTALLATION

I've seen wood stoves used in installations that would keep me awake at night though the owners never had a problem over a lot of years. It simply doesn't pay to take any kind of a chance with this, as the gasses going up a wood stove flue are exceptionally hot, while the presence of hot coals and ashes in the stove itself may create hazards.

Chimneys used for wood stoves must be of the finest quality available, whether they are the prefabricated steel models that lock

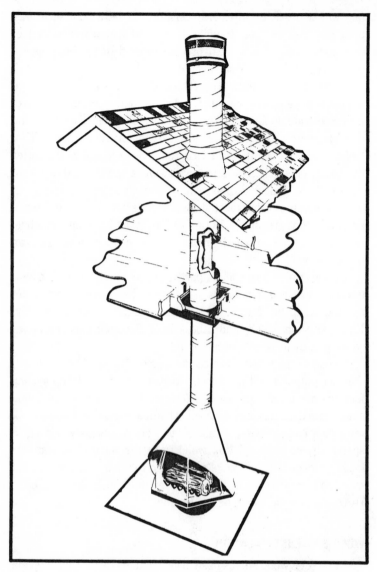

Fig. 8-29. Class A triple wall chimney. (Courtesy of Majestic Thulman.)

together and go up quickly and easily or of masonry lined with flue tiles.

A class A chimney installation, such as the Majestic triple wall shown in Fig. 8-29, can be easily made in any home. Various termination styles are available, as are various lengths and adapters (Fig. 8-30).

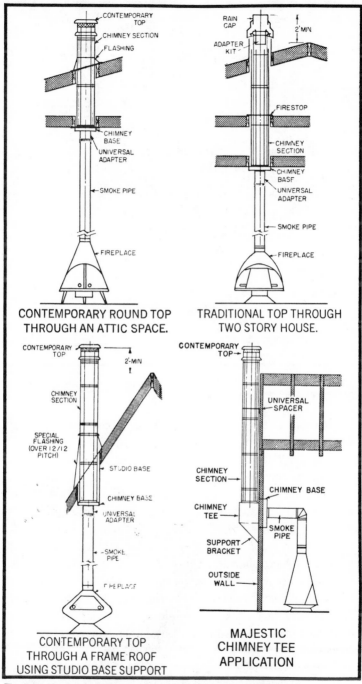

CONTEMPORARY ROUND TOP THROUGH AN ATTIC SPACE.

TRADITIONAL TOP THROUGH TWO STORY HOUSE.

CONTEMPORARY TOP THROUGH A FRAME ROOF USING STUDIO BASE SUPPORT

MAJESTIC CHIMNEY TEE APPLICATION

Fig. 8-30. Typical installations of Majestic Thulman chimneys.

203

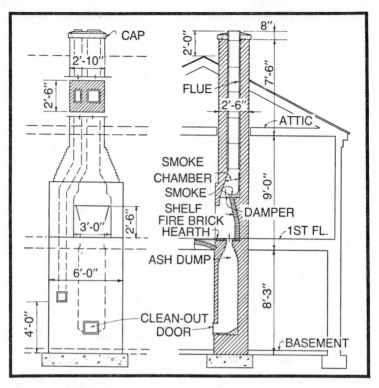

Fig. 8-31. Diagram of an entire chimney such as is commonly built to serve the house heating unit and one fireplace.

Masonry chimneys are more difficult to construct, but may prove less expensive if you do the brickwork, or most of it, yourself. Concrete block can also be used, either faced with brick or left unfinished as you desire.

The chimney shown Fig. 8-31 is designed to serve a fireplace, but could easily be adapted to a wood stove installation by simply leaving the fireplace off and running the chimney down onto the foundation and footings. Chimneys of masonry require their own footings, while prefabricated units are enough lighter that they can be supported by wall, floor, and roof framing.

Footings must go below frostline, and will then extend at least 6 inches beyond the chimney on all sides. Single story chimneys will need 8-inch-thick footings, while 12 inches is required for two story chimneys.

Correctly sized flue tile is needed to line the chimney. This flue tile is available in round and rectangular styles, and in a wide variety of sizes. Masonry chimneys must have walls 8 inches thick, and the flue liner is placed with the chimney built up outside it. Mortar joints are needed to seal one flue liner to another, and you must take care that the internal portion of this mortar joint is as smooth as possible so as not to restrict the flow of gasses.

You can put more than a single flue in one chimney, as Fig. 8-32 shows, but divisions between flues must be masonry wythes at least 3¾ inches thick. Each woodstove, each fireplace, and each furnace *must* have its own flue.

If you want to ease up the job of cleaning the chimney each year (twice yearly cleaning is recommended when wood is used as a fuel, so that creosote cannot build up and become a fire hazard), a soot pocket and cleanout door should be placed at the bottom of each flue (Fig. 8-33).

Smokepipe entry into a flue is of great importance in overall stove installation safety. The smokepipe will most often enter the chimney horizontally. It will not extend into the flue itself. Use a metal thimble to line the chimney wall where the pipe enters. These flue rings can be bought in diameters ranging from 6 inches—the most usual size with wood stoves—on up to 1 foot, with lengths of 4½, 6, 9, and 12 inches.

If a wood wall is between the stove and the chimney, the installation must provide protection for the combustible wood surfaces. Usually, it's best to cut the wall opening about 12 inches larger than the diameter of the smokepipe, then make a two sided metal

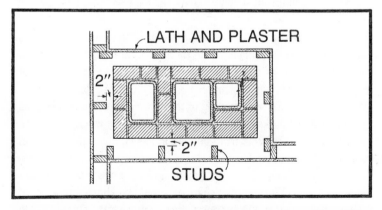

Fig. 8-32. Plan of chimney showing proper arrangement of three flues. Bond division wall with side walls by staggering the joints of successive courses. Wood framing should be at least 2 inches from brick.

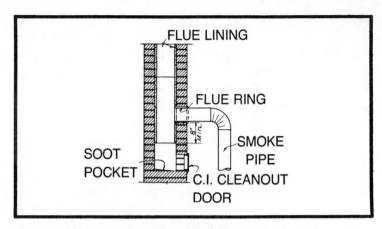

Fig. 8-33. Soot pocket and cleanout for a chimney flue.

shield to keep heat from getting directly to the wood. Don't forget to drill at least 6 vent holes of ⅜-inch diameter around the metal shield so that hot air can pass out (Fig. 3-34).

Too, no wood can come in contact with the chimney. The distance varies. Solid masonry chimneys require only a ½ inch of space between the brick and the wood, while chimneys made of hollow block require at least 2 inches of clearance. In both cases, the chimney wall must be at least 8 inches thick. The space is filled with a porous non-combustible material, not concrete or other solid material. Two inches of clearance is also needed where the chimney passes through the roof. This not only provides fire protection, but allows for the different settling and expansion rates of the house and the chimney.

Flue linings on masonry chimneys extend at least 4 inches from the top course of masonry, and are then surrounded by no less than 2 inches of cement mortar. The mortar cap should be sloped so that water runs off onto the roof and not into the chimney. Place a formed wire spark arrestor over the top of the chimney. Not only does this prevent a lot of sparks from spraying the area, but it will also serve to keep birds and squirrels from nesting in the chimney during warm months.

Chimney design includes height and distance from obstructions, as well as flue size. No chimney should be shorter than about 12½ feet or it will not draw correctly, no matter the flue size. On peaked roofs, the top of the chimney must be at least 2 feet above any point of the roof within 10 feet (and that includes such obstructions as trees), while a flat roof requires a chimney that rises at least 3 feet above its surface.

WOOD STOVE LOCATION

Whether the chimney used is masonry or metal, it is best in my mind to install it inside the house. Installing the chimney on the exterior wall of a house allows it to become a source of heat loss where the insulating values of the wall are cut away. A chimney on the interior of a house costs a bit of space but is usually a source of net heat gain.

Wood stoves have different requirements for placement when combustible walls are involved. Some require little or no clearance, while others may need as much as 3 feet. This is information included with the stove by the manufacturer and those recommendations should be followed as closely as possible.

It is possible to reduce stove to wall distance by building a shield of asbestos millboard or a form of decorative brick. Make sure the decorative brick used is of mineral and not plastic. If millboard is used, place it in such a way that there is at least a 1-inch gap between it and the wall. This allows an airflow behind the millboard and serves to keep the wall even cooler than would placing the board directly against the wall.

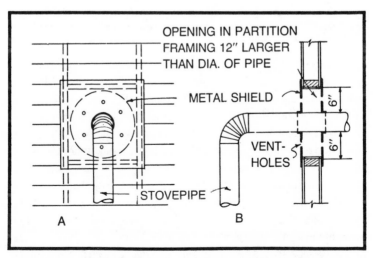

Fig. 8-34. One method of protecting a wood partition when a smoke pipe passes through it. (A) elevation of protection around the pipe. (B) Sectional view.

Fig. 8-35. Styria 130 cooking range with firebrick lining, white enamel finish, warp-proof extra thick steel cooking top, and hot water tank. (Courtesy of Styria Wood Heaters & Ranges.)

Now comes the time to protect the floor. Of course, you can make a permanent installation using slate, brick, or other masonry hearth materials under the stove. If you do, these materials should extend out beyond the front of the stove at least 1 foot so that sparks dropped during ash removal can't cause problems. Too, it's a good idea to have the hearth extend at least 6 inches back under the point where the stovepipe enters the stove. Should this pipe burn through, the coals will then drop on the fire resistant material.

If you wish the stove to be removable during warm weather, using ¼-inch-thick asbestos millboard over a piece of sheet steel is recommended for safety on combustible floors.

Stovepipe should be a minimum of 24 gauge. Use as few elbows as you can so that fewer restrictions are placed in the way of the flue gas flow. Stovepipe sections should be screwed together, using ½-inch sheet metal screws, with two used at each union, but three preferred. Since this can be a lot of work on long stovepipe runs, I would suggest you look for the type of sheet metal screw that has a head to fit a special tool for a ¼-inch drill. The screw is inserted in the driver, the tip pressed against the sheet metal, and the screw run in with the drill—a good time and effort saver.

For the true rustic, there are also cook stoves in wood and coal burning models easily available (Fig. 8-35). While these are not very good for heating much more than the kitchen, they do serve nicely in rural areas where electricity or gas, for cooking, may be difficult to get.

FIREPLACES

For the romantics among us who have to have a fireplace, there are many ways to go now. The quickly and easily erected prefabricated models available from companies such as Heatilator and Majestic, as well as several others, offer a very simple method of putting in an original fireplace, but also offer a good shot at putting one in at a later date if desirable. Too, there is now a very wide array

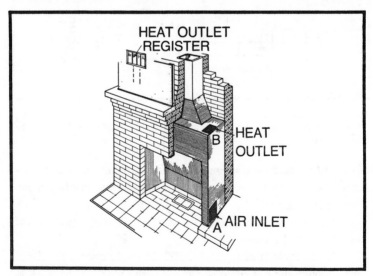

Fig. 8-36. A modified fireplace. Air is drawn through inlet A from the room being heated. It is heated by contact with the metal sides and back of the fireplace, rises by natural circulation, and is discharged through outlet B. The inlets and outlets are connected to registers which may be located at the front, as shown, or ends of the fireplace or on a wall of an adjacent or second story room.

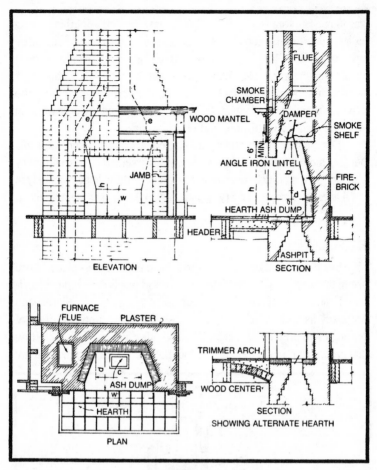

Fig. 8-37. Construction details of a typical fireplace. The lower right hand drawing shows an alternate method of supporting the hearth. See Fig. 8-38 for recommended dimensions.

of designs, from free standing cones to wall inserted heat vented models, some with power downdraft around the flue pipe to provide even more warm air.

If a fireplace is to be used, I would generally recommend one of the heat venting models (Fig. 8-36).

For the traditionalist, there is still the solid masonry fireplace, which is quite difficult to construct properly, if all firebox work is done with firebrick and fireclay. Firebrick cannot be set in ordinary mortar as the heat causes the mortar to fall apart very quickly. Modified sheet metal interiors are easily available to make masonry

| Size of fireplace opening | | Depth | Minimum width of back wall | Height of vertical back wall | Height of inclined back wall | Size of flue lining required | |
Width w	Height h	d	c	a	b	Standard rectangular (outside dimensions)	Standard round (inside diameter)
Inches	*Inches*	*Inches*	*Inches*	*Inches*	*Inches*	*Inches*	*Inches*
24	24	16–18	14	14	16	8½ x 13	10
28	24	16–18	14	14	16	8½ x 13	10
30	28–30	16–18	16	14	18	8½ x 13	10
36	28–30	16–18	22	14	18	8½ x 13	12
42	28–32	16–18	28	14	18	8½ x 13	12
48	32	18–20	32	14	24	13 x 13	15
54	36	18–20	36	14	28	13 x 18	15
60	36	18–20	44	14	28	13 x 18	15
54	40	20–22	36	17	29	13 x 18	15
60	40	20–22	42	17	30	18 x 18	18
66	40	20–22	44	17	30	18 x 18	18
72	40	22–28	51	17	30	18 x 18	18

Fig. 8-38. Recommended dimensions of fireplaces and size of flue lining required. Letters at heads of columns refer to dimensions in Fig. 8-37.

fireplace construction simpler, while also providing the heat venting features that add at least a little to fireplace efficiency.

For those who insist on a masonry fireplace, Fig. 8-37 and 8-38 may give some idea of the complexities involved. Fortunately, it isn't necessary to form one's own damper as these are available from many of the prefabricated fireplace makers—one job cut down. The rest requires careful design and construction if it is to draw properly. For more construction details, see the *Wood Heating Handbook*, Charles Self, TAB book No. 872.

Chapter 9
Insulation & Ventilation

With today's energy prices and the constant increase we can continue to expect over the coming years, all new homes, whether for vacation or primary use, should be correctly insulated. This applies unless the place is totally unheated and used only in weather where air conditioning is not desirable. In addition, proper ventilation is also needed to remove water vapor from the house before it can damage walls, ceilings, floors and other parts. With the extra tightness being built into modern homes, correct ventilation is even more important now than ever before.

Details of ventilation will vary from home to home, with most of the variation depending on the size of the house, but with at least some dependent on the area in which you are building. Positive movement of air through both the attic and any basement or crawl space is essential if you are to prevent condensation of moisture from cooking, bathing, laundering.

In houses that don't have basements, ventilation will consist of set-in screened vents, with moisture penetration of the earth prevented by a vapor barrier laid on the ground. This vapor barrier should be a plastic film 2 or 3 mils thick. The ventilation area should equal 1/160 of the crawl space area: thus a crawl space of 1,000 square feet would need 6¼ square feet of ventilator space if no ground cover is used. With the ground cover, ventilator area is reduced to 1/160 of the ground space, or 0.625 of net ventilator area. There should be at least two ventilators used.

Homes with full and partial basements are considered adequately ventilated in that area if there is at least a single window. The crawl space area of any partial basement must be ventilated to standards unless that crawl space opens into the partial basement and a window is present.

Proper ventilation of an attic area not only removes the chance of internal wall damage from moisture, but prevents the formation of ice dams. Snow along the warm edge of a roof melts, running down to the colder cornice area where it freezes, forming an ice dam that could back water up under the shingles as runoff keeps up. During summer, proper ventilation keeps a flow of air moving through the attic, thus removing some of the hotter air.

Attic ventilation is too often left to simple screened louvers at the gable ends, which leave air movement to the wind direction and force. If lower ventilators are also provided in the soffit areas of the roof overhang in addition to the louvers at gable ends. The warmer air at the top of the house will then be foreced out as natural air currents draw cooler air in through the soffit ventilators. It is essential that these soffit ventilators not be blocked when the roof and upper wall areas of the house are insulated.

Ventilator area on the upper part of the house is just as important as it is for the lower portion of the structure. Use a moisture barrier, either as it comes on your insulation or as a sheet of film covering the entire wall, and you will need about 1 square foot of ventilator area for every 300 squre feet of attic floor space. That means 4 square feet of ventilator for a 1,200 square foot attic. This figure should be divided about evenly between soffit ventilators (Fig. 9-1) and gable end louvers.

SEALING

Once the ventilators are taken care of, you need to seal your home against drafts. A check of your window and any sliding door styles is a good idea. According to Owens/Corning, the use of sliding doors is not a good idea to start with because of the thermal losses through such large expanses of glass, even when they are double glazed. If they are used, make sure they are of the type known as thermal break if they are metal units; the same type of construction should be used in metal window units, too. The thermal break style is simply a sandwich, which places the highly conductive metal window or door frame parts outside a less conductive material

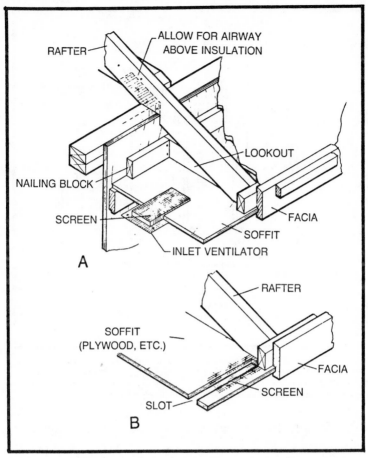

Fig. 9-1. Inlet ventilators. (A) Small insert ventilator. (B) Slot ventilator.

such as vinyl (Figs. 9-2 and 9-3).

After these, sealing starts. A poorly fitted and unweatherstripped window can allow as much as five and a half times the air infiltration as can a properly sealed unit. With a minimum of 10 percent of the house wall area being windows, this allows, in an average home, a heat loss on the order of 20,000 Btu per hour.

To maintain the correct fit during settling of even the best quality window, caulking is used. First any dirt or other material, including paint, that may have collected around the window during construction is cleaned off using a putty knife or large screwdriver. Next, if tube caulking is to be used, you draw a bead down the sides of the window and over the top and under the bottom, making sure

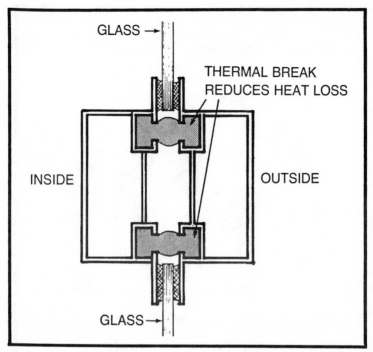

Fig. 9-2. Thermal break type windows reduce heat loss. The window frames are basically metal with some less conductive material sandwiched in between the outside and inside metal frame units to cut down on the amount of cold transmitted through the metal. (Courtesy of Owens-Corning Corp.)

the caulking bead is wide enough to adhere to both sides of the gap. This type of caulking takes a bit of practice to get the desirable smooth bead, so you may prefer to use the rope style that is simply unwound and pressed into place with the fingers.

Once the exteriors of windows and doors are caulked, you can move on to the wider gaps that may appear between the siding of the house and the foundation. If these gaps are very wide, as they may well be if you have a stone foundation, use strips of glass fiber insulation to fill in the gaps, then cover with a finish from the caulking gun.

The next job is weatherstripping both doors and windows if they were made or came without this important material. Several kinds of weatherstripping for windows are available. The thin metal springs are easily installed when the sash is in the open position, slipping into the channel in which the window moves (double hung windows). The strip for the lower sash seal at the window bottom is installed on the bottom rail, usually with brads, while the top rail strip is installed from the outside of the house. The nails here must be set in with a nailset or they'll catch on the top rail of the lower sash, eventually wearing it away and defeating your work.

Rolled vinyl is installed in a similar manner. A third type of weatherstripping is available, an adhesive backed foam strip. This type of weatherstripping works fine on windows where there is no friction, but is not good for most areas needing weatherstripping on double hung windows, the most popular type in residences.

Four kinds of weatherstripping are available for doors. Adhesive backed foam is simply measured, cut to size, and pressed in place along the areas needing sealing. Durability is poor. Rolled vinyl with an aluminum channel backing is nailed along the casing using no less than one small nail each 6 inches. Installation is easy, and durability is high. Wood backed foam rubber is also easy to install, being nailed so the foam is a snug fit against the closed door. Durability is not very great. Tin strips, actually spring metal in a V-shape, are quite simple to install, too. Nailing takes place in a slightly different manner, but durability is high and the stripping is invisible with the door closed.

INSULATION NEEDS

New insulation requirements have been developed in the past few years. With the rising cost of heating and cooling, the increase in

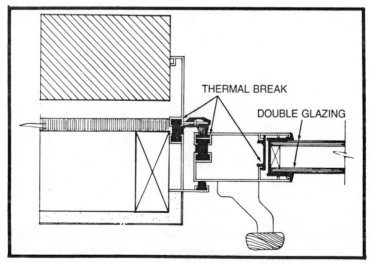

Fig. 9-3. Thermal sliding glass door jamb. (Courtesy of Owens-Corning Corp.)

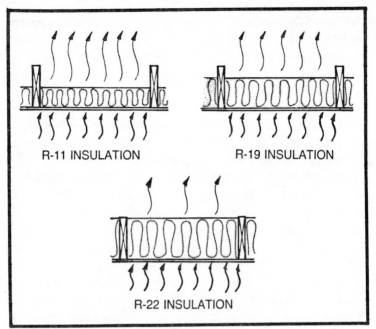

Fig. 9-4. The larger the R-value, the greater it will retard heat flow. (Courtesy of Owens-Corning Fiberglas Corp.)

the amount of insulation becomes ever more practical. There is no likelihood that we will ever again be faced with low heating fuel costs unless solar energy becomes financially feasible for a great many more people in the next decade or two. Insulation is classified by R-value, which is nothing more than a simple way to designate the particular material's resistance to the passage of heat. As an example, to get the R-value of 6 inches of glass fiber insulation, you would have to build a brick wall 7 *feet* thick, or a solid wood wall 15 inches thick. The R-value of 6 inches of glass fiber is 19 (Fig. 9-4).

Insulation comes in several styles, each with varying R-values for particular thicknesses. Figure 9-5 indicates the different R-values and the styles available. No determination of R-value for a particular type of rigid foam insulation can be provided as there are many variables from brand to brand. Generally, with the rigid foams, the R-value per inch of thickness is a fair amount higher than it is for the same thickness of glass fiber insulation, but the price is also higher and special installation techniques are needed to provide fire safety. In most cases, new home builders will go with either rock wool or glass fiber insulation in batt and roll forms. There is seldom

	BATTS OR BLANKETS		LOOSE FILL (POURED-IN)			
	glass fiber	rock wool	glass fiber	rock wool	cellulosic fiber	
R-11	3½"-4"	3"	5"	4"	3"	R-11
R-19	6"-6½"	5¼"	8"-9"	6"-7"	5"	R-19
R-22	6½"	6"	10"	7"-8"	6"	R-22
R-30	9½"-10½"*	9"*	13"-14"	10"-11"	8"	R-30
R-38	12"-13"*	10½"*	17"-18"	13"-14"	10"-11"	R-38

Fig. 9-5. Type of insulation needed for a specific R-value.

any need for using loose fill insulation in a new home, but there are several areas where rigid foam boards in varying thicknesses can help cut heating costs. In fact, as simple and economical a change as moving to 2 by 6 studded walls on 2-foot centers can cut heat loss in many homes by as much as 700 Btu per hour. This loss can be cut even further by applying ¾-inch rigid board insulation under the exterior sheathing (Fig. 9-6).

The values for the insulation needed vary from area to area because of the changing costs of heating and cooling in those parts of the country. It will cost more to heat a home in Albany, New York where I used to live, than it will in southwestern Virginia where I now live simply because the degree day difference is immense. Albany has an average—on a base of 65°F—of 6875° days, while Lynchburg has 4166, for about 60 percent difference.

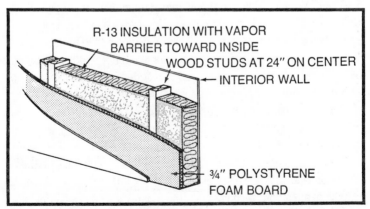

Fig. 9-6. Increase the R-value. The R-value in this case has been increased to R19. (Courtesy of Owens-Corning Fiberglas Corp.)

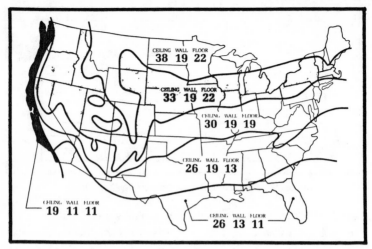

Fig. 9-7. Recommended R-values. (Courtesy of Owens-Corning Fiberglas Corp.)

Owens/Corning's map (Fig. 9-7) of recommended R-values for the United States shows the difference. In Albany, I would need 10 inches of roof insulation, 6 inches in the walls, and 6½ inches in the floor. Down here I need 9½ inches in the roof area, and 6 inches in the floors. The differences aren't great, but even the minimal cost variation wouldn't pay over the years. That is, I would not save enough extra money to pay back the cost of the extra insulation, plus a reasonable amount of yield on the money.

Actually, the cost differential here would be so little, I wouldn't worry about it, while the cost differential between Albany, New York and northern Maine is almost low enough to jusitfy applying the R38, R19, R22 values used up there. My reasoning here is simple. Fuel costs are still rising, so any extra insulation added to a home has to pay sooner or later. It doesn't deteriorate. It does add value to any home being sold at a later date. And that added value will likely go up as inflation keeps hovering over us.

In other words, I would use the Owens/Corning map as a base, then use the insulation values from the next colder area in any new home I intended to build. And I would go beyond the R19 value for walls in most areas by using rigid foam at least ¾ inch thick on them (exterior side only). This will add to cost, but will come close to eliminating heat loss through even the most widely spaced studding, while adding R6 to the R19 6-inch glass fiber already in the walls. The cost should be under $450 for most homes. Eventually, fuel oil will cost 75 cents per gallon and on that day, your investment will pay for itself in about one winter. Owens/Corning projected rate increases at a very conservative 7 percent a year, but fuel oil has risen close to 200 percent since 1972, based on my then cost of 16.8 cents per gallon versus a last delivery cost of 48.9 cents per gallon. Inflation alone continues at well over 6 percent a year. Oil reserves become lower, thus scarcer, thus more expensive. Both are due to demand forcing price up and the increased costs of extraction as we get away from the easily found and worked pools. Nope. I would go with more insulation—never less—and then burn wood.

BASEMENT & CRAWL SPACE INSULATION

Slab foundations are insulated before pouring, though we have done nothing in this book on them because of my belief that such a foundation is a money waster; the footings must still be below frost depth, yet you don't even have a crawl space into which you can stuff your lawnmower, hoses, and other such gatherings of life. Crawl spaces should be insulated, with a moisture barrier on the floor. Should you have built on piers, or over an unheated space such as a garage, the floor of the house must be insulated. If the walls of your heated basement extend above the ground, insulation should be carried down the walls, and at least 2 feet below ground level. Actually, insulating the entire depth of the wall may be a waste of money, but in very cold areas you may wish to go as much as 3 or 4 feet below ground level. At this point, the earth seldom, if ever, freezes, and insulation is not needed.

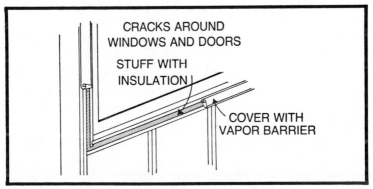

Fig. 9-8. Stuff all cracks around doors and windows and all odd shaped cavities with insulation and staple polyethylene over these areas. (Courtesy of Owens-Corning Fiberglas Corp.)

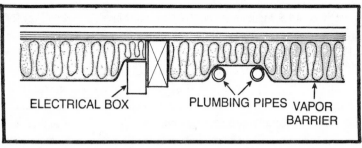

ELECTRICAL BOX   PLUMBING PIPES VAPOR
                                  BARRIER

Fig. 9-9. Insulate behind pipes and electrical boxes. (Courtesy of Owens-Corning Corp.)

Various combinations of insulation can be used if your vacation home is built with a partial basement next to a crawl space and so on.

INSULATION INSTALLATION

Glass fiber insulation installation is one of the simpler jobs in home building, with about the only tools required being a sharp knife, a heavy duty stapler, and a straightedge (as well as a measuring tape). First, check the vacation home framing, making sure you've ordered enough insulation to fill in gaps in sections such as those found around windows. Before window trim is installed, it is a simple matter to force insulation in around any gaps in the frame. This sort of sealing cuts way down on air infiltration (Fig. 9-8).

The blanket and batt insulation with a foil vapor barrier on its back is installed with the vapor barrier *always* placed to the warm side of the structure, the interior house side in most cases. Careful cutting of the batts or blankets will save on handling. Make sure that ceiling insulation extends over the top plate of the wall framing. If a gap remains, stuff any remaining space with strips of insulation.

Insulation is run behind any plumbing runs and electrical boxes (Fig. 9-9). If your home construction includes a band joist for a second story, it is insulated too (Fig. 9-10). For second stories that are cantilevered out over a first floor, the insulation must be continued into the cantilevered portion for best results (Fig. 9-11).

Crawl spaces can be insulated in several ways, always taking into account the need for a nonpermeable moisture barrier over the area of the crawl space. The method shown in Fig. 9-12 needs modification in areas where a termite shield is used, but that is usually a matter of imbedding the termite shield in strips of the glass fiber insulation as the sill is bolted on.

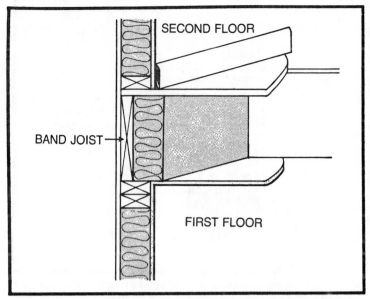

Fig. 9-10. Insulating behind band joists. (Courtesy of Owens-Corning Corp.)

SAVING ENERGY IN OTHER WAYS

Insulation is an effective means of reducing heating and cooling costs, and generally pays for itself with reasonable speed. Some other methods are applicable, and a few of these cost nothing. We've already looked at thermal break double glazed windows, which are an added cost option that also pay off in the long run. The house design can be made to save normally wasted energy. Heat loss

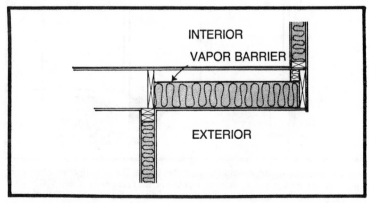

Fig. 9-11. Insulate underneath any cantilevered construction. (Courtesy of Owens-Corning Corp.)

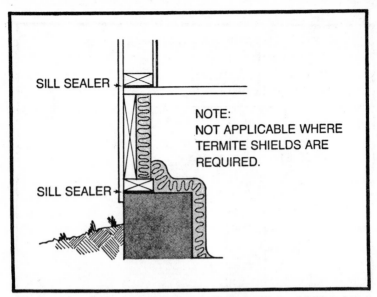

Fig. 9-12. In frame construction, a sill sealer between the top of the foundation wall and the band joist or sill plate will reduce air infiltration. A termite barrier is usually installed at the same time as insulation in the crawl space. (Courtesy of Owens-Corning Fiberglas Corp.)

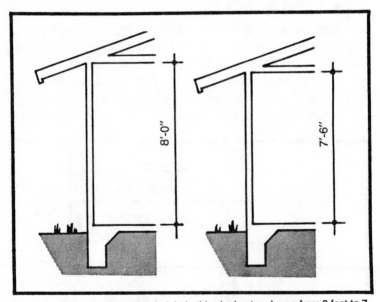

Fig. 9-13. Reducing the ceiling height in this single story home from 8 feet to 7 feet 6 inches, even with full thick wall insulation, will conserve another 400 Btu for the simple reason that lower ceilings reduce the area of the wall. (Courtesy of Owens-Corning Fiberglas Corp.)

changes in long skinny house designs are great. A single story home 32 feet by 50 feet will have 675 Btu per hour less heat loss than will a home of the same floor space that is 24 by 66½ feet long. Too, L-shaped and H-shaped single story homes have greater heat losses. To get the same area as the first example, we can take a 24- by 50-foot home and add a 20- by 20-foot L-addition. The Btu per hour heat loss goes up 1,000.

A reduction in ceiling height can also reduce heat loss by reducing wall area to be heated. The savings here for a house of about the size of our example would be on the order of 400 Btu per hour (Fig. 9-13).

Reducing window area is a good way to cut heat loss. Most window area recommendations now state that no more than 10 percent of the wall area should be glazed. Even double glazed windows lose much more heat than do windows. Any southern exposure glass should have a long eave to shade it from summer sun. At the same time, the lower angle of the winter sun will allow that to

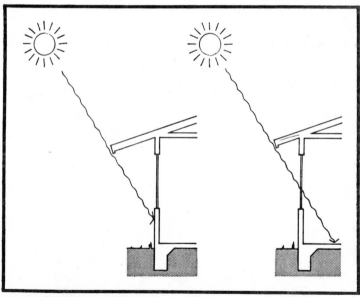

Fig. 9-14. Reducing heat gain through windows. Shading southern exposure glass with an overhang is an important method of reducing heat gain in the summer. At 35 degree latitude—North Carolina, Oklahoma, and Las Vegas—a 32-inch overhang will completely shade a south floor to ceiling window during the summer. This reduces the heat gain 50 percent on the glass. It can save 1,200 Btu in the summer while still permitting winter sun to help with the heating load. (Courtesy of Owens-Corning Fiberglas Corp.)

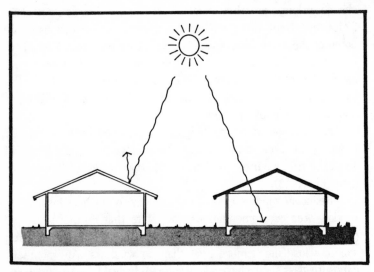

Fig. 9-15. Lighter roof colors reflect heat, while darker ones absorb heat. (Courtesy of Owens-Corning Corp.)

shine through and provide a bit of heat gain during those months (Fig. 9-14).

Selecting the correct shingle color can also save you some money on summer cooling. A lighter roof will reflect a great deal more heat than will any dark color (Fig. 9-15).

A bit of care during siting, insulating, ventilating, and overall construction will be paid back many times in savings over the years.

Chapter 10
Home Wiring

Like plumbing, wiring a home is not a job for the unwary and thoughtless person. Modern homes use a lot of electricity, and over the years safety codes have been developed to prevent major problems with wiring systems. Alternating current, which reverses polarity sixty times each second, is used for homes in this country, with generally available 120- and 240-volt circuits.

Your first step in getting ready to wire any house is to promise yourself you will never, under any circumstances, work on a live circuit. Your next step is to locate and buy a small circuit tester. By inserting the prongs of this tester's leads into a socket, or touching them to bare wire ends, you will be rewarded with a nonglowing neon bulb on circuits where the power is off. This little tool costs under a buck most places and can save a lot of problems.

Your second step is to contact your local utility company. The utility will tell you where the meter and service entrance must be located. At this point you'll also find out how to go about hooking things together. Most utility companies have the home owner provide and install, or have installed, all parts of the system in the home, up to and including the service panel, and, often, the service entrance head. Then the utility company installs the meter and the service drop lines and cuts the power on for you. You will also have to let the company know the size service you will be installing.

Next, and just as important as the first two steps, you must obtain a copy of the *National Electrical Code* (NEC). In some cases, the local utility will loan you a copy of this 600-page book, but you'll probably have to order one from the National Fire Protection Association 470 Atlantic Ave., Boston, MA 02210. Cost is $5.50. As such this is not a law or series of laws, though most areas today have local codes that incorporate all or most of the provisions of the NEC, which gives them the force of law. You'll also want to obtain copies of any local codes. Most utility companies will supply a free copy of these.

Next, check out the need for permits. Some communities will not allow a home owner to do the work in any case, but others are quite helpful. You will probably be in an area where the job is inspected periodically to make sure all is going well, with a final inspection just before you close up the interior walls. At this time, if the community uses them, you are ready to ask for a certificate of occupancy.

ELECTRICAL NEEDS

The first step in the job is to determine just how large a service you need. Most codes today require a minimum 100-ampere service panel, which should provide adequate service for almost any but the most luxurious vacation home. If part of your vacationing is something on the order of arc welding, then you'll need a 150-ampere or larger service entrance panel. The 100-ampere panel is installed with number 2 RHW (for wet or dry locations) wire, while a 150 ampere panel must use 1/0. All such installations are now three-wire cables.

The number of circuits and the spacing of outlets are set for minimums by the NEC, but you are free to add more circuits and space outlets more closely if you've installed a larger service. General purpose circuits are 15-ampere capacity, 120 volts, used for lighting outlets and all types of receptacle outlets except for laundries or kitchens. Appliance circuits supply the laundry and kitchen, and are 20-ampere, 120-volt circuits. Receptacles should all be grounded in these areas, but your best bet for all kitchen, laundry, bathroom, and other high shock possibility spots is the installation of a device known as a ground fault circuit interrupter. These units, known as either GFIs and GFCIs, are now code required in circuits in bathrooms and around swimming pools, but probably should be used in many more spots. A shock of as little as 50 milliamperes (0.050 amperes) can kill a healthy adult, but the GFCI shuts off flow within about 0.025 seconds when a leak as small as 5 milliamperes (0.005 amperes) occurs.

Appliance circuits, incidentally, are not meant for such heavy appliances as an electric dryer, which would have to have its own 30-ampere, 240-volt circuit.

Appliances such as a pump for the well, a furnace, and so on, each require a separate circuit, with capacity and voltage varying with the needs of appliances. A furnace would probably use 20 amperes at 120 volts, while a large pump in a very deep well might require 30 amperes at 240 volts.

If you make sure your circuitry meets your needs as well as NEC requirements, the installation can be planned easily from this point.

MATERIALS

The array of wiring types, sizes, boxes, and special fittings may give pause to the starting home builder, but all we have to do is remember that each job has a specific requirement, so that each material or component is designed to do that job. As an example, consider wiring types or rather cable, which is simply two or more wires covered by additional outside insulation.

Most home wiring today is done with nonmetallic sheathed cable. The two types basically used are NM and NMC. NM has paper wrapped wires inside a plastic cable sheath and is suitable for use only in dry locations. NMC has its individual wires encased in plastic before the exterior plastic sheathing is put on, so it is suitable for being run through wet or dry areas.

The wiring used in a vacation home will be designated as to size and cable contents as well as the NM and NMC typing. Thus a number 12 wire, with two wires in the cable and a ground, would be classified as No. 12-2 with ground, as the ground wire is not a circuit wire. Then, for a damp area, requiring a 20-ampere capacity cable with a ground, you would need NMC No. 12 with ground.

Cable with two wires will have one white and one black, while the ground wire may either be bare wire, green insulated, or green with yellow stripes. If your cable is a three wire type, the third wire will be red. Circuitry requiring more than three wires and a ground will be run in conduit as more than one cable is then needed (Fig. 10-1).

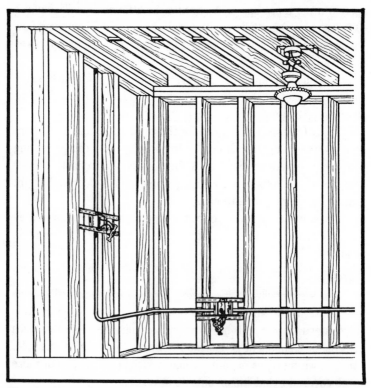

Fig. 10-1. When wiring a new home or addition, conduit wiring is preferred, but not required. This figure shows one method of anchoring conduit by notching studs. Always anchor conduit securely. Use fish tape to insert wires. (Courtesy of Sear, Roebuck & Co.)

Conduit is basically tubing through which wire or cable can be run. Rigid conduit is usually galvanized steel, much like old fashioned water pipe. Then there is an EMT, or thin wall metal conduit which is cheaper and easier to work with than the rigid conduit. Flexible conduit looks very much like the old metal armored cable known as BX (Fig. 10-2).

Boxes for various uses in wiring a home come in hundreds of styles and have nearly as many applications. Most of the time home electricians will be working with junction boxes, switch boxes, light fixture boxes, and receptacle boxes. Metal and plastic, deep and shallow, are all available, but check local codes to find out the minimum depth allowed for the number of wires installed. See whether or not the plastic boxes are allowed. The NEC requires the use of a box anytime you splice wires, or connect wires to themselves or to terminals; and the boxes must be properly supported within the structure being wired (Fig. 10-3).

Receptacles must be grounded, according to NEC requirements. This means the receptacle will have three terminals, one silver colored, one brass colored, and one green. Newer types are easier to hook up, as the stripped wire is simply pushed into the terminal to make the proper connection.

Switches today start with the simple toggle switch and move from there to silent switches, dimmer switches for controlling light levels, and on to touch switches where you need only push the top or bottom of the switch to operate it. Switches are matched to the loads required by their job, with most of today's rated as 10 amperes at 120 volts; this drops to 5 amperes on a 240-volt circuit. This rating is stamped on the switch.

Hold saw at angle. Cut through 1 section of armor then twist to break. Do not cut into wires. Allow 8 in. of insulated wires for connections in box.

Removal of armor exposes water-repellent paper around wires. Insert bushing between paper and wires. Never overlook this very important step.

Remove paper, slip connector with locknut removed over wires and armor. Be sure fiber bushing is touching front of connector, then tighten screw.

Wires, with connector fastened are inserted through knockout of box. Screw locknut to connector and draw up tightly to assure a good ground for safety.

Fig. 10-2. How to install armored cable. Note that some armored cable was made with a bond wire. In these cases it was bent back against the armor and fastened to the screw of the connector to assure a permanently low armor resistance. (Courtesy of Sears, Roebuck & Co.)

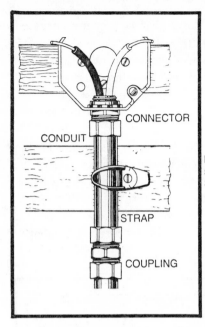

CONNECTOR

CONDUIT

STRAP

COUPLING

Fig. 10-3. Use a box each time you splice or connect wires. (Courtesy of Sears, Roebuck & Co.)

Fixtures range from simple ceiling lights to the more complex bathroom heater/light/heat lamp fixtures, with maybe even a fan thrown in. The variety is close to endless and is finally determined by your lighting needs, your taste, and your finances.

Service entrance equipment consists of a panel, or entrance box, with either circuit breakers or fuses to protect the circuits; GFCIs do not replace circuit breakers, as they are designed to protect people, not circuits. Circuit breakers and fuses come in a lot of sizes, with the most popular sizes being 15, 20 and 30 amperes, though single circuit breakers up to 100 amperes capacity are available (and expensive at over twenty bucks each). Usually the huge breakers are used as main circuit protection, but occasionally some large electrical draw will require one nearly that large (Fig. 10-4).

Once all the above are gathered together, you'll find a need for a few odd items such as electrician's plastic tape, clamp connectors, and twist-on connectors. Most local codes now allow the use of twist-on connectors—simply a plastic shell with metal threads inside—for splices. But not too many locales are ready to accept the clamp on solderless connectors yet, though their use is a great time saver when straight line splices are needed. It also simplifies the job a lot.

WIRING TECHNIQUES

Basically, you can find out just what you need in the way of planning from reading the NEC, and most of the details needed to wire residences. Just about anything else in the world is included, which is why that book is so long. Ignore the stuff on industrial and commercial wiring.

But a few techniques and tips from an old wire puller can't hurt too much. Starting with stripping solid core wires. Most people simply cut into the wire with an electrician's knife making a circle around it, then haul away at the insulation until it comes off. It works, but it isn't right, and isn't really safe. Those nicks can cause shorts and other problems at a later date—sometimes not all that later.

If the wire is of a small enough size, a pair of electrician's stripping pliers will do the job quite well. But you start to have problems with these once the wire goes past a No. 10 wire, and when you get down to those sizes used for entrance cable, such as No. 1 or 2, you can barely get the stripper handles around the stuff. Here, the old pocket knife comes out once more.

The easiest way to get the correct style of splice, with no nicks in the wire, is to shave the material away from you, using as much care as possible not to bite into the copper wire. If you are stripping stranded wire, even greater care is needed, as those little strands are quite easily cut right through by a sharp knife blade. You are looking for a taper cut in the insulation, not a straight side (Fig. 10-5).

Splicing comes in many styles. If you're lucky, the splicing chore is taken care of with mechanical connectors. Dut local codes around the country still have their own oddities and will continue to do so for quite some time. Too, some handmade splices provide much better current flow than do the mechanical and are nearly

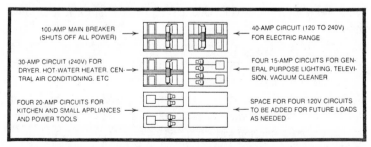

Fig. 10-4. Example of 100-ampere fuseless service entrance panel. (Courtesy of Sears, Roebuck & Co.)

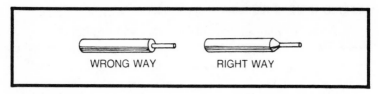

Fig. 10-5. When cutting wire, remove insulation by cutting at a slant, as in sharpening a pencil. Expose ½ inch of copper conductor. Remove all parts of the insulation, but not the tin coating, which helps soldering. (Courtesy of Sears, Roebuck & Co.)

impervious to corrosion of any kind.

The basic splice is simply one in which each free end is wrapped over the other, with the twist being made as tightly as possible (Fig. 10-6). A tap splice may take a third length of wire off this, as shown.

A pigtail splice is your next step. Properly done, the pigtail splice is a fair amount stronger than is the straight splice. Use two pair of pliers, one at the base of the splice (on the insulation, but just), and the other twisting the end.

Splice conductivity is sometimes a problem, so if local codes allow (some don't, though I have no idea what the rationale behind that particular silliness is), the splice can be soldered. For soldering wire splices, you must make sure the metal is clean. This starts with a quick wipe of the wire ends with emery cloth or very fine steel wool. Then the mechanical splice is made. After that, you have a choice. You can use a liquid flux to chemically clean, and then use unfluxed solid core solder to make the joint, or you can use rosin core solder, or you can use a flux and solder paste that brushes on and is heated. In any case, all electrical connections must be made with rosin flux as an acid flux will eventually cause enough corrosion to cut down on conductivity.

Heat is applied, using either a propane torch or a soldering iron, until the solder flows well. Use a 70/30 solder since it has a low melting point, yet retains plasticity well and flows well. Try a few times on some scrap wire, because I promise that whether you use a torch or an iron, the first three or four times you do this type of soldering you'll melt the insulation just back of the splice, or you won't get a good, solid solder joint. One is caused by too much heat for too long and the other by not enough heat (Fig. 10-7).

If you are soldering with stranded wires, the best way to go is to apply a tiny bit of solder to those wires before you make the splice. This prevents separation problems.

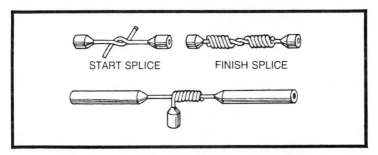

START SPLICE   FINISH SPLICE

Fig. 10-6. To make a good connection wires must be bright and clean when brought together. The connection must be tight, well fastened with solder or solderless connector, and covered with tape. In this way, the wire is as well insulated as orginally. To splice wires together (A), remove about 3 inches of insulation from each wire. Cross wires about 1 inch from insulation; then make six to eight turns using fingers and pliers. To for a tap splice (B), strip away about 3 inches of insulation from the continuous wire without cutting the copper. Strip away 3 inches from one end of the tap wire. Wrap it around continuous wire, solder, and tape. (Courtesy of Sears, Roebuck & Co.)

Once the splice is made, if you haven't used mechanical connectors, the joint must be insulated. Start about 1 inch above where you stripped the wires, wrapping as tightly as possible, and overlapping each wrap by half the width of the tape. Keep going until you have gotten 1 inch past the other end of the stripped wires. Keep making wraps until you have built up a layer of insulation no less thick than the original layers. By keeping each turn as tight as possible you assure yourself of the correct insulation value from the tape.

WIRING RECEPTACLES

Modern receptacles are among the easiest installations to make once the box is in place. Run the cable, and clamp to the correctly secured box, as directed by the NEC. If the receptacle is the newest type, with push-in connectors, you need to strip about ⅜ inch of insulation from each wire. Then the hot wire (black) goes into the brass colored terminal, and the neutral wire goes into the silver colored terminal. The green terminal takes the ground wire.

Fig. 10-7. So that the solder will flow easier when soldering, first coat the wires with electrical soldering paste. With the soldering iron, heat the wires until the solder melts and flows into every crevice. (Courtesy of Sears, Roebuck & Co.)

If the receptacle uses screw style terminals, strip the first ½ inch of the wire and using a pair of needle nose pliers make a partial loop in the wire. Screw out the terminal and slip the loop over the terminal with its open end in the direction the screw will trun to make the connection. Close the the loop with the tips of the pliers and screw the terminal down tightly (Fig. 10-8).

Switch connections are made in the same manner as are receptacles, though wiring may differ when you use three and four way switches (Fig. 10-9).

OUTDOOR WIRING

Even a vacation home, possibly especially a vacation home, can be more enjoyable with some lights and receptacles outdoors. There are a few special rules for outdoor wiring, starting with the use of ground fault interrupters on all outdoor circuits. GFCIs can be installed at the service panel in the form a circuit breaker replacement. These push-in units also contain a circuit breaker, and protect the entire circuit, while they cost some $10 less than does a single outlet outdoor mounted GFCI. The NEC now requires the use of these devices on outdoor wiring, and most local codes willl follow suit if they've been updated in the past few years. Even if local codes don't require, go ahead and install the GFCI. It's worth it.

All outdoor underground wiring must be placed below frost depth (where the frost depth is less than 2 feet, that is the minimum). Conduit is often required and is a good idea when not required by the local codes as it protects plastic sheathed cable from damage by digging tools. Only UF (lead covered) or NMC cable can be used in outdoor applications.

Use receptacles and lighting fixtures that are UL (Underwriter's Laboratories) tested for outdoor use.

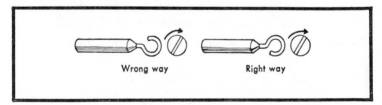

Wrong way   Right way

Fig. 10-8. When making connections at screw terminals, bend the end of the wire into a loop to fit around the screw. Be sure to attach the loop in the direction in which the screw turns when tightening as shown. (Courtesy of Sears, Roebuck & Co.)

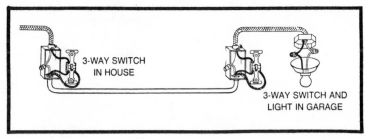

Fig. 10-9. Use of three-way switch to control garage light. (Courtesy of Sears, Roebuck & Co.)

BASIC SAFETY RULES

1. Never work on an electrical circuit that has power to it.
2. Always test to make sure the circuit is unpowered, even if you've pulled the circuit breaker, main switch, or fuse. Foul ups are possible.
3. Follow the National Electrical Code and any local codes right down to the crosses on the *T*s.
4. Use ground fault circuit interrupters on all kitchen, bath, laundry, and outdoor circuits, even if local codes do not require it.
5. Take your time and be as neat as possible. Wire nicks, burned insulation, poorly stripped wires, all are trouble causers. Neatness really does count in home wiring.
6. Have the work you do inspected even if your locality doesn't require it. A local electrical contractor should be willing to do that job for a reasonable cost if there is no local building inspector or if the utility can't or won't inspect.

Chapter 11
Finishing the Interior

Finishing the interior of a home is the last step taken before moving in. With a vacation home the job can be done in steps, doing a room at a time as money is available, or all at once as it is usually done on other homes. The interior finish includes closing up the walls, using paneling, gypsum wallboard, plastic or ceramic tile, or other materials as you choose. From there, it's a move to installing interior doors and trimming the doors and windows. We'll cover the installation of all doors and windows here to simplify things a bit. From there, you move to whatever painting is needed, and the final step is the laying down of the finished flooring and its molding.

DOORS & WINDOWS

Once your window and door units have arrived on site, assuming you're doing the sensible thing and working with ready made sections, it will pay to first measure the parts of the windows and doors that fit directly up against the rough openings. Next, check the rough openings in your framing (Figs. 11-1 and 11-2). Prefabricated window and door assemblies of wood construction must be stored on site for at least 24 hours in order to reach the same general moisture content level as the framing and any sheathing that might already be up.

If all measurements are correct, the humidity levels are right, and you have a helper around—large window units should not be

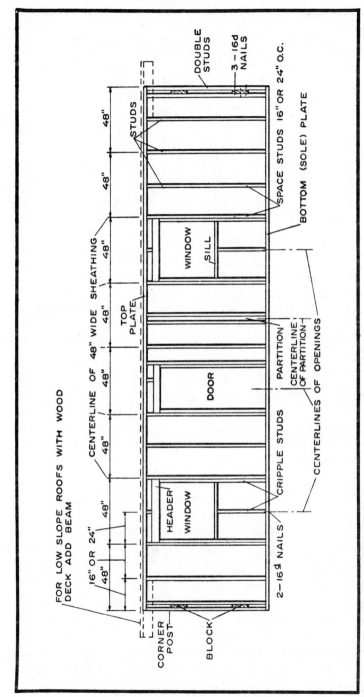

Fig. 11-1. Framing layout of a typical wall.

239

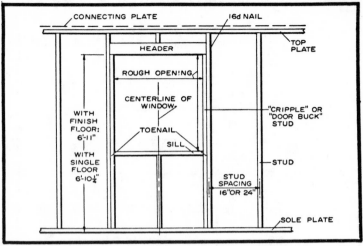

Fig. 11-2. Framing at window opening and height of window and door headers.

handled and installed by one person as that is just asking for the thing to slip and cause breakage—you can check the assemblies for damage that might have been incurred in shipping.

Leaving the corner bracing strips in place, sit the window unit in its rough opening, using strips of building paper and glass fiber insulation around the edges of the opening to cut down on air infiltration. Plumb the window frame and nail to the side studs through the blind stops, or through the casing (see Figs. 11-3 and 11-4 for details of two types of windows). Figure 11-5 gives a bit better idea of the location of the blind stop. This nailing is temporary, until the window is further checked for level and plumb and shimmed to be dead on the marks. If the window is out of plumb or not level, sooner or later it will stick, no matter the type being installed. Use great care, then, in getting this correct.

Once checking is done, continue nailing and continue with a check of plumb and level about every third or fourth nail. When nailing to the header, sill, and side studs is completed, you can remove the strips at the window corners for the window is now braced within the building's structure and will change plumb and level only if the building does.

EXTERIOR DOORS

Exterior doors require a few different operations than do interior doors, and are structurally a bit heavier and often more

240

complex. The usual exterior door will be at least 1¾ inches thick by 6 feet 8 inches high. The main door should be at least 3 feet wide, and I would recommend sticking with that size even for side or rear doors. Sooner or later one piece of furniture that is too large to work around

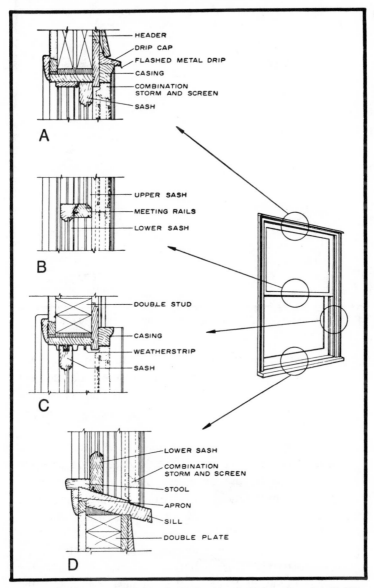

Fig. 11-3. Double hung window unit. (A) Head jamb. (B) Meeting rails. (C) Side jamb. (D) Sill.

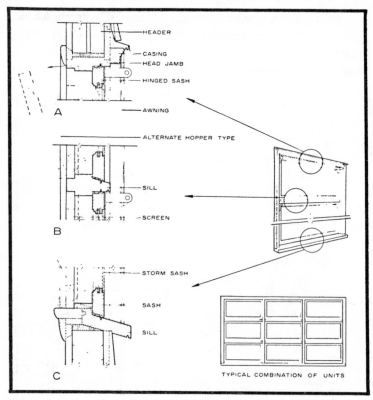

Fig. 11-4. Awning or hopper window. (A) Head jamb. (B) Horizontal million. (C) Sill.

to the front of the home will need to be taken through a side or back entrance. If you use the standard 32-inch service door size, you could end up having to remove the door, its frame, and all to get the piece through. Not too handy, so it's best to stick with the larger sizes.

If the door uses a sill of wood softer than oak, it will need a metal nosing strip to cut down on wear. Stand the door unit in place and nail, after plumbing, through the outside casing into the studs of the opening. Use one nail to a side, and leave the heads projecting. Now, plumb and level at the top and sill. For prefabricated units, the sill is installed first and is already level if you're using site built components. Make certain the sill rests solidly on the header or the stringer joist of the floor framing. If this fit isn't solid, use a hatchet or saw to trim away wood as needed. The sill must rest firmly or the door will later be difficult to open or close.

Continue the nailing after plumb and level are check, doing as you did with the windows, making sure that plumb and level don't get pulled off as you nail. If necessary, cedar shakes can be used as shims between the side jambs and the rough opening framing to prevent such movement (Fig. 11-6). Use 8d nails for door nailing.

Exterior door trim is now installed, with the edges mitered and nailed through the miter corners to prevent separation. Interior door trim is not installed until after the final work is done on paneling or wall board, including painting. This prevents slopover of paint and varnish which makes for a messy look.

If you have constructed your own door framework, the hardware installation will require some work on the plain door. The first step is to build a door jack as shown in Fig. 11-7. This item keeps the door handy and steady for any routing, chiseling, drilling, and planing operations you need to do.

Hinges are most usually of the loose pin butt mortise type (Fig. 11-8). If you need to mortise for these, you have two choices. The first is doing the job by hand using wood chisels, a time-consuming job open to a lot of possible errors. The best way to do it is to get the proper template for your size hinge and use a power router with the correct cutter. This makes the job a lot more rapid, and the template and a bit of care will cut way down on the chance of error.

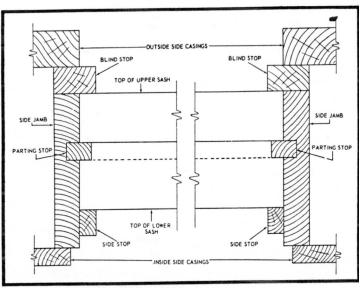

Fig. 11-5. Double hung sash installed.

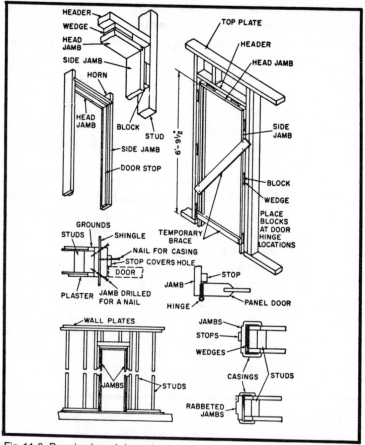

Fig. 11-6. Door jamb and door trim.

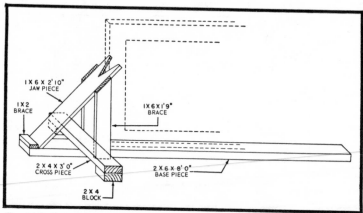

Fig. 11-7. Door jack.

To install the rest of the door hardware (locksets), you'll need an adjustable hole drill and, once more, your router. The hole drill is needed to make the hole for the major portion of the lockset. A wood drill brings in the striker hole, and the router is used to set the faceplate flush with the wood surface (Fig. 11-9).

INTERIOR WALLS

Interior walls are a good spot to add to decorative possibilities. You can use paneling, gypsum wallboard, or a combination of these, or work out just about any kind of covering you wish.

In new construction, most paneling goes up using nails or glue directly to the studs. The choice of panels and styles is so wide as to make any recommendation silly. Select to suit your tastes and price range, then just go right on ahead with the job.

Gypsum wallboard replaces plaster in new construction. Actual plaster is almost never used today, as the expensive labor costs add far too much to the price of a home. Wallboard can go up either

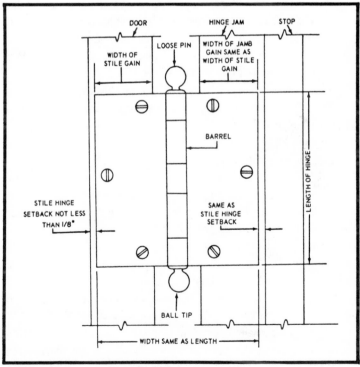

Fig. 11-8. Loose pin butt mortise hinge.

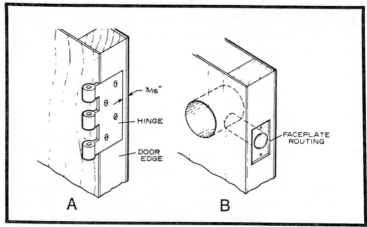

Fig. 11-9. Installing door hardware. (A) Hinge. (B) Lock.

vertically or horizontally, and is available in lengths of 8, 10, 12, and 16 feet in almost every area of the country. For single layer installation, use ½ inch wallboard.

Wallboard will be 4 feet wide and have tapered edges so that the joints can be taped invisibly. This is the hardest part of any wallboard installation for amateur builders. The last part of any major job of taping joints is going to look a lot better than the first part, so you may wish to hire a person who specializes in taping.

Wallboard edges must be centered on studs if the installation is a vertical one. For horizontal applications use a nailing block on which the bottom edge of the top sheet is centered. End joints in horizontal applications must also center on studs.

For ½-inch wallboard you'll use ring shank 1⅝-inch nails. Stick with ring shank nails, as one of the worst faults in much new construction is the popping of nails on interior walls as the framework dries out when humidity drops during the first cold spell. Nail at 6-inch intervals along the outside edges and at 8-inch intervals along inner stud lines.

Horizontal installation is best when you can apply a full length of sheet down a single wall, thus cutting out all vertical joints which don't fall on corners or at walls and windows. For me, it is easier to tape the horizontal seam so that it doesn't show.

When driving nails in gypsum wallboard use a hammer with a slight bell shape at the head. This allows you to get the needed dimple around the nailhead without cutting into the paper covering.

JOINT & NAIL DIMPLE COVERING

Use a good joint compound, with preference going to the premixed canned kind. Use a wide spackling knife. I like a 10-inch taping blade, while others prefer narrower blades, which are easier to use on nail dimples. In any case, the blade should be moderately flexible, not extremely stiff.

On vertical joints, start with the top edge and run a good coating of joint compound down the line. Now use the taping blade to press the tape into the joint compound. Once this is done, a second, thinner, coat of compound is laid on with the edge of the tapered wallboard. A light sanding after the joint compound is dry, then an application of the final coat completes the joint (Fig. 11-10).

The same principle of two to three coats is used on the nailhead dimple, with a light sanding between the second and third applications, and a final sanding once that is completed.

For interior corners, simply fold the tape down the center and treat the joint as you would any other vertical joint. You can often find

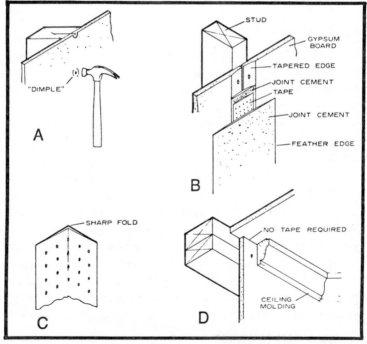

Fig. 11-10. Finishing hypsum dry wall. (A) Nail set with crowned hammer. (B) Cementing and taping joint. (C) Taping at inside corners. (D) Alternate finish at ceiling.

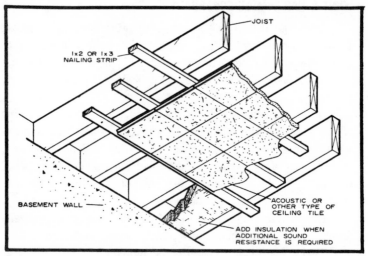

Fig. 11-11. Installation of ceiling tile.

special corner taping knife styles, though the regular one with care should work quite well.

CEILING MATERIALS

Again, great variation in ceiling styles is possible, from the open beam cathedral ceiling showing the wood of the roof planking, to various ceiling tile products installed either on wood furring strips or in frames especially made for the purpose. Ceiling tiles come in a wide array of colors and styles, with most today still being the type that are nailed or stapled to furring strips installed at right angles to the rafters, collar beams, or joists above (Fig. 11-11).

Gypsum wallboard can also be used as ceiling material, but nailing should change to 6 inches at all points all along the sheet. The minimum is again ½-inch board. For those jobs where you haven't the muscle power to lift longer sheets to the ceiling and nail them in place, you'll need a T-support of braced 2 by 4s to support one end or the middle of the sheet. Simply cut the support so that it is 1 inch or so lower than the joists, pad the top with a chunk of cheap felt or scrap of rug and use that to hold the board in place during nailing. Joint and nail dimple finish is exactly the same as for wall work.

CEILING & WALL MOLDINGS

To get a finished look at the junction of wall and ceiling, a wooden molding is a good touch. Select the design and size that best

248

goes with your style of house and carefully miter all outside joints. Inside joints should be coped. That is, a coping saw is used to shape one side of the joint exactly to the other. Narrow moldings are nailed into the upper sideplates of the wall, while wider (over 2-inch) moldings need to also be nailed into the ceiling joists where possible.

To make a coped joint, cut the first piece so that it is square cut against the inside corner. The next piece is cut at a 45-degree angle in a miter box; then the coping saw is used to finish trim along the inner line of the miter cut (Fig. 11-12).

FLOORING

Home flooring is selected for the job it has to do, and for appearance. Usually there is a fairly wide variety of materials to handle any specific job, with the choice made on the basis of cost, durability, appearance, and ease of installation. As an example, there are two major kinds of wood flooring, with subvarieties among

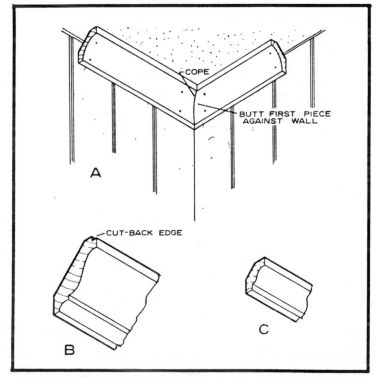

Fig. 11-12. Ceiling molding. (A) Installation of inside corner. (B) Crown molding. (C) Small crown molding.

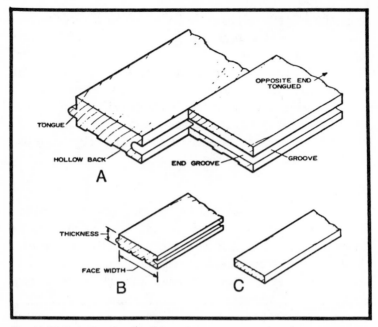

Fig. 11-13. Strip flooring. (A) Side and end matched. (B) Side matched. (C) Square edged.

these. Strip flooring (Fig. 11-13) can be considered to include all wood flooring types that come in pieces where the length exceeds the width by at least three times. Block flooring (Fig. 11-14) is that type of flooring that comes in blocks usually square or rectangular, but always with the width no less than a third the length.

Strip flooring can be tongue and groove, spline and groove, end butted, or some other joint style. Most narrow strips are tongue and groove, while the thicker, wider units used for post and beam homes will often be spline and groove. Block flooring can be just about any size from 4 inches square on up to 2 feet by 1 foot, or even larger (seldom).

Installation procedures differ for the types. Strip flooring is laid at right angles to the joists with builder's paper covering the sub-floor. The first board is placed ½ inch away from the wall, leaving room for the baseboard and shoe molding. This board is face nailed close enough to the wall edge for the shoe molding and baseboard to cover the nailing. The next board is forced against it, after the tongue of the first board is blind nailed to the joists, and the blind nailing continues on with each strip laid down (Fig. 11-15).

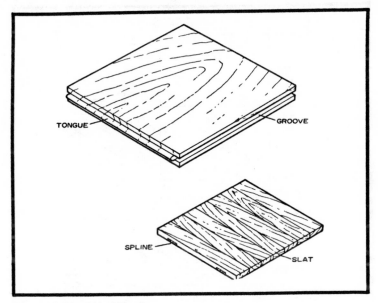

Fig. 11-14. Wood block flooring.

The last row of boards, or the last board, is forced down and face nailed to the joists. This face nailing is covered by the baseboard and shoe molding on that side of the room.

Square edge flooring is simply face nailed with finishing nails, though you can also use decorative nail styles if you wish the floor to resemble those installed in older homes.

Wood block flooring may be blind nailed in much the same manner as is strip flooring, but usually it is laid in adhesive in much the same manner as resilient tile floors.

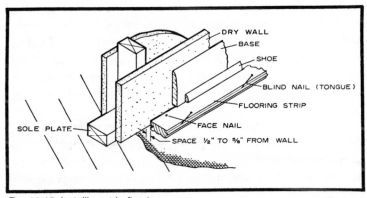

Fig. 11-15. Installing strip flooring.

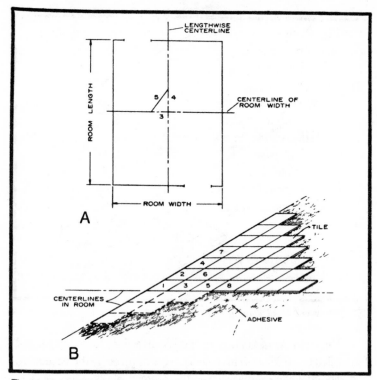

Fig. 11-16. Installing resilient tile. (A) Center baseline. (B) Order of laying the tile.

Resilient tile flooring requires some different methods than strip wood flooring. First, it is started at or near the centerline of the room, so that baselines must be snapped with a chalk line. Simply measure to the center of each wall on both sides of the room, and snap the two lines as shown in Fig. 11-16. Resilient tile flooring is laid over a subfloor specified for that purpose. In most cases, the plywood subfloor will do the job, but if you've used board style subflooring, underlayment nailed with ring shank nails every 6 inches will be needed. Adhesive is spread over a quarter section of the floor, after you've checked to see how much is to be trimmed from the tile that reaches the wall. For the time being, leave this space cl ear of adhesive.

Start laying the tiles at the juncture of the center lines, snapping them into the adhesive as they are put down instead of pushing them up to adjoining tiles (pushing them up to the next tile tends to force adhesive out of the joints, making for a lot of unnecessary cleanup afterwards).

Edge tiles should leave about a ⅛-inch gap so that expansion is possible. Place a tile directly on the last full tile row, and directly on one tile. Now take another tile and butt it against the wall. Draw it off about ⅛ inch and mark the tile on that last full row. That will provide your trim mark and give you an exact fit.

Baseboard and shoe moldings are installed in a manner similar to that used with wood floors if the moldings are to be of wood. If the cove material is to be of the same material as the tile, it is usually placed with adhesive.

Ceramic tile floors are not much more complex to lay than are resilient tiles now that the manufacturers have provided kits for do-it-yourselfers. Most such floor tiles come in sheets to allow rapid installation in the mastic adhesive used. The work is done from chalk centerlines just as it is with resilient tile, with the major difference being the cutting tools needed. While a sharp utility knife will serve for resilient tile of all types, ceramic tile requires a special tile cutter. These can be rented at quite reasonable prices, though sometimes the retailer selling you the tile will let you use one if you leave a deposit on the tool.

Edge tiles are measured in the same way as are resilient tiles. Seams with most ceramic tiles will have to be grouted, though the ones that come in sheets will have few such spots. The manufacturer will either recommend or supply the grout to be used.

STAIR CONSTRUCTION

There are carpenters who specialize in making stairs, and for most of us, the best bet is to locate one and contract the work out. If you don't wish to do that, then you need to have at hand some basic stair building information.

As a start, it is generally accepted that for safest and most comfortable stair usage, one tread and two risers combined should add up to 25 inches. Next, a single riser and a single tread should add up to 17 to 18 inches. Then, if you multiply the height of the riser by the depth of the tread, your total should be just about 75 inches. To fit in with rule one, you would take a riser of 7½ inches and add in a tread depth of 10 inches. Total for two risers and one tread is exactly 25 inches. Too, this fits rule three. But a riser that is only 6½ inches high would need a 12-inch-deep tread to make the grade. Treads are measured minus the nosing or part that overhangs the riser. For most residences, treads are seldom less than 9 inches nor more than

12 inches deep. All treads and risers in a stair run must be of the same size, else you'll find people stumbling over any odd size units. Stair width should be no less than 3 feet.

Calculating the number of risers and treads in a given staircase is done by first dividing the total rise by seven. If we assume a total rise of 8 feet, or 96 inches, then our answer is 13.71. There must be an even number of risers, so we take the closest whole number to that answer, or fourteen. The total rise in inches is now divided by that. Thus, 96 divided by 14 equals 6.85 inches height per riser. To get the correct tread height, of which there will be one less than there are risers in a given stairway, we need to have a tread depth of 11.3 inches. Thus, with a total run of 11.3 times 13 we get a total run of 146.9 inches.

From this, we can start laying out the stairwell stringers. Using a procedure similar to that for laying out rafters, we place the marking clips on the framing square at the correct spots. The rise of the stair is laid out with the tongue, while the run or tread depth, is laid out using the blade. Before any cuts are made, this layout must be checked in the stairwell opening and any needed adjustments made. One reduction is guaranteed: the bottom riser must be reduced by the amount equal to tread thickness to correct for the tread thickness increase when the first tread is installed on its riser. Most main stair treads will be 1⅛-inch-thick hardwood (Fig. 11-17).

Stair treads include a nosing with a depth of about 1¼ inches to allow for toe space.

A bit easier method of handling stair construction is available. Most stock or close to stock stair sizes are available in precut form. After you get the measurements for the job, your lumber or millwork dealer can order the parts for you, leaving you with little more to do than assemble the unit when it gets to your building site. Outside of hiring a stair specialist to build yours, this is probably the easiest way for most people.

PAINTING & FINISHING

Exterior surfaces of vacation homes are often made of woods that weather well when left to their own natural tendencies. Most durable among the woods used for these purposes are cedars and redwood. From this point, it's pretty much up to you as to what you care to put on the surface. Preservatives containing pentachlorophenol retards mildew formation, prevents water stains, and adds to decay resistance. Such preservatives are relatively easy to apply since they are brushed on much as paint is. The first application, though will seldom last more than a couple of years, though you'll find it best to slop on a new coat each year for the first three. After that all you need to do is keep a check on the color of the surface. When it starts to become uneven, retreat.

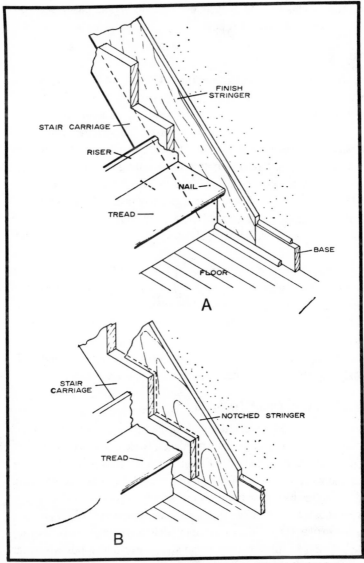

Fig. 11-17. Stair construction details. (A) Full stringer. (B) Notched stringer.

When using these preservatives, follow all the manufacturer's safety precautions as most are quite toxic to humans, animals, and plants.

Pigment can be added to these preservatives to change the natural color of the wood. Such additions help to stabilize the overall color of the finish and may add to durability. Pigmenting stains, too, lack durability when first applied. After the second year, you'll need to recoat. This second application, though, should easily see you going 8 years without a repeat.

PAINTS

Paints are excellent protectors of wood, and are nonporous. They cannot prevent decay. Generally, paints are more than a little higher in cost than are preservatives and pigmented stains.

First, protect the surface with a preservative if the siding used wasn't so treated before installation. Make sure this preservative is adequately dry before attempting any painting over it.

New wood requires a coat of primer. Don't try to get more than 400 square feet of coverage from a gallon of primer for best results. Select the primer to match the type of paint you plan to use. If you're going to use an oil base final coat, do not use a latex primer and vice versa.

The first coat of paint should go on over the primer within 2 weeks of its application to cut down on any chance of blistering or peeling. The second coat should go on within 2 weeks of the first, otherwise weathering may affect the adhesion between the coats, causing separation and peeling.

Oil base paints work best in temperatures above about 45°F., while 50° to 55° is about the minimum for latex paints.

INTERIOR WOODWORK FINISHES

Some people prefer the look of natural grain woods on their interior baseboards and ceiling moldings, while others like the look of gleaming white baseboards. Either finish is easily and successfully carried out with only a minimum of hassle if a few simple rules are attended to. First, for the greatest sheen on painted surfaces, you will probably want to use enamel, or at least a semigloss paint.

Go over the molding surfaces with fine sandpaper to rid it of any nail set marks, planer marks, and so on. For softwoods which can present a quite ugly grain problem under enamel, try sponging the wood lightly with water, allowing them to dry completely; then sand them lightly.

For hardwoods such as oak, a wood filler is needed as the wood pores are large enough to show through when enamel is applied. This goes on before the primer is applied.

Knots in pines should be shellacked after the primer is applied. Without the shellac, resin will bleed though the enamel and cause ugly stains.

Use an enamel undercoat to check on the wood surface. Apply two coats, allow to dry thoroughly and sandpaper smooth. After this, apply the finish coat of enamel.

Transparent wood coatings give a fine look over many hardwoods and some softwoods. Stains can be used to accentuate the wood grain, or the coating can be applied without the stain for a more natural look.

Again hardwoods must have a wood filler used to provide a smooth surface for varnish or lacquer. Sealers are then applied. This can be simple a very strongly thinned varnish of the type being used for the final coat.

Interior walls of gypsum wallboard require a sealer coat before the flat or semigloss finish coats are applied.

It has been my experience that the more expensive of the top brand name paints, exterior or interior, give benefits far in excess of the extra cost. First, they usually go on much more easily. Second, color saturation is greater, thus a single coat will often do a better job than as many as three coats of so-called economy paints. Finally, overall durability is a great deal better.

WOOD FLOOR FINISHES

Wood floors are usually finished with some form of varnish. As a start, the floor should be sanded to great smoothness and all dust removed.

Then start with a sealer as a base coat. Get the sealer by simply cutting the varnish to be used on the floor with thinner. Make sure you use the correct thinner for the type of varnish. I would recommend one of the polyurethane varnishes as they are reasonably simple to apply and are extremely durable, though the expense tends to be higher than for some other types.

TOOLS FOR FINISHING

A paint brush is a paint brush is a... No way. Not only are there cheap paint brushes and expensive paint brushes, there are brushes designed and sized for specific jobs, and your work will be a devil of a lot easier if you use the correct kind and size for each job.

Select the best brush you can afford for each job, without going overboard. If you care for a good paint brush it should last a lifetime, but most of us don't bother.

Wall brushes: flat, square edged, widths from 3 to 6 inches used for large surfaces, inside or outside.

Sash and trim brushes: flat and square edged; flat and angle edged; round; oval. Widths from 1½ inches to 3 inches; diameters from ½ inch to 2 inches. For painting window frames, sash, narrow trim boards, interior or exterior. The brush edge may be chisel shaped to make precise edging and cutting in around window glass easier.

Enameling and varnish brushes: widths from 2 to 3 inches. These brushes have very fine bristles shorter in length than is usual.

Masonry brushes: widths from 5 to 6 inches. Appear much like wall brushes, but have coarser bristles, resistance to abrasion.

Size the brush to the job, going neither oversize nor undersize, and all will work better. Size can vary with the person painting. If you, like me, are a rather slow painter, then a slightly smaller brush for large areas is a good idea, as it is less tiring to use, thus adds to the evenness of the coat being put on.

Paint rollers are useful for large areas, and widths can vary from 3 inches on up to 18 inches. Nap length controls the usage, but most rollers are marked as to their specific purpose. These are particularly great timesavers for applying flat paint on interior walls.

Chapter 12
Decks & Porches

Sometimes it seems as if no vacation home is really complete without at least a deck placed so the sunsets are easily viewed. A roofed porch is sometimes desired, and will most usually follow the same basic construction patterns as does the unroofed deck, with one major exception: the porch roof is usually tied into the house framing members. Decks are usually added on as structures totally in their own right. Porches can be too, but are not normally.

Low level decks require support in the form of driven poles or posts set into footings of one kind or another, as we'll cover shortly. Porches need the same sort of support. The first consideration, though, whether for porch or deck, is that of materials. Because of constant all side exposure to weather, the wood used in decks is subject to more rapid deterioration than is that used in the primary part of the house. If the wood is to be untreated, then the choice comes down to one of the three A-rated for decay resistance: cedar, cypress, and redwood. All are quite expensive, but also quite attractive in their natural states. Such wood is almost essential for untreated posts, while decking and outdoor stairs need not rate quite as high in decay resistance. Woods suitable for outdoor decking and stairs include cypress, white oak, Douglas fir, redwood, cedar, and southern pine.

Plywood for use in decks, should you desire a closed floor design, must be of exterior type. Interior type plywood, even when made with exterior glue, is not sufficient.

TREATED WOOD FOR DECKS

For the use of woods, other than the three superbly decay resistant varieties, to be used as posts or in contact with the ground or water, only one type of preservation process is really acceptable. It is pressure treatment to the American Wood Preservers' Association standards. This treatment uses an oil preservative such as creosote or pentachlorophenal in an oil or liquid gas carrier. In some cases, a salt such as chromated copper arsenate can be used; these must be nonleachable salts. Such pressure preservative treatment supplies the maximum amount of decay resistance, while simply coating the wood with the substances will provide only light penetration allowing early failure.

Nonpressure treatment is suitable for the less decay resistant woods which are not in contact with the ground. A penta solution with a water repellent is a good type. All end grains and cuts should be flooded with preservative so that penetration is as great as possible. If drilling and cutting is finished, it will not hurt at all to allow the structural members to soak for 24 hours in the solution; dig a shallow trench and line it with heavy plastic sheeting—at least 3 mils thick—for an effective soaking trench. Plywood for decking is treated in the same manner.

Fastenings are generally made with nails, as the use of screws, while supplying greater strength, is expensive and time-consuming to a degree most of us simply can't consider these days. Deformed shank nails supply the greatest holding power, and are greatly preferred over common nails. This holds true through almost all residential construction. Various other fasteners can also be used, as we'll see.

Once the basic design of your deck is set, following land contours on your property and matching the exterior room openings for the areas you desire, site preparation needs to be taken into account, just as if you were building an entire house—almost. Grade enough to insure natural runoff away from the home. No more is usually needed.

Posts below grade will provide the greatest support. Sometimes an unfooted post is simply driven into the ground but more often a foot, either of concrete block or poured concrete, will be used. Prepoured footings are also available. A third type is the concrete footing poured in place to simply fill the hole around a supported post. A fourth type is known as the pedestal footing, with the footing, either precast or poured, placed first and the pedestal poured, in wood forms, on top of that. Anchor bolts are needed in this style of footing.

Whether the support for the deck is to be a driven pole or a poured footing, it must extend below frost line. The set in gravel post or driven post will require a depth of at least 2 feet more than the frost level to get sufficient rigidity to support the loads of the deck and its traffic.

Footing size is 1 foot by 1 foot by 8 inches deep when posts are no more than 6 feet apart. Where pole spacing goes past 6 feet, footings need to be 20 inches by 20 inches by 10 inches deep.

Concrete footings allow the use of various kinds of anchors for beams. Most of these are embedded in the top of the footing as would anchor bolts be, with the beams bolted, screwed, or nailed to the anchor.

Various methods of tieing in the beams to the posts are possible when the foundation support doesn't include an anchor. Toenailing is the last choice and by far the least secure of any.

Once the beams are in place on the joists, you must consider the connection to the house. If the deck goes up at the same time as does the house, you may wish to use the masonry foundation wall, suitably enlarged. In other cases, metal beam hangers can be attached directly to the house. These metal beam hangers are best attached directly to a 2 by 10 that has been lag-screwed into the house framing. It must go into the framing and not just into the sidewall sheathing.

Bracing is sometimes required under wood decks, especially should an uneven site force the underpinnings to reach past 5 feet of surface to deck support. In every case where the deck is not attached directly to the house, as just covered, bracing will be needed to provide structural rigidity. Fasteners for braces should always be lag screws or bolts. Braces under 8 feet in length can be 2 by 4s, but if the distances grow beyond the 8-foot mark, 2 by 6s will be needed. The simplest form of single bracing is the W-brace, though the single direction brace is a close rival. The single direction brace is not as rigid as the W-brace.

Cross bracing and other forms of special bracing may be needed for posts of extreme length. Using a bolt where the braces cross will add more to stability. If your site has a very steep slope and several

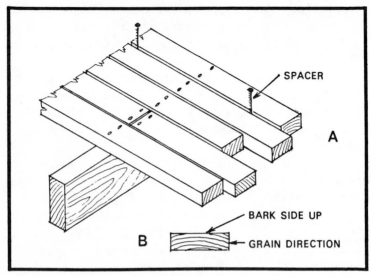

Fig. 12-1. Fastening flat deck boards. (A) Spacing between boards. (B) Grain orientation for flat grain boards.

of the posts reach up to the 14-foot mark, or higher, using a double brace saves wood while providing good strength.

Partial, or gusset braces, can be used for posts not taller than 7 feet. When braces are attached to posts, the cuts on the ends should be made to protect the end grain of the wood from extreme weathering. When braces butt as they would with a partial lumber brace, it is best to leave a slightly open joint to allow water to run through as well as for expanding and contracting forces.

When your deck beams open up beyond the 5-foot on center mark, you'll need joists between the beams to help keep the deck flooring rigid; 5 feet on center requires 2 by 4 Douglas fir, or an equivalently strong wood, as deck flooring. Joist hangers can be used to keep the tops of the joists level with the tops of the beams.

For flat laid deck boards, you will face-nail the 2 by 4 decking to the joists or beams using two nails per 2 by 4. If the 2 by 4s are on edge, a single nail per joist is used. Ring or twist shank 12d nails are used. Whether flat or on edge, the deck boards are spaced ¼ inch apart (Fig. 12-1). All end joints must fall over a joist or beam, and strength is improved if they fall over double beams or spacers are used (Fig. 12-2).

When plywood is used as a deck covering, you should leave an edge spacing of at least a 1/16 inch and end spacing of twice that.

Too, plywood covered decks are best built with a slight degree of slope to allow for water run off; the minimum is about 1 inch in 10 feet.

RAILINGS

Decks much more than a couple of feet above ground level must have a railing. Railings, though, of low strength are not a lot of use. There's nothing like expecting a railing to provide some protection, walking into the thing and falling 6 or 10 feet. Spacing of posts shouldn't be more than 6 feet if the top rail is of 2 by 4 stock, and 8 feet is the maximum when the top rail is a 2 by 6. Posts can either be extensions of the posts supporting the deck (Fig. 12-3), or they can be made of 4 by 4s for 4- to 6-foot rail on center spans, with 2 by 8s used for spans up 8 feet.

For posts not extended up from footings, bolting to the edge beam with at least two ⅜-inch bolts is essential. The size of the post

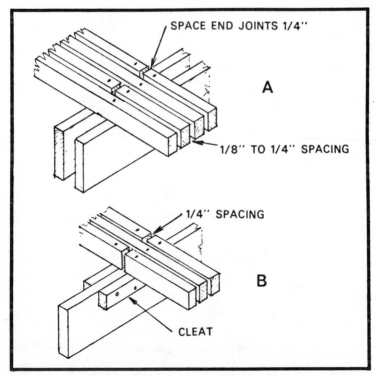

Fig. 12-2. Fastening on edge deck boards. (A) Installing over double joist or beam. (B) Installing over single joist or beam.

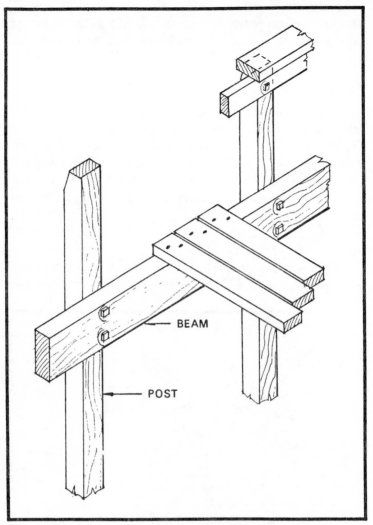

Fig. 12-3. Extension of post to serve as a railing support.

will give you the maximum number of bolts, but use as many as you can without appreciably weakening the post. As Figs. 12-4 and 12-5 show, several different designs are possible at the lower ends. To protect the end grain of the rail post tops, a cap rail, as well as a side rail, are needed (Fig. 12-6). The cap rail is nailed on with stain resistant (galvanized or aluminum) ring shank nails, 12d, but the side rail should be lag-bolted to the balusters or post rails. Too, the side rail should always be placed to the *inside* of the post rails.

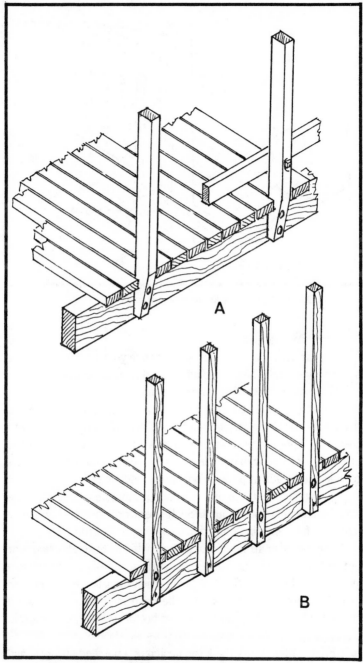

Fig. 12-4. Railing posts fastened to edge of deck member. (A) Spaced posts (4 feet and over). (B) Baluster type posts.

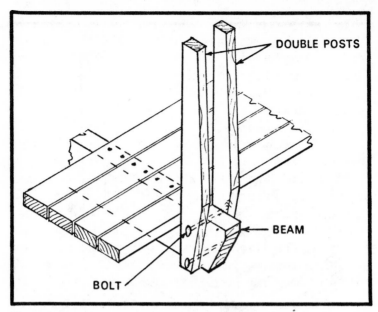

Fig. 12-5. Double railing posts at beam or joist ends.

DECK STAIRS

If your deck is any great distance above your yard, the need for a stairway of some kind is going to quickly become obvious.

The same standards for riser height and tread depth apply for outdoor stairs, but construction is somewhat simplified because you don't want to cut the stringer any more than you have to. Each cut tends to expose a portion of end grain to the weather, so the preferred practice with outside stairs is to use metal or wood cleats to hold the treads in place. Too, most outdoor stairs are without risers. You still need the distance, and it must be correct, but the actual material is not included. Such openwork construction keeps moisture from building up and causing damage to the wood.

Outdoor stair stringers can be supported by the ends of joists or beams that are no more than 3 feet apart, or they can be bolted to a ledger, face-nailed to a joist or beam, then toenailed to the joist or beam. Anchor bolts are used at the base of the stringer, and a concrete base is preferable to keep the bottom end of the stairway in place.

Figure 12-7 shows the basic design of a notched stringer, and the distances included in total run and total rise, while Fig. 12-8 shows three ways of using cleats to attach treads to the stringers. The use of nailed cleats is not a good idea, as bolts provide a great deal more strength and durability. Double treading, the use of two smaller (in width) boards to make up the outdoor stairway tread is the best practice. The gap between the two tread boards prevents moisture entrapment.

If wood cleats are used, the treads are nailed to them using 12d ring shank or deformed shank nails. With metal cleats, bolts are needed.

Incidentally, when placing any stair railings, make sure their distance apart is sufficient so that a child at the curious stage, which seems to range from about 2 on up to 12, can't get its head trapped between the railings.

Bolts are used to attach the rail posts to the stringer, and the side rails to the rail post, just as in deck railing. A cap rail serves both as a post rail end grain protector and a handhold for safe descents.

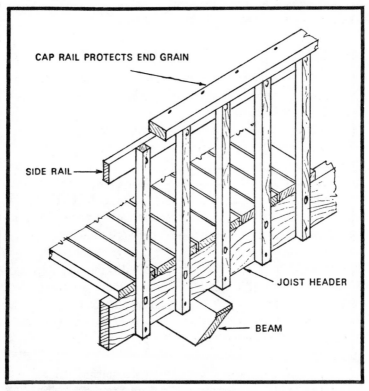

Fig. 12-6. Good railing details.

PORCHES

Porch design an construction differs greatly in detail from deck construction. Porches are almost always integral with the original house design, often with the home foundation continuing out under the porch, but most often with post foundations or pier foundations as a deck would have. The porch roof is tied to the main house structure, though the methods may vary. A house built long before a porch is added almost forces the use of ledgers bolted into the house framework, while a porch built at the same time as a house will usually have its rafters tied right in with the house rafters; the roof can be designed to continue the slope of the house roof.

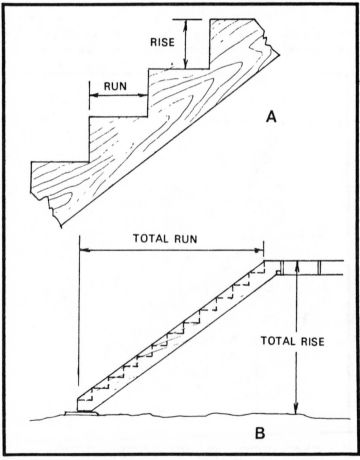

Fig. 12-7. Riser to tread relationship. (A) Individual step. (B) Total rise and run.

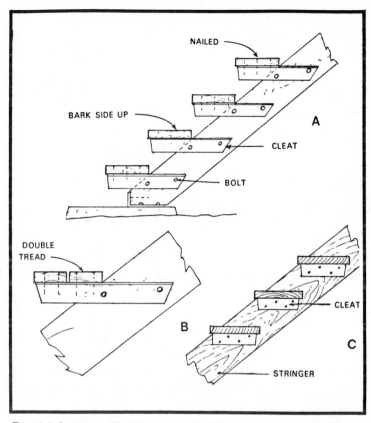

Fig. 12-8. Stairways with cleat support. (A) Extended cleat with single tread, a good practice. (B) Double tread, a better practice. (C) Nailed cleated, a poor practice.

Porch rafters can be nailed to the house top plate and rafters, whether the porch is to be open or closed.

Porch floors are solid, either of board or plywood, and always are sloped outwards for drainage unless it is a sunporch that is completely enclosed and there is no worry about the entrance of rain or snow or sleet. Framing members are of the same sizes, styles, and spacing as for the main house, with the floor slope equal to that of plywood solid decking, 1 inch in 10 feet.

Beyond this point, porch design is even more varied than is deck design, for a porch provides not only a pleasant spot to relax, but a possible future expansion of the home. It may continue across the entire front or side of the home, be only a short porch, be 8 feet deep (about a minimum for any real use), or be 16 feet deep.

Chapter 13
Prefabricated Homes

For the prospective vacation home owner who has less time, or less confidence in some of the skills needed for erecting a home and all its systems, there is an alternative. The prefabricated or manufactured home. In the past decade or so, the prefabricated home industry has worked its way from the image gained shortly after World War II—jerry-built shacks, looking exactly alike and ready to fall down within 5 years or less.

Today, the array of precut, prefabricated, modular, and otherwise manufactured homes runs the gamut from the log cabin, such as the Pioneer Log Homes model in Fig. 13-1, to the geodesic dome, such as those shown in Fig. 13-2 from Dome East. In between fall houses from such builders as Cluster Shed, Deck House, Acorn, and dozens of others, most of which can be had in price ranges starting at about $5,000 for a basic shell on a smaller vacation home and shooting on up into the $100,000 area for fully erected and equipped homes of luxuriant design and quality. Deck House offers Model 7148 with four levels enclosing a study, master bedroom, immense living room, dining room, kitchen, and breakfast room, family room mud room, laundry and sewing room, workshop, storage room, a two story playroom, four other bedrooms, a screened porch, and 3½ baths. Total living area is 6,030 square feet. In today's world of the smaller house, that's truly immense, and it appears to be the largest of the Deck House offerings. Obviously, Model 7148 is going to be far beyond the means of most of us, but here Deck House comes in with other designs ranging from about 1500 square feet on up.

More reasonable for most of us might be Model 7123. Still offering four bedrooms, this home has 1581 square feet on two levels in attractive design with many inclusions (Fig. 13-3).

Deck House, though, is not truly a prefab company. The company designs the house, starting with one of their basic series of designs, and including help with selecting the site. This post and beam style home has all interior partitions set to be nonload bearing, which gives great interior design flexibility. The use of laminated floor and roof decking over the posts and beams promises great structural stength. Panelized wall sections fill in between the posts, with final siding applied on site.

Once the individual design factors are considered, the house is manufactured in a plant. All interior doors are prehung, all interior stairs are assembled. The doors use mahogany jambs, and the stairs are also mahogany, indicating the fact that the Deck House package is not a cheapie in any way. Decking is also of superb quality since it is laminated cedar.

The package is delivered to the home builder's site, upon which the foundation has been erected by the builder (or by a contractor), and the structural assembly and enclosure begins. The foundation, well, septic field, electricity, plumbing, and heat are not included in the package so must be installed in the field, either by you or by contractors.

Fig. 13-1. A moderately large cabin from Pioneer Log Homes.

Fig. 13-2. Different exterior styling in two Dome East wood domes.

That follows one type of manufactured home through a fast sketch of the erection procedure, but there are many other styles, and many other ways to go.

DOMES

Geodesic domes have been becoming popular for some time now, and in the past few years several companies have sprung up to manufacture the components or the entire dome. Geodesic domes are considered optimized structures from an engineering point of view. That simply means that every piece used in the structure is necessary.

Because no dome will meet any building code that requires such and such an on center distance for framing, there may be difficulties

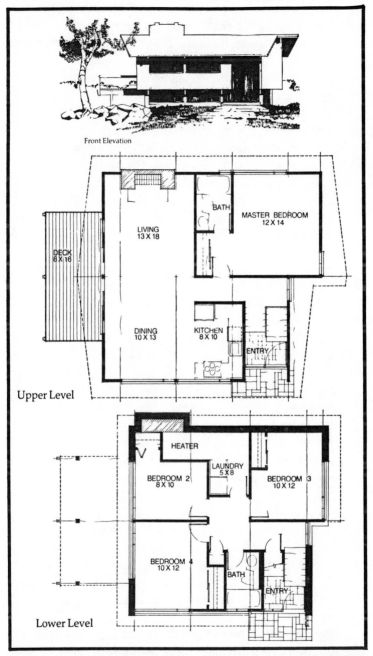

Front Elevation

Upper Level

DECK
8 X 16

LIVING
13 X 18

BATH

MASTER BEDROOM
12 X 14

DINING
10 X 13

KITCHEN
8 X 10

ENTRY

Lower Level

HEATER

LAUNDRY
5 X 8

BEDROOM 2
8 X 10

BEDROOM 3
10 X 12

BEDROOM 4
10 X 12

BATH

ENTRY

Fig. 13-3. The Model 7123 from Deck House is attractive and as large as many primary homes. Upper level is 835 square feet. Lower level is 746 square feet. Total living area is 1581 square feet.

with local codes and other regulations. So if you wish to erect one of these houses it is a good idea to make two immediate checks. First, check the local codes and the ease of getting waivers for new styles. Next, if waivers appear difficult to get, make sure the company making your dome will provide assistance in getting waivers or in otherwise meeting codes.

Dome East provides the following: they use local building ordinances to establish loading criteria, then design and check the loadings using a computer program. All critical members are then subjected to stress analysis. Their final step is to help get needed building permits and certificates of occupancy when the dome is completed.

The framing illustrations in Fig. 13-4 show why some building codes may have difficulty relating the framing of a geodesic dome to rectilinear on center distances for conventional framing.

One of the greatest problems with geodesic domes over the years has been the sealing at junctures. Dome East recommends a neoprene-Hypalon system that is applied with a spray or a roller. This forms an elastic skin over the entire structure.

Dome East supplies any one of three forms of kit, in seven sizes ranging from 30 feet, for a ½ dome, to a 49-foot ⅝ dome; the 30-foot size is also available in a ¾ dome, while the larger 49-foot dome comes in ⅜ and ½ models too. Figure 13-5 shows the relationships of the different domes: ⅜, ½, ⅝, and ¾. There is a 7-foot 6-inch difference in height between the 30-foot ½ dome and the 30-foot ¾ dome which could provide an area of as much as 1275 square feet as compared to the smaller dome's 700. The huge 49-foot ⅝ dome offers the possibility of a total of 5400 square feet in three levels. It is 33 feet tall.

Kits offered start with the complete shell, which includes everything but the elastic skin and insulation; you must also supply, or buy from Dome East, windows and door units. Next down the line is the complete structural frame as seen in Fig. 13-4. Then you can also buy only the hub kits, which come with complete cutting instructions for all struts, along with engineering and erection plans for the model you choose.

Why have domes become popular recently? The design is not one that would appeal to traditionalists, certainly. But after a time of viewing domes, the eye begins to find a certain beauty, so that other factors come into consideration. First, the skin of the dome, the

Fig. 13-4. Top illustration shows a completed frame for a wood dome, while the bottom photo shows the axle type joints. (Courtesy of Dome East.)

plywood panels filling in between the struts, imparts no structural rigidity to the framework. It is not any more than a skin. Thus, windows, doors, skylights and so on can be placed anywhere within the struts you desire—great flexibility. That same flexibility extends to interior layouts, for none of the interior walls need be loadbearing (obviously, any interior partitions supporting a second or third floor must bear loads), so that there is really no limit as to how the interior can be laid out, nor is there any limit to the interior design.

In addition to the overall flexibility of design, and the possibility of designing in superlative strength without going to immense framing members, there is one other factor that brings popularity to domes: the rapidity of erection. Once the foundation and other systems are in or provided for, the erection time of the dome itself should take no more than 2 days for small units on up to possibly 1 week for the largest ones. Two other factors deserve consideration: the half circle shape (more or less) of a dome provides less surface area through which heat can escape, thus making them easier to heat than are conventional rectangular homes. There is a possibility that savings of 40 percent are to be *expected* in similarly insulated domes, as compared to standard homes of the same size.

Of course, the speed of erection will cut any labor cost for that erection, so there is a fair cash savings there. So domes tend to be cheaper, warmer (or cooler), and more quickly erected than conventional homes, while providing great flexibility of design. As an example, the Geodesic Dome Manufacturing Company offers a 45-foot model for a base of a bit under $7,000 when shipping is considered. Adding all skylight options, wing panels, and such would probably still leave the delivered shell price under $11,000, a remarkable feat for the interior space possible with this design (on the order of possibly 2,500 square feet). That large a shell in conventional framing would probably cost 50 percent more.

PREFAB LOG CABINS

While earlier in this book I went into rather heavy detail on building one's own log cabin from scratch, the feasibility of such a program depends in large part on log availability, time available, and other factors, including the amount of time you wish to spend waiting for the structure to be completed. Today, it's easily possible to slice move-in time for a log cabin down to a matter of a few weeks, rather than the months needed for a hand-built log cabin construction (counting the time needed to season the logs at all well).

In addition, a lot of the laborious work, from peeling and notching logs to working out some way to seal out winds is done in advance at the factory.

Foundation layout and site preparation is done just as with any other vacation home, though you must pay attention to the drawings supplied by the log cabin's manufacturer in order to get lengths, widths, and sill anchor bolt distances exactly correct.

When the truck drops off your log home, the massed jumble of logs, windows, doors, and planking will be an awe inspiring sight. All logs will be marked at the factory as to use, but your job is a great deal easier if you spend some time sorting them according to length.

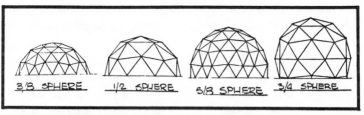

Fig. 13-5. Relative dome sizes. (Courtesy of Dome East.)

Once the sorting is completed, place polyethelene or other material tarps over the building materials (according to Green Mountain Cabins' building handbook "Pine in particular suffers from the weather, while windows usually suffer more from small boys..." an amusing point, but one to consider).

Green Mountain offers a splined section to preclude the need for chinking your cabin, and other makers have either similar solutions or logs made so they set into each other. From this point, cabin erection tends to differ as much as do the materials packages you can expect to receive. You may have a log home that uses a board for sills, while others will use logs. Northeastern Log Homes uses a board sill while Green Mountain uses a log sill. Both will do the job but it does force some different techniques which are, fortunately, explained in the manuals that come with the cabin packages.

Materials packages for shells are not at all standardized, and the wildly varying prices of packages from different companies reflect not only materials quality, but also the amount of things included. You may or may not get roof sheathing and roofing in a package. In fact, one or two makers include little more than the walls and rough framing materials for the windows. Others have package prices that are still listed as shell prices that can include all flooring, stairs, roofing, windows, interior and exterior doors, and interior partitions.

Northeastern Log Homes supplies a package that includes all but the foundation, plumbing, heating, wiring and, roof insulation. Finish detailing for the roof, such as flashing, they also expect you to pick up locally, as they do the kitchen cabinets, and any interior and exterior finish stains or paints. The price for all this material must be reflected in the cost of the package, as must the fact that the materials included are top grade, such as Andersen welded insulating glass double hung windows, Andersen permashield welded insulated glass sliding doors (where included in plans) and Morgan tempered safety glass prehung exterior doors. All interior partitions are precut, with enough V-groove knotty pine paneling to cover both sides.

Ward Cabin Company up in Houlton, Maine goes pretty much the same way with quality, using Andersen windows, with tongue and groove wall logs, sawn flat on three sides to give a flat interior wall, and ¾-inch tongue and groove pine or white cedar paneling for the interior partitions. But where Ward Cabins changes things is in the way they offer their packages. There are three.

The starter unit includes log wall material, studs for any bearing partitions, exterior doors and window units, and material needed to erect this. Next up is a shell kit including all wall material, floor framing, subflooring, studs for bearing partitions, roof sheathing, ceiling framing, stairs (where needed), prehung exterior doors, window units, and so on. Then the third choice, the complete package, includes just about everything except the finish flooring.

In more than one sense, this sort of triple option is a good idea, for it allows the buyer with a modest amount of cash to get started, get the walls up and possibly obtain a bank loan on the partially completed vacation home so that it can be completed. There is a strong price variation between the starter kits and the complete package, in most cases amounting to something on the order of $6,000 to about $10,000. If you can get such materials more cheaply locally, too, you save some there. In addition, if distances are great, shipping costs are cut by getting only the basic package, then buying the rest locally.

In any case, the person buying a log cabin kit should be aware of just exactly what is included in the price. Don't settle on a package simply because it is low in cost. Examine the features, check the materials list carefully, then decide. A lot of the difference, as you see, comes from the use of fewer materials to fill out a package, while some companies may use cheaper brands or materials to fill out what otherwise looks to be a good, complete package. Use care.

EXPANDABLE PREFABS

Starting small and growing as the family grows are good ideas, especially if the finances are a bit thin at the outset of your vacation home project. Factory precut or prefabricated buildings are no longer cheap, though they do cut on site labor and allow quick erection, while still saving a bit of money. In most cases, the houses

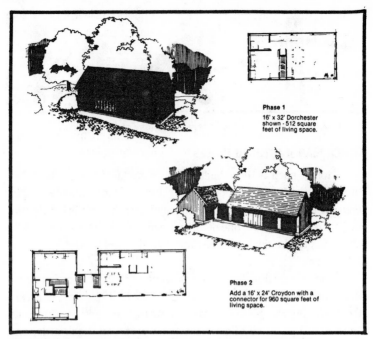

Phase 1

16' x 32' Dorchester shown - 512 square feet of living space.

Phase 2

Add a 16' x 24' Croydon with a connector for 960 square feet of living space.

Fig. 13-6. The expandable home. (Courtesy of Cluster Shed, Inc.)

involved come in small sizes, but are easily expandable, either in cluster form or using modules, to much greater size. As an example, one style of the Cluster Shed Dorchester model serves extremely well. Starting with the basic model, you have 512 square feet of living space. An addition of a smaller unit, with a deck and walkway drawing the units together, and you have two more bedrooms and a total of 960 square feet of room (Fig. 13-6).

Cluster Shed goes back to the days of pegged timbers and mortise and tenon joints, using 6 by 6 framing members to produce a rustic effect (Fig. 13-7). In addition, the framing is left exposed on the interior, and covered with a skin of insulation and siding.

Cluster Shed units come in several package options. The frame alone is available; then there is a utility kit, which does not include the insulation package, leaving the home builder the option of such things. The complete package includes the works, from the floor to the roof, with insulation package, doors, windows, and so on. For the largest models, there is about $6,200 difference between the frame kit and the complete package, with the utility kit running about $1,500 more than the frame kit alone.

Fig. 13-7. Mortise and tenon with pegs. (Courtesy of Cluster Shed, Inc.)

OTHER MANUFACTURED HOMES

Homes such as those built by Acorn are factory assembled, but there is little that goes back to the classic prefab home idea, other than the fact of factory assembly of panels. Each home is individually designed, starting with one of thirty basic models. These are seldom owner erected models, as they are sold through builder/dealers in most cases.

The standard mobile home is another form of vacation home that is relatively inexpensive and needs little or no participation from the home owner. Simply drive it onto the site where water and sewage and electricity lines have been prepared, hook it up, and watch the driver of the "bobtail" leave. You're ready to move in. The foundation can be in just about any form approved by local codes. Sizes now range from about 500 square feet on up past 1,500 square feet; these double wide units are trucked in in two parts and attached on site. Prices start at about $5,000 and now go on past $15,000 for the larger and more luxurious models.

Check local codes as there are, in some of the more snooty areas, restrictions on home size. I remember one New York county requires a minimum of 850 square feet on the first floor of any home. This requirement was instituted to keep out mobile homes without being blantantly prejudicial. With the new larger units, it no longer works.

The variety of manufactured homes is extremely wide, and can cut building time considerably. In some cases, that and the possibility of added quality, are the major benefits, for these homes can easily cost as much, sometimes more, as can homes erected with conventional on-site labor. In other cases, you can reduce house building costs a great deal by doing much of the work yourself. And the erection of precut, marked sections is definitely easier than is starting from scratch, measuring, marking, and cutting each piece yourself.

INDEX